INTERROGATING IMAGES

AUDIO-VISUALLY RECORDED POLICE QUESTIONING OF SUSPECTS

David Dixon

with Gail Travis

institute of criminology

Sydney 2007
The Institute of Criminology Series No 23

Sydney Institute of Criminology Series No 23

Series Editors: Chris Cunneen, University of New South Wales
Mark Findlay and Julie Stubbs, University of Sydney Law School

Titles in the Series:

Cunneen, C (ed), *Aboriginal Perspectives on Criminal Justice* (1992) out of print
Chan, J, *Doing Less Time: Penal Reform in Crisis* (1992)
Shea, P, *Usefulness of Psychiatric Reports in Court Proceedings* (2nd ed) (1996)
Fraser, D, *The Man in White is Always Right: Cricket and the Law* (1993)
Aungles, A, *The Prison and the Home* (1994)
Stubbs, J (ed), *Women, Male Violence and the Law* (1994)
Yeo, S, *Fault in Homicide* (1997)
McKillop, B, *Anatomy of a French Murder Case* (1997)
Cunneen, C & Stubbs, J, *Gender, Race & International Relations* (1997)
Bolen, J, *Reform in Policing: Lessons from the Whitrod Era* (1997)
Dixon, D (ed), *A Culture of Corruption: Changing an Australian Police Service* (1999)
Shea, P, *Defining Madness* (1999)
Banks, C (ed), *Developing Cultural Criminology* (2000)
Garkawe, S, Kelly, L & Fisher, W (eds), *Indigenous Human Rights* (2001)
Finnane, M, *When Police Unionise: the politics of law and order in Australia* (2002)
McNamara, L, *Regulating Racism: Racial Vilification Laws in Australia* (2002)
Woods, GD, *A History of Criminal Law in New South Wales* (2002)
Poynting, S, Noble, G, Tabar, P & Collins, J, *Bin Laden in the Suburbs* (2004)
Pickering, S & Lambert, C (eds), *Global Issues, Women and Justice* (2004)
Buti, A, *Separated: Aboriginal Childhood Separations and Guardianship Law* (2004)
Pickering, S, *Refugees and State Crime* (2005)
Chan, J (ed) *Reshaping Juvenile Justice* (2005)

Published by:
The Sydney Institute of Criminology
University of Sydney Faculty of Law
173–175 Phillip Street Sydney NSW 2000

Distributed by:
Federation Press
PO Box 45 Annandale NSW 2038
http://www.federationpress.com.au

© 2007 The Institute of Criminology and the authors

National Library of Australia Cataloguing-in-Publication data
Dixon, David, 1954 June 21- .
Interrogating images : audio-visually recorded police questioning of suspects
Bibliography. Includes index.
ISBN 978 0 9751967 4 8.
1. Police questioning - New South Wales. 2. Police questioning - New South Wales - Audio-visual aids. I. Travis, Gail. II. University of Sydney. Institute of Criminology. III. Title. (Series : Institute of Criminology monograph series ; no. 23).
363.254

Cover design by fisheye design
Typeset by Four Eyes Editing; Printed by Southwood Press Pty Ltd

CONTENTS

Acknowledgements

Chapter 1
Introduction: From verballing to ERISP   1

Chapter 2
Researching recorded interrogation   26

Chapter 3
Dramatis personae: police, suspects and others   70

Chapter 4
The interviewing process   136

Chapter 5
'PEACE' and investigative interviewing skills   174

Chapter 6
Perceptions and experiences of videotaping
the questioning of suspects   219

Chapter 7
Conclusion: the role of audio-visual recording
in criminal justice   262

References   276

Index   288

ACKNOWLEDGEMENTS

This book is the product of a series of research projects on police questioning of suspects which have been supported by the Australian Research Council. In addition, as part of an ARC collaborative project, the New South Wales Police provided funding for the project on interview practices and training ('sample 2') which is principally reported in Chapter 5. I am very grateful to the Australian Research Council and to the NSW Police for this grant support.

Many people have assisted in these projects. I am very grateful to those in the NSW Police who (among many other things) helped to get the research going, found ERISP tapes for our samples, completed our questionnaires, and answered our questions. In particular, I acknowledge the support and assistance of John Mares, Julie Stewart, Chris Devery, and Peter Smith. Above all, I owe an enormous debt to Roger Kilburn for his support, encouragement, assistance, and tolerance. NSW Police deserves credit for developing its system of audio-visually recording interviews with suspects. Much of the success of that program is due to Roger Kilburn.

I also wish to thank professionals from other sections of the criminal justice process — defence lawyers, prosecutors, and judges — who assisted us, notably in the questionnaire study reported in Chapter 6. In particular, we gratefully acknowledge the assistance and support of John Favretto.

The Law School at the University of New South Wales has been an excellent base for this research. I am grateful to many colleagues for help and assistance. Jill Hunter, in particular, has been an invaluable source of encouragement, information, and advice. Many thanks also to my editor, Dawn Koester.

Finally, I have been very lucky to have Gail Travis as my research assistant on these projects. Her skill and commitment have made this book possible.

David Dixon
Dean, Faculty of Law, University of New South Wales

CHAPTER 1

INTRODUCTION: FROM VERBALLING TO ERISP[*]

1.1 Audio-visual recording as a panacea

The Commissioners seem to have revised an old adage in the light of the television age: they think that believing is seeing (Ericson 1994:130).

If only we ... had a guaranteed tape recording, ... all our other troubles about police interrogation would go out the window.[1]

Police interrogation has long been a source of problems and controversy in criminal justice around the world. Police malpractice has ranged from unintentional inducement of false confessions, to fabrication of confessions ('verballing'), to torture. Sometimes of equal concern to the authorities have been allegations of abuse which have been false or unverifiable, but which cause delay in the justice process and harm the reputation of police. A series of connected responses developed in English-speaking countries. In the 1960s, the United States Supreme Court interpreted the Constitution to require protection of suspects' rights, notably through access to legal counsel.[2] In the 1980s, detailed statutory regulation of custodial interrogation was introduced in England and Wales.[3] In Australia, the High Court developed the law of evidentiary admissibility,[4] and Commonwealth and state statutory regulation was introduced (Dixon 1997:ch5).

In the wake of these responses, official concern about interrogation and confessions waned, partly because it was thought that judicial and statutory responses had been adequate, partly because of the shift in public concern from due process to crime control, partly because other issues became more fashionable for policy-makers, grant funding agencies, and academic researchers. However, such concern has been sharply revived in the last decade as false confessions have emerged as a significant source of the miscarriages of justice which have been disclosed by the use of DNA analysis. This is particularly the case in the United States, where the limits of judicial supervision even in capital cases have been exposed by the acknowledgment of a mass of

---

[*] ERISP : Electronically Recorded Interviews with Suspected Persons.
[1] Lord Widgery, 33 8 HL Debs 1626, 14 Feb 1973 (quoted, Lucas 1977:52).
[2] *Miranda v Arizona* 384 US 436 (1966).
[3] Police and Criminal Evidence Act 1984.
[4] See Section 1.3, below.

miscarriages of justice through use of DNA. False or coerced confessions have been a significant contributor to the wrongful convictions which should have become a national scandal (Scheck, Neufeld & Dwyer 2000; Westervelt & Humphrey 2001; Worden 2004). Similarly in England, some of the contentious disputes over alleged miscarriages of justice stemming from false confessions have been resolved by DNA analysis (Sekar 1997, 2005).

There has been a common theme in many responses to these controversies: police interrogation should be audio-visually recorded. Indeed, electronic recording is frequently presented as a solution to the ills of custodial interrogation. Interest in such recording is not new: as will be shown below, there have been calls for its use from the time that recording equipment was widely available. However, the contemporary calls for audio-visual recording are more widespread, united and urgent than before. They draw on the widespread familiarity with electronic recording as a means of social control via CCTV (Newburn & Hayman 2002; Norris & Armstrong 1999).

Notably, calling for the use of electronic recording has become a standard component of proposed programs to avoid miscarriages of justice in Canada (FPT Heads of Prosecutions Committee 2004) and the United States (Drizin & Reich 2004; Huff 2002; Johnson 1997; Leo 2001:48–49; Leo et al. 2006; Kamisar 2006; Westling 2001; Slobogin 2003). A prominent example was provided in 2003 by the state of Illinois. In response to concern about the execution of people who had been wrongfully convicted, Illinois required police to electronically record interviews with murder suspects. The reform was designed 'to restore the integrity of the criminal justice system'.[5] All too often, electronic recording is put forward as a panacea. There is little consideration of how or if it will deal with the problem: it is taken for granted that it will.

Criminal justice practitioners and researchers tend to be parochial. In Anglo-American discussions of audio-visual recording, there is little recognition that several Australian jurisdictions have been using audio-visual recording since the early 1990s, not just in field trials, research

---

[5]   Governor Rod Blagojevich, quoted 'Ill. Law 1st to order taping murder confessions' *USA Today* 18 July 2001, 3A. Maine, New Mexico, Wisconsin and the District of Columbia followed Illinois in legislating to require electronic recording of custodial interrogation in homicide investigations. In addition, taping is required in Alaska and Minnesota as a result of court rulings (Slobogin 2003; Sullivan 2004, 2005; Leo et al. 2006). Elsewhere, judges have drawn adverse inferences from the absence of electronic recording or spoken in favour of such recording (Iraola 2006; Donovan & Rhodes 2000).

experiments or selected cases, but routinely for questioning about all indictable offences. This book reports the first systematic research on audio-visual recording in such conditions. Based on a detailed case study of audio-visually recorded interrogations in New South Wales, it draws on international experience in police research, and comments on the implications for criminal justice processes in all jurisdictions facing problems and controversies in the questioning of suspects. Its conclusion is that audio-visual recording offers significant benefits to criminal justice, but is no panacea. It can even be counterproductive if it instils a false confidence that all is well. Indeed, the study suggests that there is an urgent need to acknowledge and deal with other problems in the regulation of custodial interrogation.

1.2 The problem of verballing in Australian criminal justice

In New South Wales, the introduction of electronic recording of police interviews with suspects must be set against the background of longstanding concern about the practice of verballing. As Alderson reports, 'From the 1940s to the 1970s, credible complaints of unlawful and improper conduct in detaining and questioning suspects had been a recurring feature of policing in NSW (and elsewhere in Australia)' (2001:253, see id 252–267). A history of verballing cannot be attempted here. However, the apparent pervasiveness of the practice can be suggested by reference to accounts from within the criminal justice process, allowing us not to be delayed by complaints about the motives or reputability of sources. A full history would have to include less 'respectable', but more critical voices from outside, such as the victims of verballing. As will be shown later, allegations that suspects had been verballed may have been used in attempts to discredit genuine confessions. Further, the making of allegations of verballing became problematic per se (irrespective of their veracity) because of the amount of court time consumed by voir dires and other challenges to police evidence. Nonetheless, it would be naïve to believe that there was no fire beneath all the smoke.

Philip Arantz's autobiography gives a telling insight into the practice of verballing in mid-twentieth century New South Wales. His lengthy questioning of a murder suspect attracted the ire of the chief of the Criminal Investigation Bureau who directed him to 'stop the interrogation ... Look, just give him a few words' (Arantz 1993:39). In

Arantz's account, verballing was pervasive and approved by senior officers. Sturgess suggests that, in Queensland, verballing 'started in earnest ... when physical coercion went out' (Sturgess 2001:12). By the 1960s, the latter was regarded as 'ineffective' (particularly in dealing with professional criminals) and 'a risky way of doing business. Increasingly, it became more sensible for the policeman to keep his hands in his pockets and merely allege the suspect confessed' (Sturgess 2001:12). In the opening scene of Ian David's dramatised account, *Blue Murder*, Detective Sergeant Roger Rogerson (an iconic figure in NSW criminal justice; see Menab 2006) belabours Neddy Smith with a telephone book (David 1995). According to potent popular belief in Sydney, the telephone book was a standard tool of interrogation. There were, however, ways of achieving results which required less exertion.

The rise of psychologically coercive interrogation in the US is explained by Richard Leo as a response to declining tolerance for violent methods of obtaining confessions — the 'third degree' (Leo 1994, 2004). In Australia, verballing appears to have been a common police response. Chester Porter, a Sydney barrister, notes the significance of the widespread availability of colour photography. Colour photographs displaying substantial injuries on people released on bail

> made it very difficult to bash a prisoner into confessing and then claim the signed confession was voluntary. There was a need for something new ... Verballing now became a skilled science practiced very extensively by the Criminal Investigation Bureau (CIB) and later detectives ... right up until the ERISP law just about eliminated the practice (2003:259).

Looking back, a disgraced NSW officer called Ray Peattie commented

> ... up to about 1992 [sic] when the Evidence Act changed, verballing was as common as anything ... I'm not gonna say every policeman did it, there's plenty obviously that don't ... but in my experience it was a tool used by police to, in their eyes, put away crooks that would otherwise go free ... the vast majority were accepting of it and you were ... doin' the right thing. Blokes that wouldn't do it were ostracised to the point where, for example, if I was doing a job and I knew I had to go and get a particularly hard crook or a seasoned criminal,... I wouldn't be taking someone with me that I had prior knowledge of not being willing to

verbal a bloke ... there was never any regrets with it at all because in our eyes we were doin' what should have been done. They had the edge on us all the time and still do. It was one way that we could stack the odds slightly in our favour but naturally like all things police ruined it, overdid it and abused it.[6]

Willingness to verbal became entrenched in police practice. Not all officers would do it, but abstaining was not a good way to make progress in one's career, as Arantz discovered (Arantz 1993). Queensland's Lucas Committee reported that

> Some (police officers), we are sure, would not verbal under any circumstances; some would, but only as the result of considerable provocation and with an absolute belief that the person is guilty; but some do 'verbal' persistently and without conscience (Lucas 1977:para 28).

A similar account, drawing on one of its principal witnesses, was given by the Fitzgerald Inquiry:

> Herbert said that although some police would not verbal, there was usually no need to sound out an unknown police officer to see whether he would give false evidence. It was just accepted. When a person was arrested police would sit down at the typewriter and 'You would make up the story as you went along.' ... There is virtually no risk involved for police in ... verballing and the chances of success are excellent. Ordinarily, any issue relating to disputed evidence involves a contest between an accused whose credibility will usually be questionable and who most often will prefer not to enter the witness box, and police officers who support and corroborate each other. Even in blatant cases where lies have been exposed action has seldom been taken against the police concerned (Fitzgerald 1989:206–207).

As research on police culture has shown, such attitudes and practices are neither unchangeable nor distinct from legal conditions (Chan 1997). When using ERISP became compulsory in indictable matters, 'that took a lot of pressure off you to do it [verbal suspects]' (Peattie quoted, Masters 2002:7).

---

[6] Ray Peattie, quoted in Masters 2002:7. Peattie's corrupt activities were discovered by the Police Integrity Commission's Operation Florida: see PIC 2001. Of course, his credibility may be questioned, but for an unusual character reference, see the remarks of Judge Finnane on sentencing Peattie to gaol: District Court 3 May 2002, available at abc.net.au/4corners/stories/s611827.htm.

In the late 1970s and early 1980s 'probably 80% would have been prepared to verbal' (Peattie quoted in Masters 2002:10). According to Peattie, 'there was a definite stigma there that if you got an offender into the office, and let him go you were considered weak' (quoted, Masters 2002:7). The same word was used by Roger Rogerson: 'verbals are part of police culture. Police would think you're weak if you didn't do it' (quoted, Anderson 1992:43). Arantz reported that his treatment of a murder suspect attracted criticism from his colleagues for not using 'a simple "verbal"' and instead 'employing the "dangerous precedent"' of having an independent person present during the interview and conducting an "actual" record of interview' (1993:40). Similar experiences were reported elsewhere in Australia: 'Police officers refusing to engage in the practice were derided by those who did' (Sturgess 2001:13).

The Royal Commission into the NSW Police Service reported that verballing became 'an art form within certain sections of the NSW Police Service' (Wood 1996:40). Suspicion about a disputed confession could be dispelled by making the suspect's statements realistic by including significant admissions or an account 'tying the suspect to a ridiculous story which made his defence almost impossible' (Porter 2003:259) rather than bald confessions; using appropriate language; and including information apparently known only to the culprit.[7] In Rogerson's experience, fabricating a record of interview was straightforward: 'the hardest part for police was thinking up excuses to explain why people didn't sign up' (quoted, Anderson 1992:43).

Like most police deviance, verballing is not explicable merely by reference to individual venality or malevolence. It became a widely accepted practice for structural reasons. First, there was the general cultural context in which criminals (and suspected criminals) were treated as distinct from ordinary society, so that they were seen as fair game: their conviction was a social good irrespective of how it was achieved. According to Rogerson, verballing 'was all done in the interests of ... truth, justice and ... keeping things on an even keel, and keeping the crims under control' (quoted, Anderson 1992:43). Officers justified these practices by claiming that 'You only virtually did it to

---

[7] For a lesson (from victims of the practice) on how to construct a verbal, see Zdenkowski & Brown 1982:337–351.

known criminals, you didn't do it to everyone that come in (sic)' (Peattie, quoted, Masters 2002:8).

Secondly, it is important to understand how low-level verballing could become entrenched, not from venality but as a product of bureaucratic, mundane practice. One reason for the routinisation of verballing is that a record of interview was almost inevitably a selection and paraphrase of what was said rather than a verbatim account (regardless of whether it was made contemporaneously or retrospectively). Editing is almost inevitable when spoken words are committed to writing (Gibbons 2003:31–32). At best, what is recorded is 'what a police officer hears, regards as relevant and then decides to record' (McClintock & Healey 1987:39).

> Experiments show that it is impossible for participants successfully to remember, even immediately afterwards, what was said to them in two-party conversation that lasted for as little as five minutes... Participants can typically reproduce only 25–30 per cent of the ideas contained in their interlocutor's contributions and then only in a paraphrased form (Coulthard 1992:245).

The confession or admission was recorded in the police officer's, not the suspect's voice. This created great potential problems even if police attempted to do their job conscientiously. Take, as an example, the Stuart case, in which an Aboriginal man was convicted of killing a child. It became the subject of a significant political dispute in South Australia in the early 1960s (Inglis 1961). Whatever Stuart had or had not done, his 'confession' was unreliable because it was written in language which was not his own. Moreover, as police typed an account in their own words, consciously or not, matters which strengthened the police case would be emphasised, while those weakening it would be downplayed. A typed record of interview could at best aspire to being impartial and accurate. At worst, it was not a long step from reconstructing statements to not going through the rigmarole of formal interviewing, and simply concocting a confession.

Thirdly, there was the pressure on police to produce results. Public pressure in high-profile cases was a significant source of police misconduct which led to numerous miscarriages of justice in the UK. As for NSW, the pressure on Arantz to close a case by verballing a suspect has been noted above. In Queensland, an early version of 'performance culture' was responsible for pressure on police officers to verbal: any inhibitions against verballing in very serious or doubtful cases disappeared 'in the scramble for favourable statistics dealing with clear-up rates' (Sturgess 2001:13). More mundanely, verballing assisted officers who 'simply wish to achieve a quick end to a particular case' (Rutherford 1975:2). There were pressures to verbal on investigating officers from above, and little risk attached to the practice. As Peattie explained, 'More often than not if the bloke did complain the senior officer wouldn't take any notice of it anyway and it'd never get recorded' (quoted, Masters 2002:9). As will be shown in more detail below, courts were unreceptive to complaints from 'criminals'. An officer confessed 'it was common knowledge quite frankly and I think it was an acceptable practice obviously ... the authorities got tired of it in the end, but I think it was condoned for a long, long time'.[8]

The case involving Arantz illustrated another, indirect but potent pressure. Instead of verballing the suspect, Arantz had attempted to conduct a proper interview which, because of the suspect's mental illness, became very lengthy.[9] For his pains, Arantz was castigated by the trial judge who refused to allow the record of interview into evidence. The lesson for other police officers was unmistakable: if Arantz had followed the Superintendent's order to verbal, he 'would not have been subjected to such criticism by the judge, as the case and the manner in which the evidence was tendered would have been typical and "normal"' (1993:41). The crucial context of this incident was the utter inadequacy of the law on the detention and questioning of suspects. As I have shown in detail elsewhere, governments and legislators failed to recognise that longstanding changes in the respective roles of police and magistrates made reform of criminal procedures vital (Dixon 1997:ch5). This failure continued in NSW until, belatedly and unsatisfactorily, detention for investigative purposes after arrest was authorised and regulated in 1997.[10] In the meantime, police had to work within — or find their way around — vague and inappropriate law which left them subject to the occasional burst of criticism from the judges.

8 From C Masters 'Interview with the undercover officer' abc.net.au/4corners/stories/s611818.htm.
9 The suspect was later found not guilty on grounds of insanity.
10 Crimes Amendment (Detention after Arrest) Act 1997; see now Law Enforcement (Powers and Responsibilities) Act 2002 part 9.

The courts encouraged misconduct more directly. State trial and appeal courts were often left to decide a 'swearing contest' between police and accused who, it could be argued, had good reason to lie. While in legal theory the burden of proof should have favoured the defence, in practice the prosecution could secure the admissibility of confessional evidence 'with mechanical efficiency' (Stevenson 1980:65). In the 1950s, magistrates in local or (as they then were appropriately called) police courts, favoured the police. According to an experienced (politically conservative) NSW barrister,

> The magistrate listened, or pretended to listen patiently to a long and impassioned address before finding inevitably in accordance with the police evidence ... The idea that a policeman would not tell the truth was beyond most magistrates' contemplation in the early 1950s. This gave police licence to bash and lie, and in particular to verbal witnesses (Porter 2003:21).

In notable contrast to the Royal Commission on the NSW Police Service (Wood 1997; see Dixon 1999), Porter sheets home the responsibility for facilitating police deviance:

> No experienced criminal lawyer was very surprised by the revelations in the 1997 Wood Royal Commission. The responsibility for much of what was revealed ... must rest in part with the courts that were so ready to act on police evidence while disregarding the evidence of mere citizens, even if they were of good character (Porter 2003:21).

Porter pulled no punches: 'I blame the magistrates and judges for many of the troubles in the police force, not so much those on the bench now, but rather those who sat in the past' (2003:257). Claims never to have known a police officer give false evidence 'revealed the stupidity of the speakers and the prejudice in favour of the police then common among many magistrates and police' (2003:257; see also Rutherford 1975; Alderson 2001:255–256). If lawyers accused the police of lying,

> When before juries this defence sometimes succeeded, when before magistrates it hardly ever succeeded, and only a few judges would ever accept the word of an accused against a police officer, even to create a reasonable doubt ... [F]or many years it was almost headline news for a magistrate to reject police evidence, let alone find that one was lying (Porter 2003:47, 258).

> [P]ersons in custody were ... often supposed to have made verbal admissions that they denied at their trial. The summing up in these cases

would frequently contain the message, 'Why would these policemen lie?' Often the juries knew the answer to the question that puzzled the presiding judge because they weren't so biased towards the police (Porter 2003:118).

Against this background it is not surprising that, in the cases in Stevenson's study of District Court cases in New South Wales (1980, 1982), only one 'confession' was excluded, despite the frequency of voir dires and other challenges. More recently, Presser (2001) and Talbot (2005) have demonstrated the unwillingness of Australian courts to exclude evidence which, according to the defence, was improperly obtained.

Ironically, even when courts were more vigilant, their efforts could be counterproductive: by treating any divergence between officers' accounts as suspicious, the courts encouraged police to collaborate in producing identical accounts rather than make independent notes which would inevitably differ in some particulars. Training material provided to officers advised officers to operate in a manner which invited a slip into verballing. Alderson quotes a police lecture stressing that officers' statements about an interview should be identical. This was to be achieved by collating knowledge:

> The lecture recommended against the taking of detailed notes at the time of questioning: 'just a brief written note' was preferable. Rather, full records should be produced after the event, when the matter had been 'properly discussed and the correct account established by all those involved' … [T]he practice of most detectives … was to take no notes of an interrogation at all, relying only on their memory (Alderson 2001:252 quoting *Police News*, May 1968, p20).

Verballing depended upon judges and magistrates being either naively gullible or willing to turn a blind eye to the practice. In the case of the latter, cultural attitudes towards criminals were again influential. While this may be expected of trial courts, similar attitudes infected the appellate division. Zdenkowski and Brown argue that 'a key factor' in the longevity of police verbals was 'the support given by appellate courts … which sustains the practice by accepting such evidence' (1982:345; see also Finnane 1994:89).[11] They quote Chief Justice Street's withering

---

[11]   While Zdenkowski and Brown were particularly critical of the NSW Court of Appeal, the High Court contributed: see e.g. *Burns v R* (1975) 132 CLR 258.

response[12] to an argument that uncorroborated, unsigned records of interview should not be admitted into evidence:

I find this submission unpalatable and wholly unacceptable. It denigrates, absolutely unjustly and unjustifiably, the police force of this state. This community can count itself fortunate to be served by a body of men and women who comprise a police force of which it can be justly proud and of which we are indeed proud. In the face of difficult odds and often, alas, badgered by ill-informed and unfounded criticism, our police have a fine record of achievement in preserving for the citizens of this state the civilities that are necessary for life in a law abiding community. To suggest the evidence of all police officers is inherently suspect to such an extent to require corroboration is, in my view, offensive and wholly without justification (quoted, Zdenkowski & Brown 1982:345).

In a case soon afterwards, the Chief Justice complained about defence challenges to the admissibility of evidence which wasted the court's time in 'tedious and pointless fishing expeditions'.[13] Hindsight challenges this view: the investigating officers in the case were Roger Rogerson and his well-known colleagues in the Armed Hold-Up Squad. According to Sturgess, 'Judges ...., along with magistrates, scoffed and any defence lawyer persisting with the suggestion (of verballing) risked humiliation during the summing up' (2001:11).

Scepticism about defendants' complaints was widespread in the criminal process: a Crown Prosecutor opined complacently that

to allege beatings, threats and concoction [of confessions] is so much the vogue that a genuine complaint may fail to win due regard ... The underworld may be ever keen to shake confidence in police evidence; but there can be too much smoke for any natural fire (Kidston 1960:369–370).

Such attitudes to evidence of malpractice (and public knowledge thereof) in state courts makes quite clear the commitments and priorities of many judges and magistrates.[14] It is a history which brings them little credit:

---

[12] In *Burke*, unreported, NSW Court of Criminal Appeal, 30 November 1978.
[13] *Lattouf & Carr*, unreported, NSW Court of Criminal Appeal, 287/1978, 13 March 1980.
[14] This challenges the assumption often made by police (and media) that lawyers are uniformly civil libertarians who delight in making police work impossible. A notable feature of the history recounted by Alderson (2001) is the aggressive crime

Some were silly enough to believe the police line; others turned a blind eye to the practice. Just about everyone remained silent regarding it ... In such a way was the criminal justice system made rotten. Verbals descended even into proceedings regarding traffic offences ... In every case it drags down the criminal justice system and, at the same time, implants the notion that obedience to the law is but a formal requirement to be disregarded whenever the circumstances seem to warrant it (Sturgess 2001:12, 13, 14).

Verballing provides a classic example of the insidious nature of process corruption. An officer certain of a suspect's guilt of a serious crime but frustrated by legal technicalities might justify the improper means by producing the desired justifiable end. The problem that this

conscientious officer ... failed to realize was that when, prompted by some less worthy motive, his lazy, incompetent or careless colleague began to do the same he'd discover himself to be hopelessly compromised even if, in an unlikely event, he was minded to disregard the strong internal loyalties of the police service and do something about it (Sturgess 2001:13; see also Wood 1996:46).

One of the effects of verballing was to de-skill investigators. If nothing more than a verbal was needed, the ability to conduct investigations was affected:

The practice of verballing was the cause of slapdash careless investigations. Instead of doing the careful work required by a proper investigation it was easier to find out from [an informer] who was supposed to have committed the crime, then verbal him (Porter 2003:260).

The standard response from the authorities was denial:

When the process stood at its worst the police pretended to be puzzled by the term. It was, they claimed, the talk of criminals and their lawyers and only used to discredit them; such things never, ever happened (Sturgess 2001:11).

There was bitter irony in the way that 'police stopped pretending the practice didn't exist' and were 'terrified of it' when one of their number was charged with offences (Sturgess 2001:49).

control stance taken by senior judges (including NSW Chief Justice Herron in the late 1960s). Some influential academics took a similar stance (Alderson 2001:98–99, 106–107).

1.3   The reaction against verbals

The reaction against verbals was part of a deeper change characterised by the growing concerns for civil liberties, legalisation of state practices, and effective, efficient policing in the second half of the twentieth century (Dixon 1997:ch7). Alderson has chronicled the long post-war history of complaints about verbals and assaults on detained suspects (2001:253–255). In the 1960s, Australia entered a prolonged period of investigation of its criminal processes by royal commissions, law reform commissions, and committees of inquiry (Alderson 2001:89–96). Their cumulative conclusion was clear: verballing was a serious problem which urgently required a solution.

The Lucas Report in Queensland concluded that the 'sad truth is that "verballing" ... is a device that is not uncommonly employed by certain members of the police force' (Lucas 1977:14). In 1978, the 'classic modern account of the verballer's modus operandi' was provided in the Report of the Board of Inquiry into Allegations against Members of the Victoria Police Force (Hunter et al. 2005:586; see Beach 1978). In unsigned records of interview, very different suspects were recorded as having used identical phrases. Yet these phrases could not be found in signed or taped interviews (Beach 1978:83–87). As Beach concluded acerbically, 'A person with a mind quite untouched by skepticism or cynicism might well conclude that this was, indeed, too much of a coincidence' (1978:83). What, in retrospect, is so notable is the complacency of the police involved: they apparently felt secure in these lazy practices of recycling verbals because managerial and judicial supervision was usually so lax. Subsequent inquiries were 'unequivocal as to the existence and prevalence of verballing' (Hunter et al. 2005:587). In considering the need for video-recording, the NSW Attorney General's Criminal Law Review Division concluded with 'a high degree of certainty that deliberately false evidence relating to confessional statements has been given by police' (CLRD 1984:22).

These inquiries did not just identify the problem: they also usually reported that a solution was available in the form of electronic recording. In 1987, McClintock and Healey observed that in 'Australia over the last 20 years, virtually every report which has touched on the law relating to criminal investigation' had recommended the tape recording of interviews and that the 'same concerns have been echoed in nearly every common law jurisdiction across the world' (1987:7). In Victoria, Beach expected that electronic recording's 'practical effect will be to minimize, if not do away with entirely, unfounded allegations that a record of interview is a fabrication or concoction' (1978:94). In Queensland, the Lucas Committee did not merely recommend electronic recording, but presented it as its 'most important recommendation', upon which its other recommendations were contingent (Lucas 1977:iv).

Recommending that interrogations should be recorded entailed accepting that police should be legally authorised to detain suspects for investigative purposes before charge, rather than expecting them to find loopholes in an outdated common law (Dixon 1997:ch5). Consequently, Australian legislatures belatedly began to provide a legal framework for detention and questioning between arrest and charge.[15] In some respects, the outcome was undesirable: the concentration on the issue of recording meant that there was no inclination to ensure that other protections of suspects — notably a working system of legal advice in stations — had substance.

The availability of reliable, economical audio-taping made a crucial difference in consideration of this issue. Judicial willingness to allow police the benefit of the doubt waned. There was, it could be argued, no need for any such doubt if electronic recording facilities could provide an indisputable record of what was said.[16] Lucas was blunt:

> [U]nless there exist very good reasons for believing that their use would prevent justice being done … it is little less than imbecility not to insist upon them being used by police officers when questioning suspects (1977:53).

The Press followed this logic, arguing that the police should welcome the possibility of using technology which would disprove the common allegations that police verballed and assaulted prisoners. Police reluctance to adopt electronic recording inevitably raised suspicion that they had something to hide.[17] It also sat uncomfortably with their enthusiasm for other technological developments, such as wiretapping.[18]

---

15 For example, Crimes Amendment (Detention after Arrest) Act 1997 (NSW).
16 See Sir Reginald Sholl, in *Molinari* [1962] VR 156 at 168, quoted Beach 1978:79–80.
17 See Lucas 1977:54 and *Daily Telegraph* 3 May 1963, cited in Alderson 2001:59.
18 See *Daily Telegraph* 8 May 1963 p2, cited in Alderson 2001:59.

The movement against verbals and in favour of electronic recording permeated networks of influence. The commissions and inquiries into policing were almost always chaired by judges. In this way, concern about police practices and support for electronic recording spread amongst the senior judiciary. As Alderson suggests, their interventions acted as vital triggers for reform (2001:58, 97). A symbolically and practically crucial point was reached when Justice Deane stated in the High Court:

> In the context of modern inquiries and experience, ... it would be to fly in the face of reality to deny that there is, throughout this country, a real and substantial risk of fabrication of police evidence of the making by an accused of oral admissions in the course of interrogation while held in police custody.[19]

Influenced by commission and inquiry reports (Alderson 2001:176, 252), the High Court attempted in a series of decisions to influence police investigative practices by imposing conditions on the admissibility of confessional evidence. First oral evidence of confessions, then unsigned records of interviews came under criticism. In *Williams*, the High Court restated the common law's prohibition of detention for investigative purposes between arrest and charge.[20] Williams' lawyer insisted that the case was really 'about "verbals" ... it arose because of the need to seek ... legal solutions to the factual difficulties and injustices caused by alleged police verbals' and the need 'to limit the opportunities during which disputed confessional evidence could come into existence' (Kable 1989:17, 25, 27). Then, in *McKinney & Judge*,[21] the High Court developed another tool against unreliable confessions by requiring that a warning should be given whenever a confession was not electronically recorded or otherwise corroborated. Corroboration is an unwieldy and unpredictable legal tool (Dixon 1991). The High Court's manifest purpose was to put pressure on police and state governments to adopt electronic recording.

While state trial and appeal courts continued to support police and to be hostile to criticism of them, the High Court's acknowledgment of the problem of verballing encouraged defence lawyers to be more forthright in objecting to verbals — and, indeed, sometimes to try to tar

---

[19] *Carr* (1981) 81 ALR 236 at 251.
[20] (1986) 66 ALR 385; see Dixon 1997:ch5.
[21] (1990) 49 A Crim R 7.

genuine confessions with the same brush. According to Sturgess, 'Defendants counterattacked and courts frequently became more like stages with the prizes going to the best liars' (Sturgess 2001:3). There was soon a growing chorus of calls for taping from politicians, the press, and academics (Alderson 2001:259).

The costs of verballing began to mount up. First, there was the social and political cost to the criminal justice process of declining public respect. Alleged confessions became 'subject to a much greater degree of scrutiny than in the past' and courts were 'much more cautious about evidence of this kind'. The term 'verbal' became common in popular discourse (CLRD 1984:3). As Alderson points out (referring to a dramatic account of corruption and misconduct in criminal justice), 'Television programs such as the ABC's "Scales of Justice" treated verballing as a simple reality of Australian policing' (2001:267; see Caswell 1984:99–100). Verballing also was brought to public attention by criminal justice campaigners, who organised public meetings, distribution of information leaflets to jurors, gaol 'strikes' and other political activities (Zdenkowski & Brown 1982:337–351; Anderson 1992; Alderson 2001:260–265; Finnane 1994:84–92). These campaigns had a significant effect on the NSW Labor Government in the early 1980s (Alderson 2001:269). Also in this period, Parliament was presented with examples of confessions which could be proved to have been fabricated by forensic and linguistic analysis, and by the availability of alibis (Alderson 2001:263–264).

Secondly, verballing and allegations of verballing produced increasing resource costs. What had once provided a short cut to a guilty plea now came under increasing challenge from defence lawyers, resulting in more cases going to trial and longer trials as defendants disavowed alleged confessions. Pressure on court time was not the only concern: fears were expressed that juries who did not believe police evidence would refuse to convict (Alderson 2001:273–274). At a time when the efficiency of the criminal justice process was coming under scrutiny and complaints and concern about trial delays were growing, the Australian Law Reform Commission's influential report on *Criminal Investigation* made the point bluntly. Much expensive court time was spent resolving factual disputes about alleged confessions; such disputes 'sap the confidence of the public and the courts in the integrity of the police'; and eliminating such disputes would mean that many trials would be unnecessary, either because the prosecution would be dropped or the defendant would plead guilty.

> If the court is informed of the events of the investigation by evidence which is not open to dispute or which is less open to dispute, criminal trial procedures will be improved, the reputation of the police force will be enhanced and the court will feel more confident in reaching its decision (ALRC 1975:71).

In NSW, Stevenson's study of District Court cases in late 1979 provided stark empirical evidence of the costs to the system of uncertainty about the reliability of confessional evidence. She found that prosecutions relied on confessional evidence much more heavily in NSW than in comparable jurisdictions elsewhere. In her sample, there was confessional evidence in no less than 96.6% of cases (Stevenson 1980:90). Despite the fact that complaining about fabricated evidence was risky because it 'may only paint that person in a worse light in the eyes of the tribunal of fact' (Wood 1996:40), challenges to the admissibility of such evidence were very common — and very costly:

> In the study cases nearly 50% of the trial time in which witnesses were giving evidence was related to determining the admissibility or veracity of confessional evidence: voir dire hearings in relation to the admissibility of such evidence took up approximately 19% of trial time and the cross-examination in front of the jury of police witnesses, regarding the alleged confessional material and/or their conduct during the interrogation of the accused at the police station or elsewhere, accounted for a further 29% of trial time. In addition, the accused frequently gave his or her account of the interrogation … (Stevenson 1980:4).

However, only one defendant (of 147) succeeded in having the evidence excluded at voir dire (Stevenson 1980:64, 133). An experienced commentator described the voir dire system as 'a farce … As the police system ensures that the accused is on his own and that the police always have corroboration, the Record of Interview is admitted unless the police admit to a serious error' (Rutherford 1975:7).

1.4   Delay

Despite the chorus calling for electronic recording, governments were slow to act. The reform of criminal investigation became 'a graveyard of reports' (Kirby 1979:628). A crucial factor here was that police were increasingly politically powerful and campaigned strongly against reform of criminal procedure (Alderson 2001:ch4). In the most notable and public incident, the Victorian Government shied away from the Beach Report's recommendations after sustained, aggressive politicking by the state's police (Haldane 1986:290–292). It was a sour irony that among the work to rule bans introduced in protest by Victorian Police was an insistence that 'interrogation guidelines would be strictly obeyed, including the requirement to caution the suspect' (Alderson 2001:155).

As regards taping, many police initially expressed outright opposition to mandatory recording schemes, treating the proposal as a slight on their integrity and an inappropriate interference in their business: 'Their opposition was declared to be "unalterable" and "strenuous"' (Kirby 1991:13). In NSW, this sat uneasily with the Police Association's policy that questioning of its members about disciplinary matters should be tape recorded (CLRD 1984:65). As pressure grew, the police shifted ground, stressing the practical problems of recording:

> The grounds were various, including expense, physical impracticality, the ease of a suspect faking sounds of a scuffle, and the prediction that confessions would be disputed, but on different grounds (Hunter et al. 2005:587; cf Alderson 2001:268–291).

In addition, police warned of problems relating to cost, mechanical reliability, transcription, the effect on suspects, and the recording of confessions away from police stations (Alderson 2001:259, 268–269). If electronic recording were to be introduced, some police argued that it should be restricted to recording a 'read-back' of admissions or confessions, rather than the whole interview (CLRD 1984:65) and tried to bargain for 'balancing' measures, such as abolition of right to silence and increased police numbers (Alderson 2001:270–271). This war of position inevitably delayed progress. In mid-1980s, according to the then Attorney General John Dowd, a significant cause of delay was 'obstruction from the Police Force, with a renowned verballer having been given primary responsibility for progress towards implementation' of electronic recording (Alderson 2001:273).

An additional factor was division within the reform lobby. While the Council for Civil Liberties approved of electronic recording, concern was expressed by other anti-verbal activists that it would worsen the situation of people in custody: 'police might manipulate taping by using threats and intimidation to secure a recorded confession which would then be impossible to challenge' (Alderson 2001:266). The Prisoners' Action Group's preferred option was to require the presence of an independent person during interrogation (PAG 1989). Similarly, the commissions and inquiries into criminal justice may have favoured electronic recording, but they often acknowledged the practical difficulties. There were also divisions within and between committees and commissioners about whether taping should be simply encouraged or should be required as a condition of the admissibility of evidence.[22]

These anticipated problems and doubts provided the opportunity for governments to shelve recommendations for change. For example, the Lucas Committee's recommendation of electronic recording was 'scuttled' when a reviewing committee reported that audio tape-recording should not be implemented because, inter alia, of the alleged danger that a suspect might pretend that he or she had been struck (Sturgess 2001:95–96). One effect of such arguments was that, when Australian states did implement electronic recording, they chose audio-visual and not just audio systems.

When the introduction of electronic recording eventually became inevitable (not least as a result of the High Court's decision in *McKinney & Judge*), much of the responsibility for developing and implementing systems fell to the police. In NSW, great credit must be given to the officer responsible, (Sergeant, later Inspector) Roger Kilburn whose enthusiasm, integrity and skill were largely responsible for the ERISP system. Opposition from police faded away when schemes were introduced and the benefits to police became apparent. As Hunter et al. remark, 'The standard police response nowadays is remarkably different, welcoming recording as a way of rebutting unwarranted slurs by criminals and their lawyers' (2005:587; cf CLRD 1986:13).

There was, however, a cost of the emphasis on verballing: the question of the accuracy of confessions, which undoubtedly had been made, was neglected.

---

[22] For details see Alderson 2001:96 n364.

1.5   The introduction of ERISP

While some tape recording had been used in Victoria from 1966 (CLRD 1986:3–4), more systematic trials were conducted by the Federal, Victorian and South Australian forces in the early 1980s (Alderson 2001:267–268; CLRD 1986:3–4). In 1981, despite the Police Association's continuing resistance (Alderson 2001:268–269), the NSW Attorney General indicated an intention to introduce audio-visual recording in the 'medium term' (Alderson 2001:269). This drew from (and fed into) a growing interest in electronic (primarily audio taping) in Canada, England and Scotland (CLRD 1986:5–10), as well as in other Australian jurisdictions (notably Queensland and Tasmania).

The NSW Government set up a committee to explore electronic recording which, in 1984, reported in favour of its introduction (Alderson 2001:270). The driving force was

> Concern which had been expressed by various groups within the community over the damaging effect which the continuing debate over police interviews was having upon police and criminal justice in New South Wales (CLRD 1984:np).

The need for reform was made clear: the system of collecting and dealing with confessional evidence was 'utterly unsatisfactory' (1984:2). Recommending the introduction of audio-visual recording, it expected the result to be more guilty pleas, saving of court time, reduced delays in bringing matters to trial, 'protection of police against unjustified attacks upon the truth of their evidence', and making it 'virtually impossible for false evidence about confessions to be given' (1984:i). This would have 'a beneficial impact upon public confidence in the administration of justice in New South Wales' (1984:ii).

This was followed by a more detailed CLRD report on how, rather than whether, interviews should be recorded and on the legal, practical and technological implications (CLRD 1986). By contrast to ad hoc developments in other states, these CLRD reports provided a substantial basis on which policy and action could proceed (McClintock & Healey 1987:7). This second report considered and dismissed the conventional objections to electronic recording (reduced police effectiveness, fewer confessions, manipulation by suspects faking assaults, technological problems, tampering etc: CLRD 1986:13–21). A more significant objection was that video images could be prejudicial. CLRD considered this in a limited way: would 'a record of things such as tattoos, speech, mannerism, dress, demeanour and language' be prejudicial to some defendants? (1986:15. Such factors led the Victorian Shorter Trials Committee not to recommend video.) The committee underestimated the difficulties associated with subjective interpretations of behaviour — the reading of 'body language' to detect deception.[23] As will be shown below, this meant that a potential problem of video was underestimated. CLRD's view was that prejudice to the defendant was unverifiable and that it might be counterbalanced by advantages, such as showing the pressures on a suspect (1986:15). In any case, it was expected that showing a video in court would be the exception. Most cases would end in guilty pleas. When a trial occurred, 'in many cases where not guilty pleas are entered, the audio tape will be sufficient and more easily edited and accessible' (1986:16).

CLRD recognised that 'not even video recording can stop allegations that inducements or threats occurred before the interview commenced' (1986:17). CLRD considered recommending a system in which 'there may be preparatory questioning and then an interview is recorded as if it were spontaneous' (1986:41). This (like 'read-backs') was rejected as 'only a minor improvement on the present system ... There is virtually no reduction in the capacity of the police to act illegally or unfairly, nor for allegations to be made of such practice'. Neither would 'address the disquiet about "verbals"' (CLRD 1986:42). As will be shown below, the system which was introduced is vulnerable to such criticism.

The NSW Labor Government was committed to introducing electronic recording, but it lost office in 1987. The State Drug Crime Commission (an autonomous policing agency concerned with organised crime, now the NSW Crime Commission) introduced audio-visual taping in 1989 (Alderson 2001:274). In 1991, federal legislation required the electronic recording of interviews relating to suspected offences against Commonwealth legislation.[24] After further expressions of concerns about cost and obstruction from some police, the NSW Coalition Government moved to introduce electronic recording in 1990 (Alderson 2001:274), and the ERISP program was eventually

---

[23] However, this was briefly considered in an appendix to CLRD 1986, a technical report by NSW Institute of Technology: see Tillam et al 1986:53–54.

[24] Crimes (Investigation of Commonwealth Offences) Amendment Act 1991.

introduced in 1991. Its introduction was not facilitated by legislation, contrary to what the CLRD had recommended (1984:I, 1986:75–76). In part, this was because there would have been an unmistakable irony about legislating to record questioning of suspects whom the police still had no legal authority to detain for such purposes (Dixon 1997:ch5). In addition, the law of evidence was in the process of fundamental cross-jurisdictional review and reform: the prospect of this legislation was itself a source of pressure for ERISP's introduction (NSW Police 1992:3).

There were some benefits from the initial lack of legislation: 'the absence of a legislative framework avoided negative symbolism that might have produced an adverse police reaction and delayed or diluted the introduction of recording in practice' (Alderson 2001:279). But the cost was the introduction of electronic recording to an unreconstructed legal regime.

In particular, the lack of parliamentary scrutiny allowed a crucial element of the CLRD's recommendations to be set aside. The CLRD had insisted that

> The use of electronic equipment to record police interviews should be required where the interview takes place in a police station ... [A]ll interviews held in police stations should be electronically recorded (1984:10).

> The whole of the interview from its commencement to its conclusion should be recorded (1984:28).

The authors were apparently concerned here to avoid the practice adopted in Victoria (and in many US jurisdictions) of recording only the 'read-back' of an interview. They seem to have assumed that all interviews would be recorded in full under their recommended system. However, as is characteristic of Australian criminal procedure (see below), the authorities relied upon rules regarding the admission of evidence rather than directly regulating police activity. The result has been to allow police to question suspects without electronic recording, so long as any admission or confession is subsequently 'adopted' on tape. An unintended effect of a rule that an unrecorded confession made outside a station should not be admissible unless repeated on tape was to encourage and provide a procedure for pre-ERISP interviews (see 2.4.3, below).

The CLRD had identified the objectives of ERISP as being

(1) To deter and/or prevent the use of unfair practices by the police prior to, during and after interviews. (2) To deter the making of unfair and false allegations of improper behaviour by the police. (3) To provide an objective means of resolving disputes about the conduct and substance of police interviews. (4) To provide the courts with a reliable account of statements made by persons accused of crime whilst in police custody (CLRD 1986:1).

The primary focus was not on controlling police questioning, but on providing courts with a record of a confession in a form so that, specifically, it could not be challenged and, generally, the reputation of police investigations could be renovated. The lengthy and increasingly embarrassing public dispute about verballing and 'the concerns which are widely held about' typed records of interview (NSW Police 1992:2) could be ended. The benefits expected to flow from ERISP included 'raised credibility of police witnesses in courts and the public perception; higher guilty plea rate; less time expended on interviews; less time spent on preparing and giving oral evidence of the interview; fewer voire dire on the issue of voluntariness of confessional evidence' (NSW Police 1992:2).

When ERISP was introduced, the priority was made quite clear:

The ERISP system of recording interviews will deal effectively with the shortcomings inherent in typewritten records of interview by providing courts with an unabridged account of the actual conversation between police and suspects .... The electronic recording will provide courts with a window into the interviewing process giving opportunity for an objective assessment to be made of the prevailing circumstances surrounding the interview and the substance of any confession or admission arising therefrom (NSW Police 1992:1).

Belatedly, ERISP was given some statutory bite in 1995 when a general reform of the law of evidence included a requirement that made electronic recording a prerequisite for the admissibility of much confessional evidence (Hunter et al. 2005:ch12). An admission made in the course of official questioning relating to an indictable offence (other than one that can be dealt with summarily without the consent of the accused person) is not admissible unless a tape recording of the interview is available to the court (unless the prosecution establishes that there was a reasonable excuse as to why a recording could not be made).[25] The growth of the summary jurisdiction means that electronic recording is not required for some substantial offences, including larceny up to $5000, obtaining money by deception (and similar offences), indecent assault, and assault on police. The admissibility of admissions to such offences is governed by the Evidence Act 1995 s86, which requires a record of interview to be adopted by the defendant's signature or initial.

However, in practice use of ERISP is not limited to questioning about the legally prescribed categories. Both the benefits to police of using ERISP and uncertainty about offences to which admissions might be made mean that ERISP is more widely used. (In other jurisdictions, including Queensland and Western Australia which have similar evidentiary provisions, all interviews are electronically recorded.) Our research samples (see Chapter 2, below) included numerous interviews about offences which did not require electronic recording. In some, there were specific justifications. For example, in 008 and 036, interviews concerning alleged simple assaults were recorded, probably because of the investigators' interest in gang-related activity. Similarly, ERISP was used to record interviews about several alleged drug possession offences in the hope that they might produce evidence for supply charges. ERISP may be thought appropriate to use for interviews with vulnerable suspects, such as the intellectually disabled male accused of malicious damage and goods in custody in 012. However, there was no apparent reason other than convenience for other suspected minor offences to be electronically recorded. There was, for example, the case of a youth found with a lawnmower in the street in the early hours (058). The suspected offence was at most a break and enter, but a goods in custody charge was more likely. As this suggests, recording of all formal interviews with suspects in police stations is now standard.

The result of this history is that NSW now has more than a decade of experience of routine electronic recording of interviews with suspects. This is in contrast to England and Wales, where caution led to reliance on audio taping. The sporadic interest in video is now being revived (Newburn et al. 2004). In the United States, audio-visual

---

[25] Criminal Procedure Act 1986 s281; this section was introduced as Crimes Act 1900 s424A as part of the reform of the law of evidence in 1995.

recording is widespread,[26] but has often been used only for read-backs in the most serious cases (Geller 1993). Most police departments 'have no written regulations or guidelines that govern when and how recordings are to be conducted [and] leave the recording decision to the discretion of the officer in charge' (Sullivan 2004:4–5). The experience of NSW provides important guidance for other jurisdictions considering the audio-visual recording of police questioning of suspects.

---

[26] With depressing inevitability, this development has spawned its own ugly neologism: an official report in New Jersey refers to 'electronic recordation' of interrogation (New Jersey 2005).

CHAPTER 2

RESEARCHING RECORDED INTERROGATION

This chapter deals first with technical and detailed issues of methods and samples, and secondly with broader issues of researching recorded interrogation.

2.1   Samples and methods

In this book, we report the results of a series of empirical studies of electronically recorded interviews with suspects. As noted in Chapter 1, this is the first research in the international policing literature of audio-visual recording in a jurisdiction which is not merely conducting field trials, but which requires such recording as a matter of routine.

First, we analysed two large randomly selected samples of ERISP audio-visual tapes involving interviews about suspected offences. Sample 1 consisted of 175 electronically recorded videotaped interviews conducted with 167 suspects (eight people were interviewed twice). Using a standard random number table, we selected these interviews from the NSW Police recording system which logs all ERISPs. Data on 168 variables were collected on a coding sheet which had been piloted on a separate preliminary sample. The intention was to provide a general view of how ERISP is used. We focus on how police conduct electronically recorded interviews and on the contribution of other participants including suspects, lawyers, interpreters, 'support persons' and supervising officers. Chapters 3 and 4 analyse sample 1, referring to these interviews by the numbers 01 to 175.

Sample 2 contained 87 ERISPs, randomly selected from interviews conducted over a 20 month period by officers who had received a new style of interview training, based on the English PEACE program (which is described in Chapter 5). In this case, we used a standard random number table to select interviews from a list of all interviews conducted in the relevant period by officers who were identified by the NSW Police as having attended this training program. Developed in response to both our identification of problems in interview practice and concern within the NSW Police about the quality of interviewing, this part of the study was intended to assess the impact of developments in interview training. As well as collecting general data on a coding sheet, we developed criteria for assessing interviewing. In so doing, we referred to English research on interview quality, allowing some comparative analysis. Chapter 5 analyses sample 2, referring to these interviews by the numbers 201 to 287. While interviews in sample 1 were conducted by both uniform and detective officers, those in sample 2 involved only detectives. Consequently, the offences in the latter sample tended to be somewhat more serious.[1]

The research design was for the samples to be, respectively, 200 and 100. In both cases, the attrition was due to interview tapes being unavailable either because they were still being used for criminal justice proceedings or they could not be located, or they were records of police complaints rather than crime investigations. Considerable effort was put into tracing tapes, including visits to numerous stations. While it is of course possible that a tape might have 'gone missing' because it included material which officers did not want us to see, we have no reason to believe that this was the case. Officers were generally helpful in locating tapes. Inadequate storage provision seems at least as likely to be responsible. We are confident that our sampling methods provide statistical reliability. In addition, the random selection produced temporal and geographical representativeness. The latter is particularly important: the study is not confined to material from the metropolitan region, but includes smaller towns and rural areas.

Chapter 6 presents the results from a questionnaire study of criminal justice professionals which examines their perceptions and experiences of ERISP. When the research for this book was planned, it was expected that it would be possible to provide firm, objective evidence about the benefits expected to flow from ERISP (see 1.5, above). Unfortunately, it has not been possible to do so for a number of reasons. First, data and archival material on pre-ERISP conditions were surprisingly sparse. Notably, no data had been collected on the frequency of voir dires (and other disputes about the admission of confessional evidence). Even worse, records of court proceedings did not consistently include voir dires, so that retrospective data collection was impossible. Secondly, criminal justice in NSW has been subjected to a wave of changes, notably in sentencing, which are likely to have impacted on guilty plea rates to an extent that would be impossible to distinguish from the impact of ERISP. This means that we have had to

---

[1]   See Table 2.2, below.

rely on the questionnaire study which sought the views of significant groups of participants in the criminal justice system. Their willingness to assist and their interest in the project produced valuable data on perceptions and experiences. However, we are well aware of the potential gap between subjective views and objective reality in such matters.

Throughout, reference is also made to a further study, 'the court sample' which was designed to investigate the uses of ERISP evidence in court. For this study, we randomly selected 75 District and Supreme Court cases and observed proceedings, viewed ERISP tapes, read prosecution briefs, and interviewed participants (including defendants).

2.2 Basic characteristics of ERISP interviews

While some interviews were very long, most were shorter than is often assumed. Interviews tended to be shorter in sample 1 than in sample 2. In sample 1, 70% were 40 minutes or less in length, with 15% over 40 minutes, while in sample 2, 45% were 40 minutes or less in length, with 50% over 40 minutes. While this disparity may be in part an effect of the procedure for PEACE interviewing, it also reflects the fact that sample 2 cases tended to be somewhat more complicated.

Table 2.1   Comparing the length of sample 1 & 2 ERISPs

Number of minutes	Sample 1 (N=175) %	Sample 2* (N=87) %
0–20	35	14
21–40	35	31
41–60	10	21
61+	5**	30***
Unknown	15	5

*   Figures do not total 100 due to rounding.
**   The five longest ERISPs in sample 1 were: 1 hour 21 minutes; 1 hour 24 minutes; 2 hours 47 minutes; 3 hours 4 minutes; and 3 hours 33 minutes.
*** The five longest ERISPS in sample 2 were 1 hour 50 minutes; 1 hour 58 minutes; 2 hours 10 minutes; 2 hours 36 minutes; and 4 hours 15 minutes.

Electronically recorded interview time was calculated as the period between the ERISP machine being turned on and being turned off at the end of the adoption procedure. That is, 'interview time' not only included the period of police questioning about a suspected offence, but also the period of formal (introduction and caution) questions by the police interviewer at the beginning and end, as well as the adoption procedure.

As Table 2.1 shows, for 15% of ERISPs in sample 1 and 5% of ERISPS in sample 2, the interview time is unknown. This was due either to technological problems (e.g. lack of ERISP sound or image or premature ending of the ERISP video) or human mistakes (e.g. an interviewer turning off the ERISP video during a break and failing to reactivate it, or an interviewer starting the ERISP machine in the middle of the interview). Specifying start and finish times was more difficult than may be expected: the timing device in the ERISP monitor is set to Eastern Standard Time, and seasonal variation had to be noted verbally. There were numerous discrepancies between the monitor clock, the interviewer's watch, and his or her partner's watch.

The interviews concerned a wide variety of alleged offences:

Table 2.2   Alleged offences in samples 1 and 2

Alleged offences	Sample 1[*] (N=395) %	Sample 2 (N=87) %
Offences against the person	12	34
Robbery	13	18
Theft	46	28
Property damage	5	1
Drugs	13	14
Driving	5	0
Other	6	5

*   Data relate to all allegations raised in 164 interviews: in the remaining 11, poor sound quality made it impossible to identify the alleged offence.

Sample 2 was distinguished from sample 1 by a lower proportion of theft offences and a higher proportion of violent offences. Notably, half the violent offences in sample 2 were sexual assaults. While the proportion of drug offences was similar, sample 1 offences tended to involve possession rather than, as in sample 2, supply. As will be shown below, the more serious offences in sample 2 tended to be investigated by rather more senior officers.

Some Crown Prosecutors and detectives suggested to us that the time lapse between alleged offence and police interview can impact on the quality of the ERISP, at least from a prosecutorial perspective. They argued that the suspect who faces the ERISP camera as soon as possible after the alleged incident has less time to prepare responses and rationalisations, if needed, and in turn offers more spontaneous and therefore truthful answers. It sometimes was added that suspects who were interviewed shortly after the alleged incident also appeared on tape in a similar condition (mental/emotional state, clothing, hair style, injuries, drug/alcohol affected) to their appearance at the time of the alleged offence. This allowed the court to see the sober, well-dressed defendant in the dock in a rather different light. Such benefits are not the preserve of the prosecution. It may, for example, be in the defendant's interest for the court to see his or her condition on arrest. For example, in 146, there was this exchange:

> Q. If at any time you feel you do not wish to continue or if any answers are affected by your consumption of alcohol, by all means, you tell Detective [M] or myself.
>
> A. I will tell you that.

What would not have emerged from a transcript was the visible evidence of the suspect's intoxication: indeed, he went to sleep as the interviewer tried to begin questioning him.

A Supreme Court trial in the court sample illustrated that the timing of the ERISP can be an important contribution to linguistic analysis. The fact that the ERISP had been recorded around the time of the alleged incident meant that the defence team had an accurate record of the suspect's level of English fluency on the date of the police interview. Since the police interview, the suspect's fluency in English as evidenced in the Supreme Court's witness box had developed beyond its earlier basic standard. It was important for that case that the ERISP documented the suspect's lack of English proficiency at the time of the alleged incident in question.

Table 2.3   The time lapse between the most recent alleged offence and the recording of sample 1 ERISPs

Period of time lapse	Suspects (N=167) %
Less than 24 hours	38
2 to 3 days	7
4 to 7 days	4
8 to 14 days	6
15 days to 1 month	8
1 month one day to 3 months	13
3 months 1 day to 6 months	2
6 months 1 day to 12 months	2
1 year or more	1
Continuing offences	6
Unknown*	13

*   Reasons for unknown included: technical problems, dates of incidents unknown, interviews only partially recorded on video tape, and interviews in which the suspect chose to remain silent.

Some suspects were questioned about a number of alleged offences on different dates. The date of the most recent alleged incident was considered in the calculation of time lapse. For a small number of suspects (10 in total), the most recent allegation concerned not a specific incident, but a 'continuing offence', such as cultivation of marijuana. These cases had some distinguishing features which required their separate consideration.

As indicated by Table 2.3, more than one third of suspects (38%) were questioned by police within 24 hours of an alleged offence. In fact, 7 suspects were interviewed within one hour of the incident alleged. In contrast, at the other extreme, one suspect was questioned about a burglary more than two years after it occurred.

2.3   Recording equipment and physical context

2.3.1   Technology

The ERISP system used in the research period combined video[2] and audio 'hybrid' recorders. They simultaneously record three audio cassettes and one video (VHS format) tape. More compact triple deck auxiliary audio equipment without video recording capacity is available for use when audio-visual recording is impractical (e.g. interviews conducted in remote locations or overseas). Of the three audio tapes, one (the 'security master tape') is sealed in the presence of the suspect at the end of the interview, a second is given to the suspect, and the third is for the investigator's use in arranging transcripts and compiling briefs. The cassettes are, respectively, yellow, white and blue. The audio tapes provide 45 minutes recording time, while video tapes are available in 75, 100 and 190 minute formats. Consequently, audio and video tapes do not finish simultaneously. The video tape should be left recording while the audio tapes are changed, and during other breaks, e.g. for toilet visits or drinks, or more commonly at the end of the interview while waiting for the Adopting Officer (who asks the suspect pro forma questions about the conduct of the interview: see below). A monitor on the ERISP machine allows officers to check that participants are within camera range. Earlier ERISP equipment consisted of a large box sitting on the end of the interview table. Subsequently, more discreet equipment has been installed below the interview desk, leaving only the microphones and camera in view.

Audio and video tapes are bulky, relatively fragile, and awkward to use. Manifestly, they are parts of an outdated technology. The NSW Police is developing digital technology for use in ERISPs.

Initially, the image on the ERISP video was intended to be of all those sitting at the interview table. However, for reasons to be discussed below, technology was introduced which allows the camera to alternate between a close-up of the suspect and a broader view of the interview room.

ERISP was designed in the expectation that audio tapes would be relied upon by police in creating briefs and subsequently by lawyers and courts. A transcript was to be produced (by an external contractor) when a plea of not guilty was likely or had been made. The video tape

---

[2]   Here and in what follows 'video' is short-hand for audio-visual.

was to be held in reserve as confirmation of the authenticity of the audio tape. The ERISP instructions provided:

> Police should note that the purpose of the video recording is primarily to show an independent tribunal that the interview was conducted fairly. Unless there is some overriding forensic reason or the defence mandates its use, the DPP will offer the audio master tape into evidence (NSW Police 1992:28).

In practice, however, many courts have insisted on seeing the video tapes. The fact that the ERISP machinery only makes one copy causes problems, notably for defence lawyers who wish to view tapes. They have to make arrangements to view them at police stations or Department of Public Prosecution (DPP) offices. Digital technology will facilitate making copies for the defence.

2.3.2 Seating

Jurisdictions considering the introduction of electronic recording of interviews should be aware that an apparently mundane issue such as seating position may be significant for the success of a program. Data were collected on the seating positions of persons in the interview room during the recording of sample 1 ERISPs. In some police stations, the confined space of the interview room allowed little choice in interview table position or seating arrangements. Since these interviews were recorded, NSW Police has changed the furniture in many interview rooms, providing ovular tables. Analysis of seating arrangements in sample 1 ERISP interviews confirms the benefits of such changes. Seating arrangement was seen to impact on the social interaction between interview participants, the visibility of participants, the sound quality of the ERISP tape, and the overall reliability of the recording.

In the vast majority of interviews, the participants sat at a rectangular table. There were exceptions, with examples of a round interview table (one ERISP); a square table (two ERISPs); and a small desk (one ERISP). In addition, one interview was held without a table in what appeared to be an office area (069). Typically, although not exclusively, the ERISP machine was positioned on or near one end of the interview table. The camera used to record the ERISP video tape was either in the machine (77%), or set on the wall looking down on the table (23%). Suspects in most (83%) sample 1 ERISPs were seated at the end of the interview table, facing the ERISP machine. In a few ERISPs (7%), the suspect was seated to the left or right of the interview table, opposite the interviewer, despite the ERISP instruction that the 'suspect will be seated so that he/she is full face to the video camera' (NSW Police 2002:18).

Table 2.4   The seating position of the interviewer in sample 1 ERISPs

Seating position of the interviewer	Interviews (N=164[*]) %
On the left/right side of the interview table, facing his/her partner, suspect at end of table	77
On the left/right side of the interview table, facing the suspect	7
On the left/right side of the interview table with the suspect seated at the end of the table, no partner present	4
On the left/right side of the interview table, facing the Independent Person, no partner present, suspect at end of table	2
On one side of the interview table, next to his/her partner, facing the interview room wall, suspect at end of table	2
At the end of the interview table, with his/her back to the camera, facing the suspect	1
On the left/right side of the interview table opposite both the partner and Independent Person, suspect at end of table	1
Other[**]	5

*   In 11 cases, the seating position of the interviewer was not discernible. Figures do not total 100 because of rounding.

**   There was a variety of other combinations, including one interviewer who moved his seating position in the middle of the interview (098).

Both the picture and sound quality of the ERISP recording suffered when suspects were seated away from the end of the interview table. The seating position for those suspects who were placed either at the end of the interview table or on the left/right side of the table offered both advantages and disadvantages. Suspects who were seated at the end of the interview table were facing the ERISP camera, regardless of that camera's aerial or table position. This meant that the suspect was recorded in full face picture image. Being positioned at the end of the table also decreased the likelihood that the suspect would 'lean out' of camera view, a problem when suspects were seated on either the right or left side of the interview table. The disadvantage of the end of the table position was that social interaction between interviewer and suspect was not as natural as when they were seated facing each other at the interview table. While the right/left side of the interview table seating position did allow for more natural eye contact and verbal interaction, the image was of the side of the suspect's face only. For those ERISPs with a clear picture image such side facial views may have been sufficient for interview purposes. However, in those ERISPs in which the picture quality was poor, the facial details of the suspect with head facing sideways could be less clear than the full facial view even though they were closer to the ERISP camera than those at the end of the table.

Three quarters (77%) of interviewers sat on either side of the interview table, facing his/her partner. Being seated close to the ERISP machine meant that both officers could supervise its operation and change tapes when necessary. Proximity across the interview table also could assist in non-verbal communication between partners or in the exchange of notes, if needed. If the two interviewers did adopt a team approach to questioning the suspect, being seated across from one another at the interview table could be helpful. A major disadvantage of this seating position was that, as noted above, interaction between interviewer and suspect was made more difficult. The interviewer seated on one of the sides of the same table was required to turn his/her head to make eye contact with the suspect. This motion was less natural than if eye contact and non-verbal communication could occur between persons seated opposite one another.

In many interviews, the interviewer focused on file material (witness statements, police notebooks, and interview transcripts) while the suspect was left staring into space, at the ERISP machine, or the side of the interviewer's head. This contributed significantly to the stilted and awkward interaction in many interviews. Finally, the seating positions of interviewers opposite one another could emphasise the distinction between officers and suspect. Separating the officers by placing the suspect opposite the interviewer (as opposed to the partner) should assist in enabling interaction between interviewer and suspect. As noted above, replacing rectangular with ovular tables is helpful. However, it must be acknowledged that the need to have the suspect facing the camera and as much as possible of the interviewing officers' faces on view limits what can be done in arranging furniture to maximise social interaction.

2.3.3 Vision

How efficiently does ERISP record images of interviews? In the following table, the frequency with which the facial images (from a full or side view) of sample 1 interview participants[3] could be seen is presented.

Table 2.5   How often were the faces of interview participants visible in the 175 cases in sample 1?

	Suspect %	Interviewer %	Partner %	Independent Person[*] %	Adopting Officer[**] %
Always	74	43	39	13	63
Most of the time	9	23	18	4	3
Some of the time	5	16	17	10	5
Not at all	9	15	14	6	20
N/A[***]	0	0	7	67	1
Unknown[****]	3	3	5	0	7

*   In three cases, there were 2 IPs.
**   Figures do not total 100 because of rounding.
*** N/A (not applicable) refers to ERISPs in which categories of persons were absent, e.g. 12 interviews were carried out by a single officer.
**** Incomplete or blank tapes.

In three quarters (74%) of ERISPs, the suspect's face was always visible. However, the suspect's face was not visible at all or some of

---

[3]   See Chapter 3 for discussion of these participants' roles.

the time in 14%. The visibility of the interviewer was significantly less satisfactory, with fewer than half of interviewers (43%) always visible. It is notable that, in the 175 sample 1 ERISPs, 120 participants were not at all visible by face. These comprised: 16 suspects; 27 interviewers; 28 partners; 10 Independent Persons; and no less than 39 Adopting Officers.

If the suspects' faces were visible, how clear was the image recorded? As noted above, dissatisfaction with the quality of images has led to the introduction of camera technology which alternates between a general view of the interview room and a close focus on the head and shoulders of the suspect. Only one ERISP in sample 1 employed this newer technology, so our results apply to general video images. While viewing sample 2 ERISPs confirmed that alternating images provide clear benefits in terms of picture quality, their use raises non-technological concerns which are examined in the conclusion.

The following table records the clarity of images by recording how often the suspect's facial expressions were visible. In more than one third of cases, the suspect's facial expressions were not visible at all. In this light, it is not surprising that those who were keen to use ERISPs as a means of assessing a suspect's veracity called for the introduction of alternating image technology. However, as noted above, clarity of the suspect's image was not the only problem: many other participants were not visible at all. The new technology has worsened this problem.

Table 2.6   How often during sample 1 ERISPs were the suspect's facial expressions clearly visible during questioning?

	Interviews (N=175) %
Always	44
Most of the time	10
Some of the time	5
Not at all	38
Unknown	3

Why was visibility poor in so many ERISPs? A number of factors played their part. First, there were numerous technical problems. Some ERISPs included no picture at all. In some, the image flickered or there were other technical problems. Some examples:

The quality of this recording was so poor that participants in the ERISP could be seen only for a fraction of a second from time to time. (157)

Lines ran from the top of the screen to the bottom. There was image flickering and slight image movement throughout the interview. (130)

While it would be expected that there would be some technical problems in any group of ERISP videos, analysis revealed some unfortunate patterns. Notably, there were seven electronically recorded interviews from the same police station in sample 1 which were recorded over a three month period. All seven ERISPs were of poor visual quality. In five tapes (57, 158, 159, 160 and 161) participants were seen for only a fraction of a second from time to time. The other two ERISPs from that station (166 and 167) were totally blank. It is worrying that for at least a three month period, the ERISP machine at this station was apparently defective and staff knew (or did) nothing about the fault.

Similarly, recurrent problems of poor visual quality on ERISP in relation to the suspect's image being out of focus were apparent at another police station. In this case the suspect's image was blurred in three ERISPs from this station over a nine month period. Finally, in the most extreme example from sample 1, seven ERISPs came from yet another police station. Although one was visually of excellent quality, the remaining six were poor, with the suspect's image blurred throughout the interview. These six visually problematic tapes were recorded over a period of 12 months. These findings indicate the need for simple processes of quality control designed to identify technical problems at an early stage.

In some ERISPs, the seating arrangements of participants affected picture quality. In some cases, participants were off camera. Some interviewers and their partners leaned away from the table. Some participants were obscured by others sitting nearer to the ERISP machine. Others, particularly independent persons, sat too far from the table for effective visual recording.

In a number of cases, the use of wall-mounted cameras reduced picture quality: looking down on the interview table, they provided a restricted view of participants. For example,

> *The camera angle is from an aerial position. There is no partner in this interview. Both the interviewer and Adopting Officer are seen only from the top/back of their heads. The suspect also is mostly seen by the top of his hair. His nose and eyeglasses are visible at times, depending on how he holds his head. But even these features are from a distance. (102; cf 082 & 092)*

In some ERISPs the suspect's face was obscured during the interview.

> *The suspect is holding a baby in a baby blanket throughout the interview. The baby blanket covers the suspect's chin and sometimes her lips. (099)*

> *The suspect is wearing a cap for the duration of the interview except briefly when the interviewer asks him to remove it to show his [shaven] haircut. This cap places a shadow on the suspect's face. (113, cf 163)*

If ERISP is to provide a useful image of the suspect's face, interviewing officers should ask suspects to remove headgear during interviews.

The posture of interview participants also affected the visual quality of some interviews.

> *As the suspect hangs his head in an intoxicated state for most of the interview, this impedes visibility of his face. (146)*

> *The suspect sat with his head bent over, with his hand supporting his chin. This position did not allow a clear view of the suspect's facial expression. (022)*

The lighting in one interview room affected visual quality.

> *On the wall behind the suspect there is a large window with a blind that is up. The light coming through that large window may be the reason for the faded colouring of the ERISP. The image throughout the interview is hazy. (150)*

In brief, there is no doubt that the technological advances in ERISP equipment since our sample 1 interviews were recorded have improved the visual quality of ERISP video tapes. However, sample 1 tapes suggested that technological advance alone is not enough. In a number of stations, significant technical problems were allowed to persist for lengthy periods. Simple matters, such as ensuring that participants sit appropriately and do not obscure their faces, need to be addressed. Appropriate interview rooms need to be provided so that useful camera angles are possible. Station-level monitoring of ERISP tapes is a simple prerequisite for the success of technological advances. Investigating officers should check their interview records, and supervisory staff should regularly sample ERISPs, in order to check both technical quality and interviewing performance. Finally, technological advance may help in one direction (by improving visibility of the suspect's face), but have counterproductive effects (reducing visibility of other participants and encouraging unhelpful attempts to read 'body language': see Chapter 7, below).

2.3.4 Sound

As noted above, ERISP machines simultaneously record one video and three audio tapes. Our assessment of sound quality here draws only on the video tape.

Data were collected on the sound quality of sample 1 ERISPs, that is, how clearly interview participants could be heard on ERISP video tapes. Of all interview participants, the Adopting Officer could be heard clearly most frequently (always for 85% of this group). In comparison, less than half (46%) of the suspects could always be heard clearly. It appears that sound quality is harder to ensure than picture quality. While it is relatively simple to ensure that a person is within camera range, it is more difficult to ensure that the microphone is appropriately placed and that the participants speak with sufficient volume and clarity.

A number of factors affected the audibility of sample 1 ERISPs. As mentioned above, a number of ERISPs had no picture or sound at all, or were partial recordings. Some had technical faults, such as sound distortion, interference, or background static noise. As in the case of visual faults, these were persistent problems in ERISPs from certain stations. While an ERISP machine includes an integral microphone, suspects seated at the end of the interview table often required an additional table-top microphone. Several interviewers did not place a microphone on the interview table in front of the suspect.

Table 2.7 **How often in 175 sample 1 ERISPs could the suspect, the interviewer, the partner, the Independent Person and the Adopting Officer be heard clearly throughout the interview?***

	Suspect %	Interviewer %	Partner %	Independent Person**** %	Adopting Officer %
Always	46	80	59	13	85
Most of the time	37	13	3	2	3
Some of the time	9	1	1	4	0
Not at all	4	4	4	4	3
N/A**	2	0	28	77	1
Unknown***	3	3	5	0	7

*   Where figures do not total 100, it is due to rounding.
**   N/A: this includes cases in which partners or independent persons were not present or were present but did not speak. Also, three suspects are included because they spoke a foreign language: interpreters were used in the interviews.
*** Unknown: incomplete recordings.
**** In three cases, two IPs were present.

Audibility was affected by a number of mundane factors. Some interview participants spoke over each other. Some, particularly suspects, mumbled, spoke quietly or slurred words.

> *The suspect appears to be intoxicated, at times slurring his words. It would have been difficult to hear and understand every word he said, even for persons present during the interview. (004)*

> *The suspect does not have a microphone on the table in front of him. For a portion of the interview he speaks quietly, with questions apparently interrupting his sleep. Some answers appear to be spoken while the suspect has his eyes closed and his head bent over. (082)*

> *The suspect talks at other times with his head down. He talks while laughing and while crying. Not everything he says can be heard clearly. (126)*

During the recording of some ERISPs, there was simultaneous external noise, such as that from construction work in 034, which interfered with the sound quality of the video tape.

2.3.5 Machine failure

Problems in technological operation came in two categories. First, audio and video tapes sometimes self-ejected unexpectedly from the ERISP machine. Second, there were problems in recording vision or sound. Unexpected ejection appeared to be a result either of interviewers having delayed changing tapes after a warning 'beep' that the tapes in use were almost full or of an ERISP machine fault. Some tapes ejected without any warning signal. Some warning signals arrived at an inappropriate time, directly after a tape just had been changed, for example. Some warning signals arrived at an appropriate time during the recording of the interview, when the interviewer should have expected the tapes to be full and needing to be changed.

Table 2.8   Recording problems among sample 1 ERISPs

Type of recording problem	(%)
None	46
No sound or picture at all	3
No sound or picture for a lengthy period	5
No sound or picture for a brief period	3
Some picture quality problem, but sound adequately recorded throughout	23
Some sound quality problem, but picture adequately recorded on ERISP video throughout	10
Some other sound quality problem *and* some other picture quality problem	8
'Beep' warning, but no tapes ejected	2

In 11 ERISPs (6% of sample 1) the audio tapes ejected from the monitor on at least one occasion during the recording of the interview. In 8 ERISPs (5%), the video tape ejected. Such incidents were problematic and annoying for interviewers:

The video tape popped out at the very beginning of the interview, after a 'beep' sound came from the monitor. The interviewer had not yet stated the time of commencement of the ERISP. (091)

The video tape ejected four times in a two minute period. (084)

Finally, we made an overall assessment of whether sample 1 ERISPs were recorded properly, with adequate standards of both picture and sound quality throughout the course of the interview. More than half of sample 1 ERISP video tapes (n=95, 54%) were not recorded continuously or the entire interview on ERISP video tape was of inadequate picture and/or sound quality.

A significant proportion of ERISP tapes in sample 1 were of inadequate quality. It is unclear to what extent these problems were due to human error on one hand, and/ or faulty machine operations on the other. (Of course these categories are not neatly distinguished: technical problems may well be the result of mistakes by officers, not least amateur attempts to remedy minor problems.) For example, it was unknown whether the many partial recordings that occurred were the result of mistakes or ERISP machine faults, except in those few instances in which a comment made during the taped portion of the interview indicated the source of the problem, as below.

A comment made by the suspect during the adoption (he asks the Adopting Officer, 'Have you turned the video back on?') indicates that the gap in the recorded interview was not a technical problem, but a human error. (047)

On the other hand, there is no doubt that some recording problems listed above, such as warning 'beeps' sounding without tapes ejecting, were ERISP machine malfunctions.

The tapes do not eject, but the beep warnings continue to sound. There are about 35 beep warnings during the 49 minute interview. (033)

However, the reason for the most problems remained unclear.

Unfortunately, the vast majority of interviewers appeared to be unaware that any recording problem may have occurred. There were a number of exceptions. One interviewer did change the location of the interview to another room due to an initial machine malfunction. Warning sounds that tapes were to be ejected were checked by partners.

The partner is seen staring at the monitor, checking that it is functioning in spite of the beep warning. For much of the beginning of the interview he is seen examining the monitor. By the end he ignores the warning beeps. (033)

The partner watched to see if audio tapes were going to pop out. As nothing appeared to happen, the subsequent 'beeps' were ignored. (045)

Interviewers were made aware of problems when tapes ejected unexpectedly:

Although the interviewer may or may not have been aware of some of the machine operation problems, he certainly was aware of the video tape ejecting. This happened four times in a two minute period. On each occasion the video tape was re-inserted and re-started. The first time the interviewer mentioned that the tape ejected. The second time nothing was said. The third time the partner commented that the tape kept ejecting. During the fourth ejection period ... the interviewer left the room to find an Adopting Officer to adopt the interview. The partner completed the interview in the interviewer's absence. He asked the suspect if the suspect agreed that the tapes are 'going in and out'. (084)

In short, our data do not reveal the precise extent to which interviewers were aware of recording problems or to which recording problems were due to human error rather than faulty machine operations. However it was notable, as mentioned previously, that in some instances identical recording problem reappeared in different ERISP video tapes recorded at the same police station over an extended period of months within the sample period. Technical problems were compounded by inadequate action by investigators and their supervisors. A review of the operational readiness of ERISP equipment and facilities at police stations found that

ERISP audio and video tapes were not being checked at the conclusion of interviews as a safeguard against faulty equipment; interview rooms were not being checked regularly to ensure the optimal professional presentation of ERISP interviews to the courts; identified faults with ERISP equipment were not being promptly reported to the ERISP Unit to affect repairs or replace equipment; ERISP equipment was damaged on a regular basis with no accountability by Local Area Commands for the proper care and maintenance of facilities and equipment.[4]

In consequence, new standard operating procedures were issued which include 'clear and unambiguous responsibilities of key personnel for the maintenance of ERISP equipment and facilities'.[5]

2.4　Limits of research on interview tapes

2.4.1　Competing claims about tapes

The limitations of relying on ERISP tapes in order to research the interrogation process must be acknowledged. As Baldwin comments, tapes

> can never reveal everything that has happened while a suspect is in custody, since only the 'formal' interview is recorded, and an observer can do no more than make an intuitive assessment of what might have happened off-stage. The tapes may indeed on occasion provide a misleading picture of the whole encounter and may represent no more than the final act in what might have been a lengthy drama (Baldwin 1993:328).

Researching this issue is problematic. By definition, informal exchanges are unrecorded and usually inaccessible to researchers, while the participants have incentives not to speak openly about them.

Anyone who feels complacent about police questioning practices in an age of electronic recording would do well to read McConville's disturbing account of how some English police officers evaded controls on the questioning of suspects and were able to present audio-visually recorded[6] accounts which gave no indication of the unrecorded misconduct that preceded them.

In his first case, that of 'Billy', 'the videotape appears to provide convincing evidence that Billy's confession was entirely voluntary and not the subject of police influence. All parties appeared relaxed, and questions and answers were given in a quiet, conversational tone' (McConville 1992a:538). However, the earlier interaction between police and Billy had also been recorded, in this case by cameras and microphones installed in the station as part of a documentary project

---

4　PSN 99/75, Police Service Weekly 11(30) 2 August 1999.
5　Ibid.
6　The police force was experimenting with the use of audio-visual recording.

by a television company. The officers in Billy's (and the following) case 'appeared to forget' that they were being recorded (1992a:533). It was clear that Billy's admissions were the product of a deal struck when a Detective Inspector visited Billy's cell: bail and reduced charges were offered if certain property was returned. Allegations about bail-bargaining are commonly made by suspects: but here it was the Detective Inspector himself who is recorded on camera explaining the deal to his subordinates.

In the second case, 'Clive' was interviewed about and denied involvement in six burglaries. When the police recording equipment was turned off, a Detective Inspector joined the 'interview' and offered Clive a choice: either he could persist with denials and be charged with six burglaries and be refused bail, or he could confess to two, have four TICed,[7] and police would not oppose bail This was openly discussed as a deal, in an 'unpleasant, hectoring and abusive tone' (1992a:542): 'we'd lay it on heavy or we come off fucking light' (1992a:544). These incidents occurred despite the supposedly intensive regulation and supervision of custodial interrogation introduced by the Police and Criminal Evidence Act 1984 (PACE). For McConville, this is further evidence of the ineffectiveness of PACE which, despite its 'elaborate system of internal supervision and accountability', has 'failed to penetrate police working practices and relationships' (McConville 1992a:545; see also McConville et al. 1991). Other evidence suggests that some custody officers at least do not behave in the supine way observed by McConville (Bottomley et al. 1991). More relevant for NSW than this inconsistency is the fact that procedural regulation of custodial interrogation in NSW is insubstantial. As will be shown below, pre-ERISP interviewing occurs regularly and, indeed, is facilitated by the regulatory scheme.

McConville goes on to argue that the misrepresentation effected by incomplete recording jeopardises suspects, and that far from being a protection of suspects' rights, electronic recording undermines them. As noted in Chapter 1, there have been similar concerns in NSW (PAG 1989). McConville warned that

> where the police make threats or inducements or strike deals with
> suspects in private which then lead to a confession in the formal

---

[7] That is, 'taken into consideration' at court in a procedure similar to that in the Crimes (Sentencing Procedure) Act 1999 (NSW) ss31–35.

interrogation, the position of a complaining suspect will be weakened rather than strengthened by the supporting videotaped record of the confession because of its apparent ability to capture reality and because … it is not possible to tell from the video recording whether suspects have been the subject of improper pressure (1992b:962; see also PAG 1989).

In the cases of Billy and Clive, the official records gave a misleading account of what occurred in a way that would have been convincing had not an unofficial record been available. McConville does not claim that these cases 'represent typical police practice' in England (1992a:533). What they do show is that such cases can and do occur.

In this context, it is worth noting the claim by a defendant in one of our court sample cases (C32). While there was no indication of impropriety in the ERISP, the defendant claimed that she had been 'blackmailed' into cooperation (including implicating her fiancé) by threats:

They said I had to, otherwise I'd have to go to gaol for 15 years.

Similar allegations were made in a case heard by the ACT Supreme Court: Robert Waters claimed that an officer investigating a robbery threatened (inter alia) to involve his family and to ensure that he was dealt with severely by the courts if he did not confess: while suggesting that Waters exaggerated, Justice Gray was 'of the view that what was said was enough to concern Mr Waters that unless he confessed, the police might involve his de facto wife, keep him in custody and continue to harass him' and he excluded Waters' confession.[8]

As we will show in presenting the results of the questionnaire study (see 6.3, below), there is considerable concern among criminal justice professionals about pre-ERISP interviewing and other interaction between police and suspects. It is worth noting here that more than three quarters of defence lawyers (78%), almost half the judges (49%), and, perhaps more surprisingly one quarter (25%) of police did not believe that police misconduct before interview was prevented by ERISP.[9]

The danger that video may give a false gloss of authenticity is real. A solicitor interviewed in our court study commented that, simply by virtue of the interview being on camera makes what is said compelling

---

[8] *Waters* [2002] ACTSC 13 at para.42.
[9] For details, see Table 6.17.

and accepted as legitimate (C23, Parramatta District Court). As McConville suggests, 'What seems to be on offer, for judges, lawyers and juries, is the chance to have the past replayed, enabling the viewer to look on as reality is being constructed. It is that promise which invests the video with such persuasive character' (1992a:548). If, however, the recorded interaction is the product of earlier, unrecorded questioning, then video's promise is illusory.

There is also the problem of confessions which may have been obtained entirely properly, but the recording of which raises rather than dispels doubts. One such incident occurred in sample 1 when a suspect (003) confessed on a tape in our first sample to a long series of armed robberies, including several for which he was apparently not a suspect. On tape are merely the bland confessions, with no indication of the circumstances of their production. The officers are at pains to record his statement that he had not been offered any inducement. However, incidental references to access to legal advice and admission to a witness protection program indicate that these were important factors in the production of his confession. The potential for conjecture, and for lengthy legal dispute, about the reliability of the confession is evident. In a sample 2 interview (229), the suspect claimed that police had told him 'If you help us, we'll help you'. However, when the Adopting Officer asked if any inducement had been offered, the suspect replied 'Not at any stage'. This answer was clearly the result of discussion between the suspect and police (and possibly the suspect's mother) during an interview break. However, the accuracy and propriety of its production are unknown because the vital exchanges were not recorded.

Finally, questions may be raised by the contrast between the suspect's behaviour leading up to arrest and his behaviour in interview:

> The incident involved the police pursuit of the suspect in a stolen car. The suspect admitted in the interview that he was speeding; he drove on the wrong side of the road at times; he went through a red light at an intersection; he lost control of the vehicle; and the vehicle went up onto a footpath. This vehicle pursuit was followed by a foot pursuit as the suspect fled from the car into the bush.

> In the ERISP we see a young man (22 years old) who makes admissions to the police without hesitation. He tells them that the

friend who brought the vehicle to his house earlier that evening was involved in a car scam. He tells the interviewer that he had been disqualified from driving. He admits to the traffic violations involved in the car pursuit. He did not consider the vehicle stolen, however. When the interview is adopted, all answers are 'Yes, sir' or 'No, sir.'

How did the suspect change from a desperate, reckless person willing to endanger his life and the lives of others (his girlfriend was in the car with him) to get away from police to the cooperative, submissive suspect we see in the interview two hours later? What happened in these two hours, in the time between the incident and the police interview? (021)

Uncertainty raises doubts, just as it did before ERISP was introduced.

Competing claims are made about whether malpractice preceding formal interviews can be detected from observing tapes. On one hand, McConville asserts that 'it is not possible to tell from the video recording whether suspects have been the subject of improper pressure' (McConville 1992b:962). Those who are sceptical about the ability of police interviewers to detect deception (see Chapter 7, below) should be modest in their own claims that they can identify deception by police officers. We were made to re-examine our assumptions by 067, in which a 'rehearsal' was exposed by the suspect failing to deliver his lines correctly. The flow of an apparently genuine, original interview was disturbed when the suspect stated that he did not know who lived in the house that was burgled. The interviewer interjected: 'Do you agree I spoke to you before this interview about this and you said there was an old lady living at this address?' If the 'correct' answer had been given, the rehearsal would not have been apparent.

On the other hand, Baldwin comments 'a recording is valuable in offering some insight into what has happened when a suspect is questioned and in providing a means by which an assessment might be made of whether a suspect has been bullied or primed beforehand' (Baldwin 1993:328). This may be the case: however, it is important not to assume that it is.

Baldwin also suggests that

the techniques of discourse analysis have already been used in the courts in challenges to various forms of confession evidence, and there is no reason why they could not be used to good effect to expose indications of earlier conversations from the transcripts of formal interviews (1992b:1096).

Doing so can be particularly useful in cases involving Aboriginal suspects, whose speech patterns are often distinctive. An early and much publicised example is the Stuart case, in which it was shown that Max Stuart did not speak in the way reported in his 'confession' (Inglis 1961). This would, of course only be a resort available to a small minority of suspects. For most of those who confess and plead guilty, the prospect of obtaining linguistic experts to analyse their interview will be remote, and the issues will not be as clear-cut as in Stuart's case. In a homicide case in our court study, the defence attempted to use linguistic analysis in order to determine the suspect's level of English fluency at the time of the ERISP recording and thereby question the admissibility of some answers given. Even this seemingly uncontroversial issue of whether the suspect could understand fully what was being asked of him was not straightforward. Linguistic analysis to assess whether a suspect has been bullied or primed beforehand seems likely to be even less straightforward.

One of our court study cases involved a dramatic allegation that the suspect had been pistol whipped by police prior to the recording of the ERISP. The defence argued that this claim was evidenced by the suspect's complaint on ERISP that he had a headache; his pause when asked by the Adopting Officer if he had a complaint to make about the interview; and the fact that he rubbed his head during the interview. However, the prosecution argued that the suspect did not have visible bruising on his head, but that he was drug affected, which accounted for the pausing. Both parties argued that the ERISP visually confirmed their view as to whether there had been pre-interview police misconduct. This case suggested that there was an area of interpretation involved and that the assessment of pre-ERISP police misconduct was not straightforward, even with the availability of a visually recorded police interview. The ERISP may be valuable in indicating whether or not a suspect has been 'bullied or primed beforehand' (Baldwin 1993:328), but it is by no means conclusive. It is hardly surprising that our conclusion must be that a recorded image does not tell its own story: it has to be interpreted, and its meaning is a site for legal dispute. Electronic recording is no panacea; but nor is it useless.

So, research on police questioning by means of watching video tapes extracted from their context is problematic. McConville concludes

> Whilst the analysis of official interrogation records remains of interest, it is foolish to assume that these provide a reliable account of police interrogation practices. Official records ... are useful for demonstrating deficiencies in the techniques of questioning felt by the police to be acceptable for public exposure. These however are records of *interviews* and they give no insight into the cases in which the police, off camera, resort to *interrogation* techniques (1992a:546).

We agree with this, and we do not claim that our research provides a comprehensive account of police interviewing of suspects. It should also be made clear that we are not suggesting that NSW officers engage in the practices reported by McConville: our point is that we do not know how investigative practice before ERISP is conducted in NSW, and that our research makes no claim to knowledge about the full process.

One possibility would be to observe the investigative process from the start, so that the researcher knows what went on before the ERISP began. A crucial benefit of this would be that he or she would be able to identify instances of deception by the interviewing officers when, for example, they misrepresent the nature of evidence available against the suspect. (In the period before electronic recording was used in England, some research of this kind was done by the author and colleagues: Bottomley et al. 1991.) Apart from other difficulties, doing so would involve losing one of the key benefits enjoyed by the current research — access to records of interviews which the officers involved did not at the time of making them know would be used for research purposes. Another possibility is retrospectively to collect information about the context of an observed interview. This could be done by accessing custody records and investigators' files. The subsequent history of the case could also be followed, notably by observing any subsequent court proceedings, and by interviewing those involved. Our court study showed the potential of this approach: where available, ERISPs were watched. The comments of people who were by then defendants on the interviewing process were often valuable and revealing.

2.4.2 Regulatory facilitation of rehearsals

There are obvious incentives for officers to question suspects before a formal recorded session. If electronic recording is to have a significant role in controlling police interviewing and ensuring the reliability of confessions by providing more than confirmation of what a suspect said in a rehearsed interview, then effective legal and supervisory regulation of investigative practices is necessary. In England and Wales, an attempt was made to do this through the Police and Criminal Evidence Act 1984, the related Codes of Practice, and through judicial definition of what constitutes an interview (Dixon 1997:ch4; Zander 2003). Although drawing heavily on the PACE model, the NSW provisions lack the vigour and the specificity of PACE. In contrast to the PACE Codes, which have to be approved by Parliament and which have been fine-tuned by amendments as experience and research disclosed problems, the NSW Code of Practice for Custody, Rights, Investigation, Management and Evidence (CRIME, sic) was produced by the Police Service.[10] It has less status, and is unclear on some vital points.

The CRIME Code of Practice instructs officers

> Do not conduct lengthy preliminary interviews with a suspect before a formal electronically recorded interview at a recognised interviewing facility.
>
> Preliminary questioning, other than at a recognised interviewing facility, should be conducted only for the purpose of clearing up any doubt and/or ambiguity, unless delay would be likely to: interfere with or physically harm other people; lead to interference with evidence connected with an offence; lead to the alerting of people suspected of having committed an offence but not yet arrested; hinder the recovery of property. Once the risk has been averted or questions have been put to attempt to avert the risk stop interviewing (NSW Police 1998:25).

This follows the PACE Code in its attempt to minimise interviewing away from police stations. However, whether deliberately or not, it does not restrict the purposes for which preliminary interviewing at 'a recognised interviewing facility' may be used. Furthermore, the evidence legislation provides a statutory procedure for 'adopting' on

---

[10]   On the PACE codes, see Zander 2003:part VI. Changes to the procedure for revising the codes were made by the Criminal Justice Act 2003.

tape admissions which were not electronically recorded.[11] Such a procedure is necessary: circumstances (e.g. mechanical failure, or a spontaneous, unexpected confession[12]) do arise in which audio-visual recording is impossible. The regulatory regime should provide for such exceptional circumstances, rather than weakening the impact of audio-visual recording by leaving a void in which unrecorded questioning is, in practice, encouraged. There is no requirement that 'preliminary' interviewing must be in an interview room and there is inadequate regulation of investigating officers' access to suspects. The Code states that 'Permission to formally interview a suspect can only be granted by the custody manager' (p26). How substantial is the custody manager's role in practice is unclear. Doubts are raised by practices reported in cases such as *R v Phung and Huynh*.[13]

It is most unfortunate that the statutory requirement (Crimes Amendment (Detention after Arrest) Act 1997 s356Y) that there should be a review of the new detention for questioning powers has not yet been completed, years after it should have been. What little has been done appears to have been an exercise in minimal compliance, and the opportunity for the evaluative research which has contributed so much to the relative success of PACE has been lost. As a consequence, the Law Enforcement (Powers and Responsibilities) Act 2002 consolidated an unsatisfactory legal and practical situation, re-enacting the provisions of the 1997 Act.

The recorded interview is just one stage in a suspect's detention. Its reliability and propriety depends substantially on legal regulation of the context in which interviewing takes place. Such problems can only be tackled by much more rigorous regulation of investigative practices and, in particular, by requiring that all interviews should be electronically recorded in full and that investigating officers should clearly be put under the *effective* authority of a supervising custody manager.

Characteristically, Australian criminal justice has relied on the courts' interpretation of evidence law to control investigative practices (see 2.4.3, below; Hunter et al. 2005:ch12). The control of pre-ERISP interviewing has been the subject of a series of cases in which courts

---

[11]   Criminal Procedure Act 1986 (NSW) s281 (2)(a)(ii); see Hunter et al. 2005:611.
[12]   See p 269, n7 below.
[13]   ERISPs were excluded in a murder case because of non-compliance with provisions on support persons and access to legal advice: see [2001] NSWSC 115.

have been called upon to interpret inadequately specific legislative provisions. These will be considered in our conclusion (at 7.4, below).

2.4.3 The potential of research on recorded interviews

Despite the reservations noted above, research on recorded questioning is still worthwhile and informative. Pre-ERISP interviews are often no secret. Detectives interviewed in our study were not hesitant to admit to pre-ERISP suspect-police exchanges. The pre-ERISP suspect-police exchange was treated as a routine, uncontentious facet of the interview process. Our analysis of ERISP tapes found that many electronically recorded interviews clearly follow, and are based upon, earlier questions and answers (see also Baldwin 1992:1095). This may be shown by obvious indicators (as in the second interview in 205, in which the interviewer cautions the suspect emphatically and laboriously, adding the additional warning 'you understand that what you say may result in you being charged', because he knows that the suspect has changed his story since the first interview and is going to confess), as well as by comments such as 'as we discussed previously'. Indeed, many interviews begin with the lengthy 'adoption' via 'Do you agree that you said that ...?' of questions and answers recorded in traditional style in an officer's notebook (see Chapter 4 for details). There is regulatory provision for the practice. ERISP instructions state that 'Any relevant conversation or activity not recorded on ERISP System [sic] should be detailed to the suspect for adoption during the subsequent electronically recorded interview' (NSW Police 1992:12). Similarly, the CRIME Code requires that 'At the commencement of any subsequent interview read the written record of any earlier confession, admission or statement onto the tape. Invite the suspect to comment about what has been read ... [A]dopt any relevant conversation had with the suspect before the commencement of the interview' (NSW Police 1998:26).[14] As regards interviews concerning federal offences, the Crimes (Investigation of Commonwealth Offences) Amendment Act s23V provides a formal procedure by which a written record of interview must be read to the suspect who

---

[14] There is also judicial encouragement for such recording: see e.g. 'It is important that, if no adequate recording is made at the scene, the admissions alleged to have been made there and intended to be adduced in evidence are put to the accused in a fully recorded interview as early as possible for his acceptance or denial' (Smart JA, in *R v Reid* [1999] NSWCCA 258 at para 67.)

must be given an opportunity to draw attention to any errors or omissions.

Almost three quarters (74%, n=126) of suspects in sample 1 and 39% (34) suspects in sample 2 were identified as having been subject to some pre-ERISP interviewing which went beyond being informed about the allegation in question, the caution and the option to participate in an ERISP. Pre-ERISP interviewer-suspect conversation was revealed when prior admissions, denials or other statements made by the suspect or interviewer were referred to during the ERISP. In England, Baldwin reported references to pre-taping exchanges in 40% of his sample (1992:1096). Of the detective sergeants whose answers to our questionnaire are analysed in Chapter 6, 63% (n=77) reported that, in their most recent case, they had questioned the suspect before the beginning of the ERISP.

Officers who rehearse interviews have to be aware that the suspect may refer to this on tape (Baldwin 1992b:1096). They therefore need to be confident that any mistreatment of, pressure on, or deal struck with a suspect is going to be effective enough to ensure that there is no embarrassing outburst. Similarly, suspects may allude to other pre-ERISP misconduct or unprofessional behaviour. In 078, the ERISP may have helped the suspect by recording his apparently genuine outrage on discovering that $650 was missing from a wallet seized from him by police on arrest.[15] In other circumstances, interviewers may attempt to 'cool' their suspect. In the same ERISP (078), the interviewers made much of addressing the suspect as 'Sir', possibly to undercut his allegation that one them had called him an 'animal' before the ERISP. When the suspect in 043 referred to the officers being 'bloody pissed off' when they arrested him, the interviewers seemed uneasy, and quickly moved to another issue.

When police have pursued and captured a suspect, interviewers usually question the suspect about what happened as part of the 'legalisation' process which will be discussed in Chapter 4. However, in 065, the interviewer noticeably failed to elicit details of the police chase of a stolen car: perhaps this was related to the fact that the chase ended with a 15 year old crashing at high speed and injuring the

---

[15] 'I'm just a criminal, people won't believe me. And you wonder why people come back and do stupid things … If it wasn't for us criminals, you wouldn't have a job. How can we trust the police when they are pinching money out of your wallet?' (cf Maher et al. 1997).

occupants. Some matters are conventionally kept outside the interview room: when the suspect in 057 tried to initiate discussion about his willingness to plead guilty to other possible charges on condition that they were dealt with before Christmas, the interviewer was clearly uneasy and deflected the inquiry. (This suspect was interviewed in prison: a guard's presence may have limited the interviewers' ability to come to an arrangement informally.) Similarly, in 078, the suspect appeared to embarrass the interviewer by referring to a pre-ERISP discussion of the availability of bail.

From a police perspective, it should also be acknowledged that there is a danger that a genuine confession might be jeopardised by a suspect subsequently making false allegations of mistreatment before ERISP. As noted in Chapter 1, one of the intended benefits of ERISP was to prevent confessions being lost in this way. There is a real danger that the focus of costly and time-consuming curial investigation of police practices simply shifts from the formal interview to pre-interview questioning and interaction between suspects and police.[16] ERISP's achievement in validating what happens in the interview is negated if suspicion hangs over what preceded it. This emphasises the general points that closer and more effective regulation of the context of questioning is needed and that such regulation should be regarded by police as a potential benefit rather than a threat.

Police officers' interest in pre-interviewing should not be overstated. We should not focus too closely on the minority of cases in which officers are so committed to getting a result that they will cross the line. Our sample represented the mass of cases in which the offences are mundane, suspects are cooperative, and officers have no need or desire to behave inappropriately. There remains a need to demythologise everyday investigative practice, just as, many years ago, researchers exposed the reality of police patrol (Reiner 2000:116–118). The fact is that most investigative work is routine and undramatic, and is carried out by officers who need to be understood not as zealots, but as workers whose commitment is no more or less than that of workers in other occupations. If some ERISPs are clearly rehearsed, others are not, for very good reason: our file-note on 206 commented, 'there is no

---

[16] See e.g. *Blades ex parte Attorney General* ([2001] QCA 384) in which a defendant claimed that her recorded confession was untrue and had been induced by police in a conversation preceding the recording of the interview.

way that this laborious process of detailed factual inquiry was rehearsed: no-one could stay sane having to do this twice'.

As regards suspects, most cooperate because there are strong inducements and pressures outside the interview which make them do so. These range from the informal and formal rewards for early confessions and guilty pleas (from granting of bail to the statutory guarantee of a reduced sentence) to the individual desire for immediate release from custody on bail, whatever the long-term cost. An example came in case 267:

> *Throughout both interviews the suspect seemed to be obsessed with whether or not he would receive bail. He began to ask about bail eligibility at the beginning of ERISP I. Both interviews end with the suspect asking about bail. In ERISP II, the interviewer, when asked once again about bail by the suspect, replied that that decision was up to the Sergeant, '... as I have explained to you about eight times'.*
>
> *At the end of ERISP II, the suspect repeated his plea to the Adopting Officer.*
>
>> *Can I get bail on this? I have been cooperative and the video [referring to a CCTV surveillance video from a petrol station at which there had been an armed robbery] don't show nothing.*
>
> *The threat of not getting bail and the suspect's perception that the interviewers could influence the bail outcome appeared to be a powerful influence on this suspect's cooperative behaviour.*

The assumption that pre-ERISP questioning routinely involves attempts to coerce confessions appears to distract attention from a less dramatic reality. Officers talk to suspects to find out how the suspect will respond to formal questioning. As one detective openly explained,

> *I speak to them, first, get their position. Usually I would put it in my notebook, even if it was only a brief allegation in relation to what the situation was about. Then I'd put them on ERISP. (Detective, Parramatta District Court, court sample C11)*

In 244, the suspect had clearly admitted involvement in a robbery: however, the interview was no mere formal repetition, but involved the collection of substantial, detailed, additional information about the offence.

This perspective on interviewing practices may help to explain what might otherwise seem a rather anomalous finding. The rates at which the 123 (74%) suspects in sample 1 who had experienced pre-ERISP interviewing confessed, made admissions, denied, or refused to answer questions were not significantly different from those of the sample as a whole.

Table 2.9   Pre-ERISP interviewing and confessions in interviews

Response to offence allegation(s)	All sample 1 (N=175) %	Sample 1 cases in which pre-ERISP interviewing was identified (N=123) %
Full confession: total	26	28
Partial admissions: Total	50	55
Denial: total	12	14
Refusal: total	5	2
Unknown	7	1

Informal interviewing is part of the process of planning and preparing for the ERISP. At its simplest, it tells an officer how much work he or she is going to have to do for the interview to be successful. In interviews for our court study, a detective answered our query about the purpose of the informal interview:

> *Basically to find out what their answers are going to be, whether they are going to admit it or deny it, you know, so you can then structure your interview accordingly. Things are going to be a lot easier if they are admitting things. Where if they are not, you are going to have to put a lot more questions to them about trying to pinpoint their places, you know, what they were doing at the time, and putting to them the evidence that you know that we have got on our — that we have been given by witnesses and informers and those sort of people. There is a lot more planning that is going to go into an interview where there is denying*

something than an interview where, you know, it is just free-and-easy. You know, 'I now wish to interview you about an armed robbery that occurred at such-and-such. What can you tell me about that?' 'Oh yes, I did it. I went and stole a car from here and got a gun.' Basically that is tied up. But if they are denying things, it does take a lot more planning to formalise things. (Detective Constable, Parramatta District Court)

This same detective continued to emphasise the advantage of the informal interview in structuring the recording of the ERISP.

Basically, as I said, the only reason why I bother to do a pre-interview interview, I suppose, would be to find out what tack they are going to take, whether they are going to admit it or not, so you can then prepare your questions and plan how you are going to approach the formal interview on the tape. (Detective Constable, Parramatta District Court)

This functional aspect of the information gathered during the informal pre-ERISP interview allowing the interviewer to prepare adequately for the circumstance of the formal interview was mentioned to us throughout interviews with detectives in the court study. In this regard, the informal interview took on a mundane aspect. The informal interview made the interviewing detective's job easier. It allowed him/her to prepare adequately for questioning. An example is 098, in which

There is a sense of 'rehearsed' questions and answers and 'unrehearsed' ones. The general outline of the main body of questions had apparently been explored. Other perhaps 'new' questions in relation to this main body of burglary-focused questions could be anticipated and therefore may have been expected. These 'new' questions were asking for further details.

At the end of the interview, however, there was a brief series of questions that asked about the suspect's possible involvement in other break and enter offences in the area. Hesitancy and concern shown by the suspect in response to being asked these questions appeared to be spontaneous. There was a sense of viewing the suspect as he was responding to these questions on the spot rather than how he could regurgitate responses or how he could respond to expected questions.

This sense of viewing a spontaneous reaction by the suspect also highlighted how infrequent such moments of spontaneity seemed to be within our sample.

Similarly, in 114, much of the interview concerned 'Do you agree ...' questions about allegedly stolen property which the interviewer had shown to the suspect before the ERISP. However, the interviewer had clearly kept one exhibit back for the ERISP — a false cheque, which the suspect's response clearly showed was unexpected.

As importantly from a police perspective, perhaps, knowing what the suspect would say in the ERISP allowed the interviewer to appear more professional in the ERISP recording by being more prepared than going through questioning 'cold'. Interviewers are of course aware that the ERISP could be shown in court. Naturally, there was concern that they appeared professional. One detective, after seeing himself on an ERISP which was shown to a jury, was critical of his appearance.

I moved around on the tape. I was fidgety. You are supposed to be investigating, but you don't know you are fidgeting until you see it. You are supposed to look official. (Constable, Parramatta District Court)

The pre-ERISP police-suspect exchange assisted the interviewer to appear 'official' and in control of the interview situation.

Some officers suggested that pre-ERISP interviewing was also functional for some interviewees.

It is usually what you call a smart-aleck sort of situation where they are trying to find out basically what you know. Sometimes you will say something... and they... realise you do know what they are talking about, but other times (officers) are probably just fishing for a bit of information or something you know. And they can probably sense that, at times, that these coppers haven't got enough evidence so they are not going to give you anything in reply. (Detective Constable, Parramatta District Court)

Some suspects may be prepared to speak informally, but not to cooperate during the ERISP. One detective suggested to us that most experienced criminals will talk to the interviewer informally, but will not cooperate when what they are saying is recorded. For this type of suspect, the informal aspect of the interview offered valuable investigative information that could not be gathered in any other way.

Basically, it comes down to, in a formal interview situation, there is usually in my experience, I have found that most crooks will talk to you initially, even if it is to say they deny it. Once anything is formal, once it looks like you are writing down something or you are recording something on the typewriter like in the old days or put in front of the ERISP, if they don't want to say anything, that is when they won't. They won't say anything, nothing. (Detective Constable, Parramatta District Court)

Perhaps more significantly, suspects may well be reluctant to talk on the record about other people's involvement in offences, or indeed their own involvement in offences other than that for which they were arrested. While conducting research on police questioning in England, the author observed several cases in which it was the suspect who insisted that sections of the interview dealing with these matters should not be recorded (Dixon et al. 1990:135–136).[17]

This raises a fundamental problem in the use of electronic recording as the primary means of controlling police interviewing of suspects. There are matters that suspects will be reluctant to discuss on tape, which are indirectly yet crucially involved in the investigation of the offence for which the suspect is arrested. A suspect's cooperation may be negotiated through discussion of the implications for him or her of providing the police with information about other offences or offenders. There is simply no incentive for either party to have such exchanges recorded (Dixon et al. 1990:133–135).

These accounts from detectives of their uses of pre-ERISP interviewing are not presented naïvely. Clearly, such statements are, to some extent, self-serving. Equally, it would be wrong to dismiss their perspective on the interview process. They do indicate that there is more to pre-ERISP interviewing than deals and coercion.

Concentrating on coerced confessions may divert our attention from more mundane but significant issues. It would be valuable to pay close attention to cases in which pre-ERISP interviewing is openly acknowledged. For example, from a psychological perspective, the compliant and responsive role allocated to the suspect by adoption

---

[17] In *Nicholls*, the High Court discussed the admissibility of statements allegedly made by a suspect while the recorder was, at his request, turned off: [2005] HCA 1 (3 February 2005). See also *Hill* ([2005] VSC 503), a case in which the suspect was prepared to cooperate with police off-camera, but who exercised his right to silence when the video recorder was activated.

procedures may have significant effects. In one extreme instance in our sample, the suspect was asked no less than 96 'Do you agree ...?' (DYA) questions in 15 minutes, all of which were answered 'Yes'. The repetition of questions in this form is highly conducive to compliance. Psychological and linguistic analysis may demonstrate the subtle reconstruction of statements in these processes. In his linguistic analysis of ERISP interviews, Hall reports a 55:1 affirmative response rate (1998:62).

Hall also draws attention to the potential for this questioning style to lead suspects to adopt statements that they did not make. As discussed above, it is almost inevitable that a DYA question will contain the officer's paraphrase of the original exchange, even if an attempt was made at contemporaneous note-taking. (This was demonstrated by the difficulties observed in English policing between the implementation of PACE and the introduction of electronic recording: see Bottomley et al. 1991.) In any case, notebook interviews are often, by necessity, written up after the exchange rather than contemporaneously. The result is that a DYA question 'allows paraphrased speech to be represented as quoted speech, which it then accompanies with an on-the-record agreement to the quotation from those being misquoted' (Hall 1998:65).

For example, in 031, police asked the suspect a series of DYAs, including one about a cheque. He was then asked 'Do you agree you said "What, the one at the [X] place? I was going to pay it back."' Similarly, in 123, the suspect denied knowing that some material in his possession was stolen. The interviewer confronted him with his pre-ERISP admission:

> When I spoke to you earlier do you agree I asked you if you knew it was stolen and you said, 'I had a sneaking suspicion it may have been.' The suspect visibly was shaken as he answered, 'Yes, I did say that, yes, sir.'

Such admissions may have been accurately recorded, but they echo verballing styles and raise (possibly unfounded) concerns about police integrity which ERISP was intended to allay. The suspect is asked to confirm an account which has been constructed by the police officer. Inevitably, this involves a process of selection and emphasis: it may also involve distortion.

Similarly, in 216, the suspect insisted that another person had stolen some electrical equipment and that he was not involved. However, the interviewer then sought to adopt material recorded earlier in his notebook. This included the suspect's statement 'We just went to the clinic for needles. And we walked back and saw a girl and guy and we asked to look at their stereo.' The interviewer asked 'Is that right?' The suspect appeared hesitant, but said 'Yes'. The suspect was linked to the offence indirectly, via the officer's representation of words which conflicted with his earlier account and which he accepted hesitantly.

Hall argues that this technique elides the difference between pre- and post-ERISP questioning. Before ERISP, 'interviewing officers would write a paraphrased first person recount of a suspect's version of events and then ask the suspect to "adopt" this paraphrased version by signing in the margins of the document' (1998:60). From this perspective, presenting the suspect with statements which he/she is asked to adopt by answering a 'Do you agree ...?' question is very similar. (Hall notes other possible questioning modes, such as asking 'Did you say ...?' rather than 'Do you agree ...?' 'The former would constitute an enquiry about an event, whereas the latter would be enquiry about the perception of an event' (1998:61).) The result, according to Hall, is that 'the suspect goes on record as having made statements (orthographically represented as quoted speech) which have been recorded no more or less accurately than they would have been prior to the introduction of electronically recorded interviews, the key difference being that, now, the suspect's adoption is less arguable by virtue of her/his agreement being captured electronically' (1998:63). Only the universal employment of hand-held field recorders will provide a potential resolution to this problem, although problems of technical reliability and transcription loom large in any consideration of field recording.

The issue of preparatory or rehearsal questioning has attracted considerable attention in England. With exception of Irving and McKenzie (1989), 'all of the major post-PACE studies have found substantial evidence that informal interactions have a significant role in police investigations (Leng 1994:174). The Royal Commission on Criminal Justice recommended CCTV of custody areas. This is widely available in England (Newburn & Hayman 2002) and in NSW. Having CCTV in interview rooms would provide additional protection for all concerned. However, its extension through other areas of stations is more problematic. Cells have often been used as sites for unrecorded questioning, but the privacy of prisoners makes introducing CCTV problematic. One alternative is to have CCTV surveillance of corridors outside cells and to make custody officers control 'welfare visits' by investigating officers.

2.5 Comparative issues in interview practice

This study draws upon research and commentary from Australia, the UK, and North America (principally the USA). Assuming that lessons learnt in one jurisdiction are straightforwardly applicable in others is a basic error (Newburn & Sparks eds 2004). They may be relevant: commonalities in basic policing functions and cross-fertilisation by transfers of policy, technology, and skills are important factors here. However, it is important to note some particularly important differences.

2.5.1 Persuasion-inducement

First, the dominant response of police in the US to restraints on the use of violence in interrogations was not verballing (as was the case in Australia: see above), but psychological techniques of deception and persuasion (Leo 1992, 1994). A key influence came from interrogation manuals and field-guides, notably Inbau et al.'s *Police Interrogation and Confessions* (2001; first edition 1962). According to Richard Leo's work, the product is a system of police interrogation which is similar to that represented in TV fictions. The intimate relationship between fiction and reality is exemplified by *Homicide*, a HBO fictional series based on David Simon's outstanding journalistic study of Baltimore's Homicide Squad (Simon 1991), and *NYPD Blue* (Bandes & Beerman 1998; Thomas & Leo 2004).

One scene from *NYPD Blue* illustrates persuasive strategies. A black man suspected of shooting a police officer is interviewed by two NYPD detectives, one black (Baldwin), the other white (Medavoy). When he blatantly lies, the suspect is punched from his seat by Baldwin. The violence is controlled and specific: its purpose is to assert authority, although it remains as a threat. Baldwin seeks to persuade, not beat, the suspect into confessing. His key tactic is helping the suspect to help himself. The message is clear: if you 'lawyer-up' and don't talk to me, I can't help you by putting your side of the story, and you will be executed. So Baldwin provides the suspect with an 'out', an explanation of the shooting which minimises his responsibility. The suspect was not accustomed to the gun, and it went off unexpectedly: the death was the gun's fault. The significant threat to the suspect is the death penalty, presented as the inevitable outcome of recalcitrant no-cooperation. But if he accepts the lifeline thrown by the detective's reconstructed account of events, the detective will speak for him in court. The suspect's naïvety is bounded: he responds to the offer with a heavily ironic 'Will you, my brother?' But there is no option, and he confesses. From behind the viewing-room window, another detective comments 'That was a nice interview'.

Bandes and Beerman suggest that such tactics are standard:

> During the interrogation, the detectives imply that they can assist in a number of important ways. They suggest that only they can ensure that the prosecutor, judge or jury will hear the suspect's version of the story. They create the impression that if the suspect cooperates he will walk out of the station a freeman or at least be charged with a lesser crime, be acquitted at trial, or receive a lighter sentence. Sometimes they imply they will obtain help — such as psychiatric or financial assistance — for the suspect or his family (1998:8–9).

No examples of this kind of persuasive interviewing were observed in our samples (although it would be naïve to assume that they never occur in pre-ERISP interrogation). Even setting aside the violence, it is likely that a confession or admission produced by these means could not be used against a defendant on the grounds that it was obtained by an improper inducement.

US police have developed persuasive skills since the 1960s with a clear objective: discouraging the suspect from relying on Miranda rights to legal counsel, which, it is assumed, will lead to a refusal to answer questions. (This, incidentally, is an assumption in the US literature which deserves more critical scrutiny: a similar entrenched belief in England that legal advice leads inexorably to silence has been shown to be a myth: Dixon 1997:ch6.)

2.5.2 The use of deception by interrogators

Along with persuasion, the other key tool in the US interviewer's approach is deception. It can be argued that all interrogation involves some deception, e.g. when 'interrogators lie to create a rapport with a suspect (or allow) the suspect to believe that it somehow will be in the suspect's best interest to undertake the almost always self-defeating course of confessing' (Magid 2001:1168). However, the issue here is the narrower one of lying about available evidence, for example when an interviewer inaccurately tells the suspect that identification or forensic evidence is available, or that a co-accused has confessed, implicating the suspect. A related tactic is lying about the consequences of confession, for example stating that the suspect will be charged with a lesser offence.

In the US, most deception is permitted. Despite disapproving of deceptive practices, the Supreme Court in *Miranda* 'imposed few limits on their use', relying instead on the prophylactic effects of the right to silence and to counsel (Magid 2001:1175). Since *Miranda*, the Supreme Court has 'repeatedly declined the opportunity to place any specific limits on the use of deception during interrogation' (Magid 2001:1176; see also White 1979).

> American law permits interrogators to pretend they have evidence when they do not, and police often confront suspects with fabricated evidence such as nonexistent witnesses, false fingerprints, make-believe videotapes, false polygraph results, and so on (Leo 2001:39).

By contrast, in Australia, there is a history of legislative discouragement of evidence obtained by deception. The Uniform Evidence Act 1995 s138(2) deems a confession to have been improperly obtained if it was made during or in consequence of questioning by a person who 'made a false statement in the course of questioning even though he or she knew or ought reasonably to have known that the statement was false and that making the false statement was likely to cause the person who was being questioned to make an admission'. In such circumstances, the burden is placed on the prosecution to defeat the presumption in favour of exclusion by demonstrating that 'the desirability of admitting the evidence outweighs the undesirability of admitting evidence that has been obtained in the way in which the evidence was obtained'.[18]

In NSW, this provision replaced the Crimes Act 1900 s410 which 'had extended the common law definition of involuntariness by

---

[18] This was part of a general reform of the law relating to confessional and other evidence (Hunter et al 2002).

requiring the exclusion of a confession "induced" by any untrue representation made to the person confessing by a person in authority' (Aronson & Hunter 1998:373). Even if literally true, a statement 'could be false for the purposes of s410, if uttered in a manner and context deliberately designed to convey an untrue additional implication' (Aronson & Hunter 1998:373; cf *Hawkins* [1994] 181 CLR 440).

There is a perhaps surprising lack of a similar provision in England: 'there is hardly any English guidance on the propriety of deceptive practices in investigations' (Ashworth 1998:108). PACE and its Codes 'do not deal specifically with the use of deceptive practices … there is no legislative statement that suspects have the right to truthfulness from law enforcement officers at the interviewing stage' (Ashworth 1998:109, 126). In a number of cases, evidence obtained by deception has been excluded: notably, in *Mason*, police falsely told the suspect that his fingerprints had been found at a crime scene. The subsequent confession was excluded.[19] The fact that Mason's solicitor had also been deceived was an aggravating factor. Similarly, in *Heron,* investigators wrongly told the suspect and his legal representative that a witness had identified him.[20] However, the situation is not clear. Courts insist that the particular circumstances of each case are relevant. There are numerous cases in which evidence resulting from deceptive conduct (not in interviews, but in undercover operations) has been accepted (Zander 2003:341–345).

What are the arguments against using deception? First, there is the danger of producing false confessions which 'can surely result from trickery no less than from coercion' (Ashworth 1998:116). The English case of *Stagg* illustrates how an apparently false confession can be produced: by misrepresenting herself as being interested in sexual violence, an undercover officer elicited a confession from a suspect in a murder case.[21] Secondly, there is the need to preserve the integrity of a system which has to maintain standards and public confidence: 'police officers, above all, should be expected to uphold the values of truthfulness and probity' (Ashworth 1998:127). Thirdly, there is a crucial weakness in the consequentialist reasoning that deception is justified if it produces results. This assumes that police have the ability

---

[19]   [1988] 1 WLR 139.
[20]   Unreported, Leeds Crown Court, 1 Nov. 1993; see Dixon 1997:172–176; Gudjonsson 2003:96–106.
[21]   *The Times*, 15 September 1994.

to identify a truth, which then just needs proof. Even on a consequentialist calculation, 'Whether the end (more convictions) can be said to justify the use of tricks and other deceptive practices depends ... on a whole range of factors about which we have little hard evidence, such as the effect on public confidence, the effect on the conduct of the police in other situations ... and so forth' (Ashworth 1998:127).

Our study could not detect deception. This needs to be addressed in future research because of suggestions that deception may develop to take the place of coercive techniques as happened in the US (Leo 1994; Skolnick & Leo 1992; Ashworth 1998:108).

2.5.3 Regulation

In England and Wales, a bifocal concern to protect suspects' rights and to extend police powers led to a major reform of investigative detention in the Police and Criminal Evidence Act 1984. Detailed regulation of powers to detain suspects for questioning was introduced, including supervision, substantial suspects' rights, and contemporaneous recording (first on paper, then on audio tape). In considerable contrast to the US, the English authorities sought to regulate police practices prospectively, rather than relying on retrospective judicial exclusion of evidence. However, impetus for reform in questioning practices came later, as a series of convictions were shown to have been miscarriages of justice cases (Walker & Starmer eds 1999). The outcome is a widespread acceptance that coerced confessions are not reliable: the point at which people can be coerced or persuaded into confessing is also the point at which their confession becomes potentially unreliable. Ironically, this is one of the messages that the Supreme Court was trying to convey in *Miranda* in 1966.

The major general differences between Australia and England and Wales are pointed out by Aronson and Hunter:

> Australia differs from England in two significant respects. First, we place a great deal of reliance on evidence law's exclusionary rules and discretions (of which we have more than the English). We look to evidence law as the primary vehicle for ensuring that police comply with the rules governing their investigative practices. Second, we are lagging

well behind the English in the move to articulate those investigatory rules and to put them onto a statutory footing (1998:331).

While there has been widespread legislative activity on detention for questioning, Aronson and Hunter's point continues to be valid. Australian legislation lacks the regulatory bite of PACE (see 2.4.2, above), and much (too much) continues to be left to the courts.

Australian criminal justice has traditionally relied upon the courts to supervise investigative practices. It should now be clear that the courts' capacity to take this role effectively is limited. As the Royal Commission into the NSW Police Service pointed out in relation to objections to fabricated evidence,

> the trial process is an inappropriate forum for such complaints to be determined. Often this is because it is perceived that it may not be in the best interest of an accused to complain, either formally, or during the course of the trial process. To do so may only paint that person in a worse light in the eyes of the tribunal of fact. Alternatively, if such an allegation is maintained, it is commonly discounted as the standard response of a guilty accused (Wood 1996:40).

The Royal Commission went on to point out that the practical limits on complaints encouraged the proliferation of verballing and other misconduct (ibid). While ERISP may have dealt with straightforward verballing, it has also allowed legislators and policy makers to ignore the need for effective and comprehensive regulation of policing practices in the detention and questioning of suspects.

CHAPTER 3

DRAMATIS PERSONAE:
POLICE, SUSPECTS AND OTHERS

In Chapters 3 and 4, we examine the sample 1 interviews in detail, drawing some material for contrast from sample 2. In Chapter 5, we examine sample 2 more closely, assessing changes in interview styles. In this chapter, we focus in turn upon the participants in the interview process — interviewing officers and their partners, suspects, family members and other 'support persons', lawyers, interpreters, and 'Adopting Officers'.

3.1.1 Interviewers

The 175 ERISPs in sample 1 were conducted by 173 principal interviewers. In two instances in which the suspect was questioned twice, the same interviewer conducted both ERISPs. In six other instances in which there were two interviews with the same suspect, different officers conducted each ERISP. The vast majority of interviewers were male: 83% in sample 1 and 92% in sample 2. Almost two thirds of interviewers (65%) in sample 1 were Senior Constables. This group included uniformed, detective and plainclothes officers. In sample 2, all but one were senior constables: the group was spread almost evenly across uniformed, detective, and plainclothes officers.

Usually, two officers conducted interviews, with a clear division of responsibility between primary interviewer and partner. In 12 (7%) sample 1 ERISPs, there was only one interviewer. In an additional six (3%) sample 1 ERISPs, three officers were present. In each of these instances, one person played the standard role of partner, taking notes, for example, while the third either simply observed or assisted with physical evidence shown to the suspect. In nine ERISP tapes, it was unclear whether or not a partner was present because of either the ERISP's poor technical condition or incomplete recording. In all, there were 153 partners present during the recording of sample 1 ERISPs. As might be expected, their rank profile was slightly lower than that of primary interviewers.

Table 3.1   Interviewers' rank*

Rank	Sample 1 (N=173) %	Sample 2 (N=87) %
Probationary Constable	1	0
Constable	21	0
Senior Constable	65	Detective 26 Plain clothes 38 Uniform 34
Sergeant	3	Detective 1
Other**	1	0
Unknown***	10	0

*   Figures do not total 100 because of rounding.
**   One interviewer introduced himself as a Senior Transit Police Officer.
*** Reasons for data being unknown included sound quality tape problems, partial recordings and ERISPs in which the interviewer did not introduce him/herself by rank.

Table 3.2   Partners' rank in sample 1

Rank	(N=153) %
Probationary Constable	3
Constable	27
Senior Constable	62
Sergeant	3
Unknown*	5

*   Rank was unknown rank when, for example, the interviewer used an imprecise term such as 'detective' when introducing the partner, or referred to the partner inconsistently: one interviewer referred to his partner as 'Constable', 'Senior Constable' and 'Sergeant' during one ERISP.

Partners were slightly more likely than interviewers to be women: 18% of sample 1, 15% in sample 2.

3.1.2 The interviewer's manner

We identified the predominant manner exhibited by interviewers in sample 1. During the course of sometimes long interviews, more than one manner was adopted: however we have identified here the manner which best characterises the interviewer overall. The most common approach was for officers to be neutral/matter of fact in their manner for most of the interview.

Table 3.3   The predominant manner of interviewers during the recording of sample 1 interviews

Predominant manner	Interviews (N=175) %
Neutral/matter of fact	41
Focused/concentrated	9
Inexperienced	6
Persevering/persistent	5
Understanding	5
Awkward/lacking confidence	4
Relaxed	3
Friendly	2
Confident	2
Energetic/busy	2
Aggressive	2
Other*	9
Unknown	10

*   Others included: frustrated, disorganised, patient, annoyed, cautious, hurried (2 cases of each); sarcastic, tired; loud, and thorough (1 of each).

The following are characteristic examples of interviewers who were neutral/matter of fact in manner.

Both of these detectives are dressed in white shirts and dark ties. The interviewer does not need to refer to the printed forms in order to deliver the caution and ask the preliminary format questions. He faces the suspect and speaks with expression. His questions are wide-ranging and fairly evenly paced. He changes tactic in the middle of the interview when the suspect increasingly denies knowledge. Then he informs the suspect that one of his co-offenders has been charged. His questions were extensive, but not confrontational. He was relaxed throughout. While his partner was asking questions, he spent the time reviewing paperwork in front of him and looking again through his police notebook, apparently to ensure that all questions had been asked. (063)

The interviewer appears to have organised her interview (open-ended question, questions stemming from the complainant's statement, and another open-ended question: 'What do you claim happened?'). She delivered questions in a manner that was matter of fact and confident. Throughout the interview she sat looking through papers that were in front of her as she formed her questions. She had little eye contact with the suspect. (101)

The matter of fact, business-like manner of these interviewers can be compared with another interviewer who appeared inexperienced.

This may have been the first time this interviewer had questioned a suspect using ERISP. He asked the caution questions at the beginning, reading from the text provided in a way that suggested unfamiliarity. Then in the middle of the interview he asked, 'Prior to this interview, do you agree that I cautioned you?'. (074)

In one in 10 (9%) of sample 1 ERISPs, the interviewers were classified as being predominantly focused or concentrated in manner. For example,

The interviewer in this ERISP does not look up from paperwork as often as many other interviewers. He appears less concerned with rapport with the suspect than with forming questions and listening to answers. He takes notes during the interview. His questions are asked with a somewhat forceful tone. He speaks quickly. He is serious in his manner. He takes time to read paperwork in front of him before forming some questions. In general, he appears much more stressed in manner and in voice tone than the suspect. (125)

In only four interviews (2%) in the sample were interviewers assessed as having a busy/energetic manner most of the time.

The interviewer sat opposite the suspect at the table. At first he sat with arms outstretched on either side of his paperwork. Then he changed position and sat holding his notebook and turning pages as he asked a lengthy series of 'Do you agree?' questions. He appeared busy during the interview as he handled exhibits, maintained eye contact with the suspect and glanced at the monitor. (101)

This interviewer's manner may be explained by the fact that he had no partner present to assist with the ERISP machine and organise exhibits.

Notably, only three interviewers (2%) were aggressive in manner most of the time.

The interviewer is out of camera range for most of this interview. He sounds forceful and aggressive. He speaks very quickly when he reads the preliminary cautionary questions. He interrupts the suspect while he is answering questions several times during the interview. (150)

3.2   Partners

As noted above, the interviewer operated alone in 7% of cases. A two-person team is normal. Are partners necessary? It might be thought that resources could be saved by interviewers operating alone, with the ERISP taking the corroborative role previously assigned to partners. It is certainly the case that single interviewers should be able to deal with many mundane matters. However, partners will continue to be a necessary safeguard against false allegations from suspects so long as recording of interviews is less than complete (see Chapter 7). More positively, in more complex matters, the partner can be useful, and could be encouraged to be more active. He or she has the opportunity to be more reflective during interviews, checking on what needs to be asked or challenged. More generally, a useful role that partners can play is to take notes, for example checking on the legal points covered, recording the time of significant admissions in order to facilitate subsequent use of the ERISP tape, or charting the interviewer's progress through an interview plan. In 93% (n=129) of interviews in which a partner could be seen on the ERISP, he or she took some notes. The extent of this activity varied. At one extreme, the partner appeared to note only starting and ending times of the ERISP. At the other (more frequent) extreme, partners were seen taking extensive notes.

In most interviews, the division of labour between the primary interviewer and the partner is clear. The interviewer directs the interview, and the partner takes some notes, keeps an eye on the ERISP machine, asks a couple of questions to clarify matters when invited to do so, and, often, looks bored and disengaged. In 35% of sample 1 interviews (n=52), the partner did not participate in questioning at all. By contrast, however, in 24 (28%) of sample 2 ERISPs, the partner's contribution was judged to be significant. In these cases, the division of labour was more equal, and partners took a greater share of the questioning, often initiating a line of inquiry. Active partners were particularly helpful when the primary interviewer missed a legal issue, failed to challenge an inconsistency in the suspect's account, or was unsure of the next step:

> *The partner in this ERISP really did assist the interviewer with questioning, in particular in relation to the second allegation. After the interviewer had asked the suspect if he would agree to participate in a line-up in relation to an armed robbery of a bottle shop, the interviewer asked if the suspect wished to say anything. When the suspect responded 'No', the interviewer appeared to pause, seemingly undecided what to ask next. It was the partner who continued with questioning, asking the suspect if he had any knowledge of that offence. Similarly, at the beginning of the interview when the suspect had difficulty understanding the reference in the caution to an inducement or offer of advantage, the partner explained. (239)*

> *The partner played an important role in this interview about an alleged sexual assault. (The partner, a Detective Sergeant, was senior in rank to the interviewer, a Detective Senior Constable.) Towards the end of the interview, she tried to clarify the crucial issue of mens rea. She asked the suspect whether he knew the act he did was wrong. She tested his understanding of 'doing things*

that were wrong' by asking him to give her an example of an activity that might come to police attention.

She made a second important contribution to this interview. The interviewer often used vague, colloquial language to refer to the allegation. For example, she mentioned that J allegedly 'sucked your doodle' and then asked 'Did you ask J to do this thing?' While the suspect appeared to understand what he was being asked, the partner, at the end of the interview, ensured that there was no uncertainty about this by using explicit, descriptive language: she referred to the two boys sucking one another's penises. The partner's approach was confrontational in its bluntness, but limited the potential for misunderstanding by the suspect or challenge in court. (257)

This partner played an important role in the interview, although he did not fully compensate for the lack of detail in the questioning approach used by the interviewer. The partner largely restricted questions during the interview proper to whether the suspect had invented the names on the various bank accounts. However, towards the end of questioning he specifically asked the suspect, 'Why did you open all these accounts?' This important question focused on the suspect's intention. Although the interviewer had asked about intent, this had been as part of confusing double-barrelled questions. The suspect's response did not deal with the issue sufficiently, but the interviewer did not follow-up. It was the partner who stepped in to address the question of intent specifically. (263)

These are examples of the more active role that partners could usefully be expected to play. However, most were passive. There would appear to be room for partners to do more in assisting primary interviewers by staying alert in order to identify points of weakness in the suspect's account.

In some interviews, the partner's intervention was timely and helpful: indeed, the contrast between interviewing styles of lead interviewer and partner provides one of the best guides to distinguishing between good and bad interviewing. An example is 164:

The main questioning approach in this ERISP is an extreme example of an interviewer who treats a complicated matter — a difficult domestic relationship and an alleged breach of an AVO — in an over-simplified manner. He accomplished this by ignoring the content of most responses offered by the suspect and ploughing through question after question introduced by either 'Do you agree?' or 'I also have been told that ...' These questions all stemmed from the complainant's statement. (164)

The partner raised important issues concerning the origin of the AVO, the suspect's awareness of it, and the serving of it upon him.

Not all ERISPs showed the partner's contribution to questioning in such a favourable light, as exemplified by 104:

The suspect's nervousness contrasted with the mood of the interviewers. The partner appeared uninterested in the interview. Most of the time, he leaned out of camera view. When visible on camera he was seen fidgeting with his pen. He did ask the suspect some questions about uncontentious matters when the interviewer invited him to do so. (104)

However, several of these had already been asked, and some had been answered by the suspect. The partner simply appeared not to be paying attention.

There were many examples of interviewers and partners working together as a team in questioning suspects.

The interviewer and his partner also may have anticipated a full confession as they gestured to one another in order to share questioning (taking turns) and appeared to work hard to maintain a steady pace of questions directed at the suspect. (108)

In some ERISPs, there was an apparent fluidity between interviewer and partner roles.

In the second interview of this suspect, the detectives exchanged roles. The interviewer in ERISP I became the partner in ERISP II and vice versa. (003)

It must be acknowledged that a more active role for partners may be problematic unless there is a clear understanding between colleagues. In a number of interviews (e.g. 105), the primary interviewer appeared to be a little offended when the partner asked more than a few clarificatory questions. If too little involvement could be read as unhelpfulness, too much could be read as criticism of the primary's performance.

Towards the end of most ERISPs, the interviewer would look at the partner to signal or ask if he/she had additional questions for the suspect. The partner then did one of three things: (a) he/she did not ask any questions; (b) he/she asked a few questions; (c) he/she asked a longer series of questions. Tension between interviewers most often appeared to develop in situations (a) and (c). If the partner did not ask any questions, this could be because the interviewer covered all the ground and there was nothing more to ask. However, it could be taken as a sign that the partner was uninterested in the interview or was uncomfortable to ask questions (as in the case of some probationary constables). If the partner asks a long series of questions, he or she was more likely to be seen as either responding to a perceived major inadequacy in the primary interviewer's approach and suggesting that the interview could be 'saved' by the partner's further lengthy questioning. The approach least likely to cause tension between interviewers is circumstance (b) in which a few questions were asked by the partner. This suggested to the interviewer that the partner was interested enough to make some contribution to the interview and to be part of a team.

In 29% of ERISPs in which a partner was present and visible, he or she prompted the interviewer during the recording of the ERISP. The majority of prompts were made by partners non-verbally. Most frequently, the partner wrote a message on paper and showed it to the interviewer. Other prompts that were used included: eye gestures; signals in which the partner pointed to paperwork; and a word stated aloud by the partner as a cue, as in 121, when the partner said 'caution' to remind the interviewer. Hand waving or holding up a finger were used occasionally to get the interviewer's attention. Partners were also seen pointing to the interviewer's manual on the table and performing a charade to prompt the interviewer to ask the suspect to speak more loudly. Head nods, facial gestures and pointing in general were used as well. In a small number of interviews, the interviewer suspended the interview to allow for him or her to confer in private with the partner. Consequently, data presented above on questions and prompts understate the contribution by the partner to interviews.

The manner of partners as a group was narrower in range than that of interviewers. While all interviewers were heard speaking and asking questions and were seen interacting with the suspect, almost one third of partners remained mute throughout the interview. Such partners often appeared bored, yawning, picking nails, cleaning ears, or staring blankly at the ERISP machine. Also, partners who were heard questioning the suspect, by virtue of their role in the interview, often focused on gaps in earlier questioning, and consequently could appear more pedantic in manner than the interviewer.

Table 3.4   The predominant manner of Sample 1 partners

Predominant manner	Partners (N=123) %*
Neutral/matter of fact	37
Busy	20
Alert/interested	12
Bored/disinterested	11
Concentrated	6
Confident	3
Tired	3
Other**	7

*   Figures do not total 100 because of rounding.
** Other included: friendly (3 cases); awkward (2 cases); inexperienced, nervous, angry, and persistent (1 of each). 12 ERISPs were one-officer interview. Data were unavailable because of technical failure or camera or focus in 40 ERISPs: numerous partners sat with their back to the camera or out of camera view.

In more than one third (37%) of sample 1 ERISPs, the partner's manner for most of the interview was neutral or matter of fact. Thirteen partners (11%) appeared bored.

> *The partner's intonation sounds bored, as though he is asking questions to complete some bureaucratic form rather than questioning a suspect. (084)*

> *The partner appears to be bored and uninterested. He has one elbow on the table, leaning his chin on his bent arm. He fidgets briefly with the wires of the radio [exhibit]. He stares ahead and stares at the interviewer's notebook. He is seen rubbing his eyes. He does not have any questions for the suspect. (112)*

During the first part of the interview the partner appeared bored. He sat yawning, with his mouth wide open. He examined his fingers, his finger nails and at times bit his nails. After his partner stared at him, he appeared to try to suppress these yawns and when one did emerge, he covered his mouth discreetly. And, rather than focusing on his nails, eye contact was made with both the suspect and the interviewer more frequently than at first. (037)

The partner, a young constable, seemed uncomfortable during the interview. Unlike many other partners, he did not take notes. At the beginning of the interview he looked tired and sat biting his fingernails. He continued to check his fingernails. In the middle of the interview he rubbed his eyes before leaning back from the table with his hands behind his head. (106)

3.3   Suspects

3.3.1   Demographics: gender, age, and employment

The vast majority of suspects were male: 86% in sample 1, 88% in sample 2. (The suspect's sex was unknown in 6 defective sample 1 ERISPs.) Reflecting the more serious nature of the matters in sample 2, there was a lower proportion of juveniles (13%) than in sample 1 (21%). In each sample about a third of suspects were in their twenties.

Four-fifths (134) of sample 1 suspects were asked about their employment status. Of these, 45% (60) were unemployed, 30% (40) were employed, and the rest were students, receiving benefits or pensions, or in prison or juvenile detention. Questions about employment were used for general information gathering, but also in some cases as a basis for questions about illegal income generation. In this respect, there was a significant overlap between introductory demographic questions and investigative questions: a suspect who began answering apparently innocuous questions about their employment status could find that this turned quickly to more serious matters.

Table 3.5   Suspects' age*

Age	Sample 1 (N=167) %	Sample 2 (N=87) %
10 – 15 years	10	3
16 – 17 years	11	9
18 – 19 years	9	7
20 – 29 years	33	36
30 – 39 years	11	16
40 – 49 years	9	16
50 – 59 years	2	3
60 – 69 years	1	3
70 – 79 years	1	1
Unknown: not asked	3	5
Unknown: interview introduction not taped	2	0
Unknown: poor tape quality	7	0

*   Figures do not total 100 because of rounding.

3.3.2 Suspects' response to questions

Language used in the caution questions at the beginning and end of the interview appeared to be problematic for some suspects. Concepts such as 'offer of advantage', 'inducement' and 'free will' needed detailed explanation on occasion (although they seldom received it satisfactorily). Some suspects' lack of understanding was demonstrated by their 'inappropriate' response to certain questions. For example, some suspects who are apparently habituated to agreeing with police reply 'yes' when asked if a threat, promise or offer of advantage had been made to them. In 225, the interviewer calmly replied: 'I'll ask that again'. The suspect accepted the corrective prompt, and answered 'No'. By contrast, in 240, the suspect became understandably confused when the interviewer, who was trying to adopt a pre-ERISP exchange, asked him 'Do you agree that I asked you if any threat, inducement or promise had been offered?' The suspect replied 'No', apparently referring to the making of a threat, inducement or promise, not to the asking of the question. It could, of course, be that these suspects meant what they said, and were trying to complain about their treatment. However, there was nothing in their demeanour or subsequent responses to suggest that this was the case.

Similarly and not surprisingly, the use of legal terminology caused some problems, as in these examples:

> The partner asks the suspect what his 'intention' had been when he took the item. The suspect needs clarification of what he is being asked. (156)

> The suspect, a Year 10 school student, was uncertain whether she had 'assaulted' the complainant. She had agreed earlier in the interview that she had held R's leg and R had fallen to the ground. She denied that she had kicked R in the head. But later in the interview when the legal phrase 'assault' was used by the interviewer, the suspect was uncertain whether or not she had assaulted R. This remained unclear to the suspect at the end of the interview. For example, the interviewer asked:

> Q: You are telling me that at no stage you assaulted her?

> A: Is touching her part of it?

> The interviewer then asked the suspect if in her opinion she assaulted R. The suspect answered, 'No, not really'. The suspect, in response to the next challenging question which referred to what other witnesses had seen, stood and demonstrated, 'I was holding her with pressure.' She knew what she did, but did not know whether, legally, this constituted an assault.

> Q: It was a very serious assault against this young lady. You were there at the time and I believe you were involved in it. What have you got to say about that?

> A: I don't think I did anything. (032)

In McConville et al.'s terminology, these were 'legal closure' questions, attempts to get a suspect to adopt an incriminatory account of action without understanding the implications of doing so (1991:69–71). This example shows how matters may be less controlled by police and more complicated than McConville et al. suggest. The officers could have obtained an account of the suspect's actions and intentions in her own words which would have been incriminatory. However, the suspect appreciated the implications of the interviewer's introduction of the legal concept: this made her provide an account which constituted a denial. The attempt to 'legalise' the suspect's account was counterproductive in this instance.

Poor interviewing skills prompted some misunderstanding. Occasionally the interviewer's question was ambiguous:

> *The three questions asked in a row by the interviewer that the suspect found difficult were:*
>
> *Q: Do you agree that Constable D and I first spoke with you about 10.15 am today?*
>
> *A: Yes.*
>
> *Q: Can you tell me what happened? (The suspect remained silent.)*
>
> *Q: When we came and spoke to you, do you recall what happened then?*
>
> *When the interviewer asked 'What happened?' was he referring to what happened when police spoke to the suspect or to the allegations for which the police were called to the suspect's address? The last question was even more confusing in light of the suspect's non-response to the previous question. (109)*

The most common misunderstandings stemmed from the enduring police tendency to use excessively formal language and sentence construction:

> *Q: Can you tell me your movements on [date]?*
>
> *A: Do you mean what happened?*
>
> *Q: Yes. (143)*

The use of such stilted language indicates the significance of the occasion and the authority and status of the questioner. However, it is increasingly recognised that such symbolism is counterproductive if the suspect does not understand what she or he is being asked.

While some officers 'attended an address' where they 'executed' a search warrant and 'seized' property, others went to a unit where they carried out a search and found some property which they took to the station. Nothing is lost (and much is to be gained) by speaking plainly.

In one ERISP, the suspect mocked the interviewer by aping police language in his replies:

> *Q: Can you tell me where you got that cheque from?*
>
> *A: I obtained them from an unknown person or persons. (057)*

Further examples of 'police-talk' are discussed on pages 196–196, below.

We attempted to assess suspects' understanding of the questions which they were asked. By necessity, this involved subjective judgment based on how often the suspect had difficulty. Such difficulty was, for example, signalled by the suspect asking for a question to be repeated or explained, or answering in a way that suggested misunderstanding.

A suspect's pause before answering was not considered an indication of difficulty. Although that may have been the case, it may also have been that the suspect was using the pause to think about and prepare a response rather than think about and try to understand a question. Secondly, on occasion the interviewer did not wait for the suspect to hesitate or to ask for clarification of a question before rewording the question or explaining what was being asked. As a result, it remained unknown whether the suspect understood the original question or not.

> *Twice the interviewer rephrased questions when the suspect did not answer almost immediately. For example, he asked, 'Did she transfer it (referring to a wallet) to anything else after that?' When the suspect hesitated, the interviewer asked the leading question, 'Did she put it in the baby carriage?' Had the interviewer given the suspect more time to answer, would she have had difficulty with the original question? (157)*

Thirdly, in a few interviews a support person became involved in questioning in a way that did not allow proper assessment of whether the suspect had understood a question.

> *When the suspect hesitated or when his mother anticipated some difficulty, the latter would intervene. For example, when the interviewer asked one question, the mother rephrased that question immediately. The mother's control over such 'interpretation' did not allow assessment of how much the suspect understood himself as she would interject without his asking for assistance or even before he hesitated. For example,*

Q: Do you know the address at all of the house?

MOTHER: The house you broke into. Do you know where it is?

The suspect then answered the question. (103)

Fourthly, some interviews were overburdened with closed questions that simply required a yes/no response: the structure of this type of questioning restricted the opportunity to assess the suspect's understanding of what was being asked. A suspect's responses may be unreliable if closed questions are used carelessly.

Finally, it was recognised that some suspects' inappropriate response or request for a particular question to be repeated were merely examples of a mode of speech:

Q: What were your movements on 14th May?

A: The 14th May? My movements? I woke up, had brekkie and went to court. I told Mum what had happened and stayed home since.

Q: What time did you get home from court?

A: From court? ...

Q: And what did you do that evening?

A: That evening? Just stayed home and smoked the funny stuff. (160)

On other occasions such responses, 'echo questions', suggested that the suspect understood, but sought to evade, the question. Sometimes, this made the interviewer focus questions more sharply, as in this example from the same suspect who echoed questions increasingly as the strength of the police case against him unfolded during the interview:

Q: How do you survive on $20 a fortnight?

A: How do I survive? What do you mean, how do I survive?

Q: How do you live?

A: How do I live?

Q: How do you afford all this marijuana? (160)

With these reservations about the subjective judgment required, we assessed how often sample 1 suspects had difficulty understanding questions. As indicated in Table 3.6, more than half (59%) of the suspects did not appear to have any difficulty understanding questions.

More than one third of suspects (39%), however, did appear to experience at least some difficulty understanding some questions.

Table 3.6   Suspects' understanding of questions

How often the suspect appeared to have difficulty understanding questions	Suspects (N=152) %
Always	1
Most of the time	1
Some of the time	37
Never	59
Undecided	2

It was undecided whether or not three suspects had difficulty understanding any question. In 082, it was noted that understanding was not the real issue:

> *It is not that the suspect has trouble understanding questions per se. The problem is that he appears to be asleep or almost asleep.*

Similarly, some answers from another suspect could not be deciphered, but it was not clear whether this indicated she had not understood the questions asked or she simply had difficulty communicating her answers. Lastly, it was not clear whether another suspect repeatedly asked, 'What do you mean by that?' because he did not understand a question or as a means of cockily provoking the interviewer.

Two suspects in sample 1 who always had difficulty understanding were, respectively, a person with significant intellectual disability (027) and a person whose understanding of English was very poor (002). Some suspects who had difficulty understanding most or some of the time included others with mental illness or intellectual disability, who were affected by alcohol or other drugs, who were juveniles, or who were from non-English speaking backgrounds. While recognising that these characteristics may have impacted on comprehension of questions, they did not fully explain the difficulty that suspects appeared to experience with some questions rather than others. When the focus was shifted from the suspects to the questions, it became apparent that problems originated more from the nature of the questions than from specific suspect characteristics: suspects without these characteristics also had problems with these questions.

3.3.3 The suspect's manner

Claims that police have to deal constantly with suspects who are uncooperative and antagonistic have been found elsewhere to have little foundation (Dixon 1997:ch6). In fact, surprisingly few are obstructive or difficult. In collecting data here, we attempted to capture the suspect's *predominant* manner during the interview while recognising that many suspects could be seen experiencing a variety of moods and behaviours.

Table 3.7   The predominant manner of sample 1 suspects

Predominant manner	Suspects (N=158*) %
Cooperative	49
Awkward/ difficult to interview	18
Cocky/ self-assured	11
Remorseful/ fearful	6
Depressed	3
Nervous	3
Light-hearted/ amused	2
Angry	2
Relaxed	1
Talkative	1
Other	3
Undecided	2

*   Excluding 17 cases in which the video image was absent or inadequate. Figures do not total 100 because of rounding.

Our analysis here is inevitably based on subjective interpretation. For example, in 240 the suspect was superficially polite and cooperative, but appeared to be lying (denying a break and enter at which his fingerprint had been found).

In half of these interviews (49%) the suspect was predominantly cooperative. In a further 18%, the suspect was awkward or difficult to interview: this includes suspects whose personal characteristics rather than their response tactics made them difficult to interview. In only three ERISPs was the suspect angry. Baldwin's study reported 74% cooperative/submissive, 6% remorseful/tearful, 7% cocky/self-assured, 14% awkward/difficult to interview (1993:332). The problem with both our and Baldwin's classification is that they understate the significance of combinations. For example, the suspect in 097 was cocky, but also fully cooperative. A suspect might be awkward, but still cooperative, and so on.

As was the case for the sample of interviewers (see above), we examined whether the suspect's manner changed during the course of the ERISP. Suspects were more likely than interviewers to change. This was due particularly to the fact that (as detailed below) a number of suspects appeared to be affected by alcohol or other drugs at the time of questioning. It was assumed that this was responsible for some suspects' mood change. In 22% of interviews, the suspect's manner appeared to change.

> *The suspect was apparently affected by marijuana during this interview and showed mood changes. He was laughing aloud at the beginning of the interview. In the middle of the interview the constable asked him a 'Do you agree ...?' question about having conducted a notebook interview earlier that afternoon. The suspect replied, 'No words can tell you how I feel now. I feel like crying'. And cry he did, only to be laughing again a few minutes later. (126)*

Other examples included suspects who initially were tired at the beginning of the interview, but became alert by the end, as well as the reverse situation of suspects who were alert initially, but appeared exhausted at the completion of questioning. Other suspects became increasingly relaxed in mood as the interview progressed.

> *The suspect became less nervous as the interview progressed. This was heard in his speech pattern. Initially, his words sounded clipped and disjointed. By the end of the interview words were being strung together in complete sentences. (104)*

Others, in turn, became increasingly nervous.

> *The suspect appeared to be more stressed during the second, confrontational part of the interview. He gestured more, he moved more, he held his hands over his mouth. (130)*

A few suspects appeared depressed as an outcome of an apparent mood change.

> *Initially the suspect appeared to be apprehensive. He paused in particular when asked about M (one of the two alleged co-offenders). Then he began to answer 'Don't know' to questions. After being told that M had been charged (which the suspect said he did not know), he continued to pause at times, but appeared more depressed than apprehensive. When the partner questioned him, the suspect did not remember some information that he had already provided. However, he continued to be depressed. The mood change went from apprehension to depression. (063)*

A few became remorseful as the interview evolved, as in the following example.

> *The suspect initially approaches questions in a somewhat matter-of-fact way ... then there is a four minute break. The suspect continues the interview, but is crying. She cries briefly while asked about her partner's involvement at other times when the baby was injured. At 2.11 pm the interviewer again cautions the suspect and spends the remainder of the interview focusing on how the suspect responded to known injuries to the baby. The suspect becomes increasingly upset and, when asked if she has anything else to say, she cries continually while blaming herself. (039)*

More commonly, however, sample 1 suspects who did show change in mood were likely to become annoyed or angry as the ERISP progressed.

> *His voice becomes louder. He becomes argumentative. He shows frustration that police will not accept his offer to pay 'the lady' for the panel van window and finalise the whole problem. At the end of the interview he appears to be angry. He tells the interviewer, who asked him if he had anything more to say,*

> *'Nothing, but I'm innocent. And I wish to go home. And that is all.' (010)*

In another interview,

> *The suspect becomes visibly angry at the end of the interview. This outbreak from the suspect occurs after he was told by the interviewer that the interviewer wanted to take his shoes and jeans for forensic testing. The suspect responded,*
>
> > *'You make problem to me too much. No good. No good. You make me problem, you know. Everybody say, you know, my family say, shy, but, you know, seriously, I'm a good boy, but, you know, you don't believe me, all right, OK?' (052)*

In 158, the suspect showed annoyance:

> *In the second interview the suspect became annoyed at the end of the interview when, after telling police his version of events in relation to his possession of his neighbour's property, the interviewer told him that he was to be charged with a break and enter at the conclusion of the interview. Then when asked if he wanted to make a hand-written statement the suspect said he could not spell. His answers became curt, snappy. (158)*

While this variety of responses deserves mention, it should not divert attention from the most common response displayed by suspects. They are cooperative for good reasons. They are on police territory and many are well aware that the criminal justice process sanctions resistance through the availability of bail, the level of charge and, ultimately, the severity of sentence.

3.3.4 The suspect's response to allegations

Suspects were confronted with a total of 395 alleged offences in sample 1 ERISPs (see Table 2.2, above). This section considers the suspects' response to each allegation and the timing of any confession or admission.

Table 3.8 (below) shows that while a quarter of suspects in sample 1 made a full confession, half of the sample made partial admissions (i.e. they made some self-incriminating statements not amounting to a full confession to the offences being investigated). This distribution is affected by a particular characteristic observed in relation to drug investigations. In interviews concerning illegal drug cultivation or possession, some interviewers went on to question the suspect further about supplying drugs. However, others did not do so, irrespective of the amount of drugs involved. It may be that suspects in these cases would have faced further interviews about supply offences. However, this seemingly random inclusion of supply allegations reduced the number of full confession interviews. While many suspects admitted possession offences, none admitted supplying drugs. A suspect's response to allegations was affected by the interviewer's tactics and style. Put simply, the wider the range of allegations made by the interviewer, the less likely he/she was to elicit a full confession from the suspect.

Table 3.8   Confessing, denying and staying silent

Response to allegation(s)	Sample 1 (N=175) %	Sample 2 (N=87) %*
Full confession from the outset	24	22
Full confession during the course of the interview	2	2
Partial admissions	50	16
Denial throughout	12	53
Refusal to answer questions	4	3
Refusal: other**	1	0
Unknown or N/A***	7	3

*   Figures do not total 100 because of rounding.
**   Cases of 'Refusal: other' were one suspect who refused to be interviewed electronically, but agreed to participate in a typewritten interview; and one suspect who told police she wanted to remain silent, but who then proceeded to answer questions about her property, its fence boundaries, who resided on the property and the like.
*** This includes both cases of mechanical failure and those where the allegation was so unspecific that it was not possible to categorise the suspect's response.

The notable feature of these results is how few suspects 'crack' during the course of interview, shifting from denial to full confession. This is consistent with the findings of other researchers (Baldwin 1993; Moston & Engelberg 1993). If suspects are going to confess fully, they will do so. This will very rarely be the result of police interviewing (at least interviewing captured on ERISP). Research in England has consistently shown that the crucial factor is the strength of evidence collected in pre-interview investigative activity (Williamson 2006:147). Many suspects will stick to their denials. Indeed, more than half of suspects in sample 2 did so. The increase in denials at the cost of partial admissions between samples 1 and 2 is less significant than it appears: it is a function of the greater seriousness of cases in sample 2, and the incidence in sample 1 of cases in which suspects admitted drug possession while denying supply.

In one quarter (25%) of sample 1 ERISPs, the suspect made a full confession. Ninety-seven per cent of full confessions were made at the outset of the interview, as in the example below.

> *Straight confession from the outset: in reply to the first question the suspect said, 'Yeah, I took it'. (120)*

In half of sample 1 ERISPs, the suspect made a partial admission to the allegation(s) raised by the interviewer. Again, partial admissions were more likely to be made from the outset of questioning rather than during the course of the interview. In 12% of sample 1 ERISPs, the suspect denied the allegation(s) throughout the course of questioning.

While many suspects made either a full confession or partial admission from the outset of the ERISP, the crucial issue of how they came to do so was beyond the scope of the present study. However, almost three quarters of sample 1 suspects (see Table 2.9, above) were known to have been interviewed by police before ERISP recording began. It would be naïve to think that there was no relationship between 'preparatory' interviewing and early confessions.

3.3.5 Silence

Contrary to entrenched police mythology, very few suspects refuse to answer questions. The exercise of the 'right to silence' by suspects during police interrogation has long been the subject of controversy. In 1994, the right to silence in England and Wales was drastically reduced by the Criminal Justice and Public Order Act. Surrounding this legislative change was a vigorous dispute about how often the right to silence is exercised and how quantitative assessment should be made (Dixon 1997:ch6).

Like other researchers (McConville & Hodgson 1993; Leng 1993), we found that identifying and counting instances when the right to silence is exercised is a more difficult and subjective task than many may expect. There is considerable potential for expanding or contracting the category of silence, as close examination in some variations of non-response reveals. While superficially trivial, these matters are of considerable potential significance when policy makers seek empirical evidence on which to base possible legal change. The most contested area is when a suspect answers some, but not all, questions.[1] The way in which some interviewers in our samples questioned suspects made it difficult to determine whether or not the suspect should be regarded as having refused to answer a specific question. For example, one interviewer's mode of questioning did not allow a reliable assessment of the suspect's response:

> *Strictly speaking, the suspect did not answer all questions that he was asked. But this was not due to him refusing. Rather, it was a product of the interviewer's questioning technique. Occasionally he asked two questions, back-to-back, without giving the suspect an opportunity to answer the first one before posing the second. In each instance, the second question essentially rephrased the first. While the interviewer's intention may have been to clarify the first question, the result could be recorded as a failure of the suspect to answer some questions. For example, the interviewer asked,*

> > *'Now, do you have any knowledge of the break, enter and steal offence that occurred at ... video shop? Do you know anything about that? (014)*

In another ERISP (087), the suspect, when asked if he wished to say anything about the allegation, replied 'No'. The interviewer then proceeded to ask a series of closed questions, all of which were answered. As the interviewer did not clarify the initial response, it was unclear whether the suspect initially refused to answer questions about the alleged offence or whether he simply indicated that he was prepared to answer specific questions, but not to make a general statement.

---

[1]   While the Evidence Act 1995 s89 (NSW), does not permit an unfavourable inference to be drawn from a refusal to answer one or more questions, such an inference may be drawn from a 'pattern of answering or conduct in answering — from evasiveness, selective answering or apparent fencing with the police to determine the extent of their knowledge' (Hunter et al. 2005:621–622, discussing relevant case law).

In some ERISPs, the suspect paused and the interviewer did not clarify whether the suspect was taking time to consider an answer or was refusing to respond.

Again the dilemma in interpretation was whether the suspect paused and intended to answer, but was asked another question before he could do so, or the suspect did not intend to answer. This was not clarified by the interviewer. (96)

This interview offered another example of the situation where: (1) the suspect paused when asked a question; (2) the interviewer asked another question without clarifying the reason for the pause; (3) it remained unclear whether the suspect at that stage of the interview was refusing to answer a question or whether he/she simply was hesitant and would have answered had he/she been given more time to do so. (109)

Other interviewers assumed that they knew why suspects paused. For example, one detective took the pause as a cue that the suspect did not understand the question and needed further assistance. This came in the form of more focused, closed questions:

The interviewer seemed to respond to the pauses as a cue (warranted or not warranted) to facilitate the answer by rephrasing the questions and leading the suspect to the type of answer being sought. For example, 'When you were with M, were you pushing anything?' became 'Was there a baby at the scene?' And, 'Did she transfer it [a wallet] to anything else after that?' became, 'Did she put it in the baby carriage?' (157)

Yet another interviewer treated the pause as a linguistic difficulty:

The suspect does not answer all questions. However, his non-responses are treated by the interviewer as English language problems, not as refusals.

Q: Let me ask you this question. Would you assist my, our, inquiries into this matter by taking part in an identification parade?

A: (No response.)

Q: Do you know what an identification parade is?

A: No. (52)

Another ambiguity in the assessment of whether the suspect refused to answer a question arose in sample 1 ERISPs in relation to some negative answers.

> *In the first ERISP when the suspect is asked if he could tell the interviewer where he got the cannabis from or when he got the cannabis, he said, 'No'. This 'no' was not clarified as either 'No, I don't want to tell you' (a refusal) or 'No, I can't tell you as I don't know', for whatever reason. (160)*

A small number of suspects who did not refuse outright to answer any question may have used 'I don't know' responses as a substitute for refusals. Some interviewers, in turn, did not clarify the meaning of their response.

A few suspects avoided answering in other ways. For example, in 082, the suspect replied to a question about the alleged offence by saying 'I'm tired. I'm very tired.' His fatigue may have been alcohol related, but this was not clarified by the interviewer.

> *The suspect did not refuse to answer any question, but neither did he answer them all. At the beginning of the interview, he did not respond to questions: he appeared to be asleep. The interviewer repeated one question, told the suspect to speak up, and proceeded to another question when the suspect did not answer. This was not so much a deliberate refusal to answer as an attempt to sleep. (82)*

It was obviously inappropriate to interview a suspect in these circumstances.

Unless interviewers clarify the suspect's intention in cases such as this, it is impossible to distinguish confidently between deliberate refusals to answer questions and other reasons for lack of response. Consequently, there is a category of 'undecided' cases in the following table. Subjective interpretation and classification of such cases could lead to expansion or limitation of reported instances of suspects using the right to silence, as occurred in the English controversies over the right to silence (Dixon 1997:ch6).

Table 3.9   The number of sample 1 ERISPs in which the suspect refused to answer one or more questions about the alleged offence

Was a question not answered and this non-response was a refusal?	Interviews (N=175) %*
Yes, one question	3
Yes, some questions	10
Yes, all questions	3
Undecided	6
No refusal	67
Unknown	10

*   Figures do not total 100 because of rounding.

As this table indicates, while only 3% of suspects refused to answer any questions, 16% refused to answer at least one. Which figure attracts attention will depend on the interest and purpose of the reader. We define 'non-response' as either silence or a clear refusal to answer a question ('no comment'). We do not include evasive responses. Doing so would increase the non-response rate,[2] but it would involve subjective, even speculative, assessment of what is an acceptable answer to a question.

As Dixon (1997:ch6) argued, suspects' reasons for refusing to answer questions are more complex than is often assumed: attempted evasion of guilt is only one possible motive. Some suspects in our sample provided reasons for their non-cooperation. Twenty-six suspects were involved in the 28 sample 1 ERISPs in which there was at least one refusal to answer. Eleven of these offered reasons for their refusal. These were: the suspect had received legal advice to remain silent (2); it was not a convenient time to answer questions (1); the story had been told to the police previously and did not need to be repeated (2); the suspect did not know the answer (2); the suspect was

---

[2]   This was one of the means by which alarmingly high rates of suspects using the right to silence were produced in England and Wales before the Criminal Justice and Public Order Act 1994 (Dixon 1997:ch6).

concerned about possible negative repercussions (4); and 'Everything was done illegally' (1). This last suspect offered the Adopting Officer a list of complaints that accounted for his problem with the ERISP and his lack of cooperation with police:

(1) I don't want to be interviewed. (2) I shouldn't be here. (3) I have been taken against my will. (4) Was it a legal search? (5) Was it legal for him to draw his weapon on me? (6) Was it legal to stomp me on the back? (075)

Other researchers (e.g. Moston et al. 1992) have noted the significance of interviewers' often unskilful response when suspects refuse to answer questions. In our samples, interviewers' responses reflected the perceived importance of the refusal. In 016, the suspect's refusal was apparently considered significant, and the interviewer responded by changing tactics. The substance of the interview began with the suspect failing to answer an open question. The interviewer asked a second question, again unsuccessfully, as the suspect offered a response that avoided answering the question.

Q: Can you tell me what you were doing at that location tonight?

A: I walked past it. (016)

In response, this interviewer shifted to asking more specific, closed questions.

On other occasions, interviewers appeared understandably nonchalant about a refusal:

The interviewer did not appear concerned that one question was not answered in an interview that otherwise involved a full confession and included names of the co-offenders in two other break and enters. (067)

Some interviewers appeared to expect refusal, and phrased questions accordingly:

The interviewer seemed to anticipate that the suspect would refuse to give information about accomplices. He asked, 'Do you wish to tell me the names of the other persons in the car ...?' Other questions were worded in a more direct manner. (110)

From the wording of the interviewer's question, a refusal was anticipated. Indeed, the wording virtually prompted it. The interviewer asked, 'Do you want to tell us his name?' (131)

It is possible that officers had been made aware in pre-ERISP interaction that the suspect would refuse to answer questions about accomplices. Alternatively, it may be the result of their experience of similar suspects' unwillingness to answer such questions. However, it should be noted that many suspects (53% of sample 1) did offer police some information about or implicated another person.

A couple of interviewers in sample 1 responded to refusals by initially continuing with other questioning, but later returning to the topic of refusal, at the end of the interview, and attempting to gather the information then. In 137, the interviewer did so by using a different approach.

> *The interviewer asked directly for the fifth person's name. The suspect said, 'I'm not telling.' Then the interviewer asked for the name indirectly, 'When that car came to pick you up, who was driving it then? When you started driving, who was driving the car?' (137)*

In another ERISP the interviewer similarly used indirect questions to get around a refusal:

> *The interviewer continued to ask the suspect questions about 'time' but in a roundabout way. He asked the suspect, for example, to describe a sequence of activity that occurred before the alleged sighting of the suspect in a stolen car. But he did not ask at what time each activity had occurred. He did not ask 'how long' the suspect had talked with friends. (163)*

Most interviewers, however, responded to the refusal by simply continuing with questioning, asking about issues other than the topic of refusal.

> *They simply continue with questioning on other aspects of the offence. (011)*

> *The interviewer does not ask any further questions about the names of persons who the suspect was with, but continues to ask other questions about the incident. (008)*

Some interviewers suggested an alternative way of getting the suspect's account:

> *The interviewer pursues the suspect's request to 'write it down', cautions the suspect that he does not need to make a hand-written statement unless he wishes and then suspends the interview for*

15 minutes to allow him to write his version down on paper. He has the suspect sign and adopt the hand-written statement by asking 'Do you agree ...?' questions about it. This statement then becomes the focus of questions. (020)

If, however, the refusal concerned a matter central to the investigation, officers in sample 1 usually confirmed the refusal and terminated the interview. Only one interviewer in sample 1 continued to question the suspect after refusal in a manner that was problematic because of its unrelenting persistence.

The interviewers recognised that the suspect did not want to answer questions about the 107 cannabis plants found on her property. But when the suspect said that she was not even certain what had been found by police on her lot (initially police said that 'a number of cannabis plants' had been found), they took the opportunity to review what had been found in detail and to ask if the suspect wanted to say anything about each item found. She did not. However, this series of questions then led into another series of general questions about who lived with the suspect, how the suspect used the property (whether she walked around her lot), how some items (including a crossbow) came to be in her shed, etc. (151)

More problematic examples of attempts by officers to challenge a refusal to answer questions occurred in sample 2, and are discussed below in Chapter 5.

While some suspects refused to answer questions, others went to the other extreme: 9% in sample 1 provided self-incriminating evidence which went beyond the allegations raised by the interviewer. Most of these 9 suspects had made partial admissions, while three had made a full confession and a further three had made unswerving denials throughout the course of their ERISPs. Some unprompted self-incrimination was of a minor nature. One suspect told officers that he used heroin daily; one person stated the amount stolen was somewhat greater than that suggested in the allegation; another suspect said he did not hold a driver's licence. However, other self-incriminations were of a serious nature. One suspect confessed to a number of armed robberies. Another suspect told police that she had previously fought the girl whom she was now suspected of assaulting

I grabbed her head and slammed it against the wall. (032)

And yet another suspect mentioned that she had been a criminal for a long time. She added that when she did steal, she got rid of items right away (050). These examples of self-incrimination contributed to the total of 82% of sample 1 suspects who made some self-incriminating statement during the police interview.

3.3.6 Suspects and ERISP

Contrary to some of the fears expressed about the potential impact of ERISP (see Chapter 1), most suspects gave no indication that electronic recording affected their behaviour. Even in an exceptional case in which the suspect acknowledged that he was being recorded, the effect was not detrimental.

> *At one stage the suspect pointed to the (wall-mounted) camera and spoke to it directly.*
>
>> *'Admittedly I wasn't fucking blind, but I was a little intoxicated. Not fucking heaps, though, right? I still know what I was doing. (Pointing to the camera.) Get that for the record'. (004)*

It was clear that this suspect had had previous experience of ERISP interviews, and of their use in court proceedings:

> *When asked towards the end of the interview if he had known the victim before this incident in the bar, the suspect ranted on about him. He then commented that he didn't want to 'bag him' any more as that might mean to the judge that 'I am totally against this person'.*

Suspects' familiarity with police procedures and the unobtrusive nature of ERISP equipment appear to have minimised any impact on suspects' responses. There was no evidence in our research of suspects who were intimidated or inhibited by audio-visual recording.

If a suspect refuses to participate in an electronically recorded interview, police should attempt to record this refusal. Some suspects refuse even this level of participation. The difficulties which non-cooperative suspects create for people were lessened somewhat by the NSW Court of Criminal Appeal's decision in *R v Sophear Em*.[3] A suspect in a murder inquiry refused any participation in a recorded interview, telling police 'I'm not going to say anything to you if you

---

3   [2003] NSWCCA 374.

turn that on. I don't want to look like a dickhead'. After releasing him without charge, the investigating officers wore concealed recording equipment when they interviewed Em in a park. His confession was held to be admissible, even though it would not have been made had he known he was being recorded. The deception by the officers did not constitute unacceptable unfairness.

3.3.7 Suspects, or victims/witnesses?

By the end of some interviews, the interviewee was no longer (if he or she ever had been) a suspect. For example, the interview in 094 concerned a fire in the interviewee's garage. It soon became clear that he had an alibi and no motive — on the contrary, the business was doing well, and two cars which were destroyed were uninsured. There was also a pattern of break and enters followed by fires in the area. The interviewer did not even bother to have the interview adopted, finishing with the words 'That's it mate. We'll just seal this master copy.' Presumably the interviewee was not under arrest — there was certainly no evidence of reasonable suspicion to justify it — and this interview was taped with the possibility in mind that some evidence of wrongdoing might emerge.

By contrast, in 039, the interviewees went from witness (of child abuse by her partner) to suspect (of child neglect or complicity in assault). Of course, these categories are not mutually exclusive. In assault cases such as 054 and 101, the interviewee came to be considered as a victim of assault: however, this did not preclude them from also being considered as suspects. They had been involved in drunken arguments involving violence on both sides. Cases such as these may well not result in charges: particularly in 'domestics', apprehended violence orders may be more likely. Other outcomes may be possible: for example, in 102, the suspect had arranged to return property to the victim.

3.3.8 Aboriginal suspects

The over-representation of Aboriginal people is a defining characteristic of Australian criminal justice (ABS 2005). Concern about the special vulnerability of Aboriginal suspects in police detention has led to the introduction of specific provisions for their treatment.[4] Notably, an Aboriginal legal aid organisation must be notified that an Aboriginal person is in custody, and a representative of that organisation may attend the interview. Nine suspects in sample 1 were identified as being Aboriginal, primarily by the attendance of an Aboriginal support person. There may have been others who were not so identified. Five of these nine were juveniles. One was the youngest suspect in our samples, aged 10 years. Three were 15 years old and one was 16. The remaining four were adults (21, 23, 29 and 36 years old). One ERISP had been recorded in Sydney, at Liverpool Police Station. The remaining interviews were conducted in country NSW locations: one at each of Casino, Inverell, Tamworth and Taree, and two at both Narrabri and Queanbeyan. Unfortunately, two of the recordings (160 and 157) were of particularly poor visual quality.

The problems identified in interviews with Aboriginal people were problems which were also found in interviews with non-Aboriginal suspects. These included the controversial presence of a disruptive support person and the excessive use of 'Do you agree ...?' questions. However, it clearly must be acknowledged that factors shared with other suspects may nonetheless have a particular effect upon Aboriginal suspects.

One source of concern can, ironically, be lack of attention to the implications of 'welfare measures' for Aboriginal people. For example, Powell (2000:190) suggests that when an interviewer is faced with a silent Aboriginal suspect, he/she should ask, 'Why are you not talking? ... How can I make it easier for you to talk?' The latter is an inappropriate question for a police officer to ask *any* suspect, because it suggests the making of an inducement.[5]

3.3.9 Mental illness and disability

An unmistakable lesson from the history of miscarriage of justice cases in England and Wales is that psychologically vulnerable suspects may make false confessions — with or without pressure from interrogators (Gudjonsson 2003:ch18). Consequently, measures must be taken to minimise this risk, including a requirement that mentally ill and

---

[4]   *Anunga* (1976) 11 ALR 412; *Dumoo v Garner* (1997) NTLR 129; Crimes Act 1914 s23(H) (Cth); Law Enforcement (Powers and Responsibilities) Act 2002 (NSW) s112; Law Enforcement (Powers and Responsibilities) Regulation 2005 Division 3.

[5]   See Evidence Act 1995 (NSW) s85(3)(b)(ii).

intellectually disabled people should not be interviewed in the absence of a competent support person.[6]

It was not feasible to identify all suspects in our samples who suffered from mental illness or intellectual disability. Other studies indicate that such disability would be identified by an expert in up to a quarter of suspects (Gudjonsson 2003). The need to assist police to identify intellectually disabled suspects so that they can be accompanied during interview by a support person will be discussed below. The potential problems are illustrated by notes on one case (027) in which a support person was not present despite a suspect's substantial (and evident) incapacity.

This suspect appeared severely mentally incapacitated, possibly from advanced alcoholism. Although asked to do so several times by the interviewer, he appeared unable to explain his condition. His confusion and incapacity were extreme. He was asked by the interviewer five times whether he agreed that he had been told he would be asked some questions. He finally agreed he had been asked. When asked his address, he did not seem to know it. He could not state his occupation or with whom he lived. He rubbed his eyes at times, had his hands on his head and appeared upset. The suspect repeatedly said that, if the detective wanted to know something, he should ask his wife.

When the suspect gave an inappropriate answer to a preliminary question, the interviewer interrupted him by saying, 'Hang on. You are not answering my question.' He paused, looked away, and then repeated the question for the fifth time, in a raised, angry voice. At times he shook his head disapprovingly while the suspect spoke. As the interview progressed, the detective appeared to realise how severely incapacitated the suspect was. He calmed down and simplified his questions. However, this change did not affect the inability of the suspect to respond.

The suspect continued to be confused during the entire interview. He wanted to cooperate with police. He tried to answer questions. His wife could answer questions. He didn't know. He 'didn't know anything'. He strained. He agonised. He wanted

---

[6]   The Law Enforcement (Powers and Responsibilities) Regulation 2005 (NSW) refers to 'persons with impaired intellectual functions' cl24 (1) (b).

bail. At the end, he was mumbling pathetically when told he would be charged with attempted murder.

In another case (243), the suspect reported that he had brain damage and had attended a 'special school'. He could not read or write and had evident difficulty understanding the interviewers' questions. The interviewing officers tried unsuccessfully to determine the extent of his problem, but did not arrange for a support person to attend.

Similarly, officers appeared to be insufficiently aware of the need for caution in interviewing mentally ill suspects: in 206, a suspect displayed clear indications of paranoia, expressing fears that he was being followed and threatened, and that people whom he did not know were trying to kill him. No support person was present.

One of the difficulties here is, of course, that suspects may well not raise the issue of their disability or illness. On the rare occasions when a suspect did so, there was sometimes room for scepticism. Two suspects in sample 1 reported during questioning that they had suffered brain damage, but in both instances the reliability of this information was questionable. It may have been a technique to obstruct their interviews.

> *The two ERISPs conducted with this suspect ... show how obstructive a suspect can be when he/she chooses. ... Faced with 'Do you agree?' questions, the suspect again started to obstruct the interview. He could not remember. He gestured that he did not know in spite of being asked to respond verbally aloud. He remained mute at times. He said he had brain damage with short and long term memory loss. (075)*

> *The suspect appeared to be going through the motions of answering questions. He could 'not remember' many things. This, he explained, was due to being in a car accident that resulted in 'a class of brain damage which affects me memory'. However, the suspect also stated that he and his friends were wary of police. It was implied that this attitude also affected his willingness to answer police questions honestly. (142)*

So, while there may be scepticism when some suspects raise the issue of intellectual disability or mental illness, genuine sufferers may be unable or unwilling to do so. This suggests the need for special training for custody officers to help them to identify suspects who need the support of an independent person (and whose confessions may subsequently be regarded as worthless by a court if no such person is present). Research in England indicates that custody officers grossly underestimate (by a factor of 6) suspects' need for the presence of a support person or 'appropriate adult' (Gudjonsson 2003:68). While identification may be difficult, custody officers can improve matters greatly by the simple step of asking suspects who give any indication of vulnerability about their condition: Gudjonsson reports that this has had considerable success in London (2003:72).

3.3.10 Alcohol and other drugs

While numerous suspects in both samples were affected by alcohol and/or other drugs, quantification would again be both difficult and potentially misleading. Some interviewers did question suspects who appeared to be visibly drug affected during the interview about their drug use. However, it was unusual for them to do so adequately. Interviewers who asked whether the suspect was affected by drugs at the time of the interview were unlikely to seek information on a range of relevant issues: which drug(s) had been used; how much had been used, and when; and whether illegal drug use had been combined with medication and/or other substances, such as alcohol. Limited questioning meant that even though it may have been known that 'some drug' had been used by the suspect who was visibly drug affected, its effect on his or her ability to understand and answer questions was difficult to evaluate. Questioning by one interviewer exemplified this problem:

> *The suspect was visibly drug affected during the interview. At one stage he 'nodded off'. The interviewer roused him and asked:*
>
> *Q: You had some methadone this morning?*
>
> *A: I am a bit drowsy as I am on other medication as well.*
>
> *Q: But you feel ok to continue the interview?*
>
> *A: Yes. (114)*

The interviewer did not ask the suspect what other (legal or illegal) drugs he had taken, how much he had taken, or when he had taken them. It was unknown how much methadone had been consumed or how long ago this had occurred. The interviewer left the decision to continue the interview to a suspect who was manifestly drug affected. Similarly, in 203, the suspect's mother commented, he 'looks drugged out to me now, from his eyes'. This comment was simply ignored by the interviewer.

In another sample 1 ERISP, the interviewer chose not to explore the clear possibility that the suspect was significantly drug affected.

> *The suspect in this interview had his head leaning against the wall for much of the interview. He looked as though he was falling asleep some of the time. He paused between some answers. He spoke slowly, mostly in monosyllables. The interviewer never attempted to clarify the suspect's state. Was he intoxicated or drug affected, or both? Or was he showing disdain for police practices? The admissibility of evidence from this interview could have rested on the suspect's state at the time of the interview, but this matter was left unexplored by the interviewer. (145)*

Similarly, in 256, an Aboriginal woman who described herself as 'a junkie' hung her head down in a way that suggested she was 'nodding off' from time to time. However, the suspect was not asked about her drug use during the interview. In 286a, the suspect, who described himself to the interviewer as 'just a junkie, man' displayed unmistakable signs of 'hanging out'. Ten minutes into the interview, the detective told him that the interview could be delayed, but the suspect said he preferred to continue answering questions. At times, it seemed as if he would agree to anything in order to complete the interview. He did not even look at the exhibits being shown to him. Once again, the interviewer did not ask about the timing or quantity of drug intake, and left the suspect to decide on his fitness for interview. Only one sample 1 detective clarified the suspect's drug/alcohol state as a preliminary question (156).

The ERISP tape can be a useful tool for the defence in identifying some drug affected suspects whose words in an interview transcript might not indicate that the speaker was apparently half-asleep (e.g. 082). On the other hand, an ERISP 'may enable the prosecution to show that the behaviour of the accused (and the police) indicate that the police acted properly and that the suspect was fairly treated' (Anderson et al. 2002:287, citing relevant cases). The poor quality of many images in sample 1 reduced the utility of ERISP. However, the alternating image technology adopted in many sample 2 ERISPs is more helpful (particularly to suspects) in this respect.

In relation to the suspect being drug affected at the time of the ERISP, interviews fell into five categories. First, a number of suspects were visibly drug affected, and often acknowledged this:

> *I've had ten Rohies [Rohypnol] today plus me 'done [Methadone]. Mate, I go off in la-la land. (038)*

In a second group of ERISPs, it was debatable whether or not the suspect was visibly drug affected or whether an unusual display of behaviour should be interpreted differently, for example as alcohol use or as a mental health issue. Other suspects were not visibly drug affected on ERISP, but reported having used drugs prior to the interview. A fourth group of suspects were not visibly drug affected during police questioning, but these suspects reported that they were regular drug users, implying that there had been some drug use recently. Finally, some suspects admitted to offending in order to obtain money to purchase drugs. It was unclear what portion of these persons were drug affected at the time of questioning.

Suspects affected by alcohol were easier to identify, not least because of the greater willingness of suspects to refer to their consumption of legal drugs.

> *At the time of the interview the 17 year old suspect was intoxicated. This issue of how many beers he had consumed that day (with drinking having started at 9.30 am and the interview commencing at 11.36 pm) was addressed. The youth estimated that he had fewer than 20 beers. When he had 20 or more it made him 'spew' and as he was not 'spewing' he thought he had had 14 to 15 midi size beers. Regardless of what estimate of number of beers offered by this suspect, he appeared to be significantly affected by alcohol at the beginning of the interview in particular. His voice sounded hoarse and he spoke in a staccato mumble. (272)*

In 004, the suspect stated towards the end of the interview,

> *'I am a bit fucking pissed.' He said that he had consumed four schooners of beer and two Wild Turkeys. He described his condition earlier as being 'pissy ... Admittedly, I wasn't fucking blind, but I was a little intoxicated. Not fucking heaps though, right? I still know what I was doing'. (004)*

This suspect's comments illustrate another issue about drugs and offending: the fear of some legal, political and media commentators that criminals rely on their drink- or drug-affected state to evade responsibility is not borne out by cases in these samples. On the contrary, such suspects were keen to insist that they were in control of their actions.[7]

Swearing was often the sign of a drunken suspect: in 054, the suspect was overtly intoxicated and was difficult to interview as he would not elaborate or explain his answers. He answered in single words or brief sentences. For example,

Q: Could you tell me how did your day start today?

A: Shit.

As in the case noted above involving illegal drugs, some officers' attempts to check on the degree of intoxication were merely presentational. In 267,

the suspect was visibly and audibly drunk. His speech was slurred and his gestures suggested he was very intoxicated. He was interviewed less than two hours after an alleged robbery. He had spent the day in the park where he had been drinking with a group of about eight Aboriginal persons. (The suspect himself was not Aboriginal.) The suspect estimated he had consumed four litres of Moselle cask wine in the park. He assessed his condition at that time.

'I was pretty pissed. I wasn't sure what was going on.'

The interviewer did ask the suspect about his state of intoxication at the time of his arrest and immediately prior to that. But the interview had been in progress for 38 minutes before the interviewer (appearing belatedly to appreciate the need to address the issues) asked the suspect how he felt then, during the interview. The suspect's response was successfully controlled by a leading question:

Q: You totally comprehend what's being asked of you, do you?

A: Yes.

---

[7]   For a discussion of these issues, see VLRC 1986.

Similarly, in 275, an interviewer asked a suspect who was taking prescribed drugs for pain relief

It doesn't affect your ability to think?

However, while this was a leading question, its context was an appropriate investigation of the source of the suspect's discomfort (swelling from an ulcer), the medication in use, and its effect upon the suspect's thought processes. By contrast, several other interviewers (e.g. 276a) were aware that their suspects were regular illicit drug users and/or had recently used such drugs, but they did not ask any questions about any effect that drug use might have had on the suspect's ability to answer questions. Similarly in interviews such as 079, the interviewers made no effort on ERISP to elucidate the reason for the manifestly inebriated or drugged state of the suspect. In 127, the interviewer struggled through the adoption of a pre-ERISP notebook interview with a suspect who was heavily affected by marijuana: he told them that he lived 'with God' and got 'stacks' of dole money, laughed at the formalities, and pulled faces at the ERISP camera.

As in the case of illegal drugs, some officers inappropriately put the responsibility to decide if an interview should proceed on a suspect who was clearly alcohol-affected.

When the suspect commented that his answers could be affected by his state of intoxication, the interviewers looked at one another and simply continued with questioning. After a few more questions, the suspect was asked if he wanted to continue the interview. With the overt imbalance of power between police and suspect, the need for a suspect to be assertive in order to terminate an interview, and the possibility that doing so might be taken as an indicator of guilt, it is unlikely that most suspects would terminate an interview. The partner then advised the suspect to tell the interviewers if his answers were affected by alcohol. This 'advice' may have been seen by the partner as 'covering himself', but it seemed quite preposterous in light of the previous comment by the suspect that his answers 'could be' affected by alcohol. It was as though that response was being dismissed or glided over. And it treated the suspect as a person who could consider this option rationally, rather than having to make that decision in a drunken state. Later on, the interviewer again repeated the advice to the suspect that he could terminate the interview at any stage. While the interviewer was out of the room to find the Adopting Officer, the suspect fell into such a deep sleep that the partner had to shake his shoulder to arouse him. (146)

Taken in isolation, such cases may seem surprising. However, they have to be set in context of officers' (and courts') recurrent experience of dealing with people who are in some way drug-affected (and, similarly, intellectually disabled). From this perspective, normality has a different hue, and officers' lack of interest in the suspect's personal characteristics becomes more understandable. However, it is not acceptable, given the need for police interrogation to produce material which meets evidentiary standards.

The Evidence Act 1995 (NSW) provides that confessional evidence is not admissible unless 'the circumstances in which the admission was made were such as to make it unlikely that the truth of the admission was adversely affected'. In making this assessment, a court must take account of relevant factors, including 'any relevant condition or characteristic of the person who made the admission, including age, personality and education and any mental, intellectual or physical disability to which the person is or appears to be subject'.[8] There are also discretions to exclude a confession if 'having regard to the circumstances in which the admission was made, it would be unfair to a defendant to use the evidence[9] and to exclude improperly or illegally obtained evidence.[10]

Admissibility of a confession by a person who was affected by alcohol or another drug is subject to the Evidence Act 1995 (NSW) s85 which requires a court to take into account 'any relevant condition or characteristic of the person' in deciding whether the truthfulness of the admission was affected by the circumstances in which it was made. Intoxication or the effects of drugs should be considered in this context. The CRIME Code simply instructs officers to 'Defer questioning suspects affected by alcohol or drugs until they are no longer affected' (NSW Police 1998:23). In England, PACE Code C is more specific: 'No person, who is unfit through drink or drugs to the extent that he is unable to appreciate the significance of questions put

---

8   Evidence Act 1995 s85(2) and (3)(a) (NSW).
9   Ibid. s90.
10   Ibid. s138.

to him and his answers, may be questioned about an alleged offence in that condition' (12.3) (except in exceptional cases of need, for which special authorisation and reporting requirements are imposed). Officers are advised to seek medical advice on fitness for interview (Note 12B).

However, the real issue is not the wording of rules, but their enforcement. The NSW instruction appears to be a largely presentational rule which invites disobedience, not least because of the permissive attitude of NSW courts towards receiving evidence obtained from drug-affected suspects. For example, in *Esposito*,[11] the Court of Criminal Appeal agreed with the trial judge's decision to accept evidence of admissions from a suspect who, on the day of interview, had taken heroin, methadone, rivotril, and alcohol. Blood readings showed that she had 80 to 90 times the therapeutic concentration of clonazepam. Not surprisingly, there was expert evidence that her memory and cognitive ability were affected. By contrast, the English rule is at least inhibitory: officers know that there are potentially significant consequences of ignoring it.

3.4 NESB suspects and interpreters

An interpreter was present in three sample 1 and two sample 2 interviews. The need for interpreters was illustrated by 002:

> The suspect's limitation in the English language became apparent at the outset of the interview, when he was asked the preliminary questions. The interview acquired an almost farcical tone as it appeared the suspect (who was there to be interviewed about an assault) became confused both by the caution and by questions about the alleged assault. When he was asked by the interviewer, 'Have I threatened you in any way?' he responded, 'Yeah, I got threatened.' Some time was needed to clarify that the threats to which he referred were not made by the interviewers. Later, when the interviewer asked 'I haven't given you anything?', the suspect said, 'Me? Give it to who?' Then when asked, 'Have I?' by the interviewer, the suspect pointed, in apparent bewilderment, to his eye. When the partner tried to clarify the question by asking 'Did the constable said he will hurt you in any way at all?', the suspect appeared totally baffled

---

[11]   (1998) 105 A Crim R 27.

(perhaps confusing expected questions about the assault for which he had been arrested and this adapted preliminary question) and replied, 'I don't understand this question'. At this point, the interviewer decided to suspend the interview in order to find an Arabic interpreter.

The interview was suspended for two hours and 43 minutes while officers attempted to find an Arabic interpreter. This proved unsuccessful. The interview was resumed, with the interviewer saying 'The Arabic interpreter is no longer attending.' He then went through a briefer version of the preliminary cautionary questions with the suspect. The question about inducement and 'police threats' was omitted.

At the end of the interview, the Adopting Officer had to experience the problem of communicating with this suspect. His frustration was complete when it was realised that the ERISP audio tape had not been turned back on, and the procedure had to be repeated.

In this case, the interviewer tried sympathetically to communicate with this suspect: but the proper course was surely to arrange for the suspect to return for interview when a reliable interpreter had been identified. (Providing Arabic interpreters in Sydney should not be impossible.) Persevering was not only frustrating and time-consuming for all concerned: the answers given by the suspect would presumably be regarded legally as unreliable. Hunter et al. note several cases in which 'confessions have been excluded for involuntariness because their makers' poor grasp of English prevented them from understanding their right to remain silent' (2005:644). Similarly, in *R v Mohammed*, the Victorian Supreme Court excluded a record of interview in a murder case because of the suspect's problems in understanding and expressing himself in English. An unsuccessful attempt had been made to secure an interpreter's attendance: thereafter, the interviewing officers decided to go ahead with the interview rather than defer it until an interpreter became available.[12]

Similarly in 052, a potentially significant interview about apparently gang-related violence was compromised by the lack of an interpreter for a 21 year old suspect of Vietnamese background. The

---

[12]   Unreported, 1410/2004, 24 August 2004.

interview proceeded as a series of negotiations around the suspect's claimed inability to understand what was being asked (or perhaps his attempts to avoid answering). Interviewer and suspect talked back and forth until the interviewer was satisfied he had an adequate response. A brief example of such negotiated passages was this:

Q: Do you agree there we took possession of your father's car?

A: What do you think, yes or no?

Q: Do you agree we took your father's car?

A: Me? I'm not afraid, so ... It's up to you. You say yes or no.

Q: No, it's up to you. Did we take your father's car?

A: Yes, yes, yes.

The presence of an interpreter would have allowed the interviewer — and the ERISP's audience — to make a better judgment about whether the suspect understood the questions and the implications of the answers that he gave. The interview took place in the early afternoon: there appears to be no reason why an interpreter was not present.

A common problem is that people may be competent in everyday conversation in English, but not able to deal with more complex or unusual words and phrases which may be crucial in police interview. For example, in 215, it was difficult to assess the level of English fluency of this suspect. While he did use some colloquialisms and he did appear to be able to communicate his version of events, the term 'free will' caused difficulty. On one occasion, he said that he did answer of his own free will, but later he said that he did not understand what this meant. The interviewer had allowed the suspect to decide against having an interpreter

Q: Do you understand English, Mr X?

A: Yeah, but not that good.

Q: Do you want an interpreter?

A: Let's just see what we can do.

The interviewer may have regretted this when the suspect, at the end of the interview, claimed not to understand the meaning of free will. Similarly, in 250, assessing the Tongan suspect's standard of English comprehension was not easy. While he could converse with the interviewer about certain matters, he did not understand some key terms, such as the word 'promise' in the adoption sequence. It was not possible to tell whether this was due to language limitations, or to apparently low intelligence.

Only one suspect in sample 2 was accompanied by an interpreter. This interview (about an alleged sexual assault) demonstrated the difficulty of interviewing via an interpreter. Establishing rapport seemed quite unrealistic: simply achieving an adequate level of communication was difficult enough. For example, the interviewer followed up one response given by the suspect as a possible expression of guilt. The suspect said that when the complainant became upset and a passer-by stopped to talk with her, he, the suspect 'ran off'. The interviewer asked the suspect why he chose to 'run off'. At this point in the interview the interpreter interjected and said that there could be different meanings in Turkish for the word used by the suspect and first translated by the interpreter as 'ran off'. He could have meant that either he had 'run off' or that he had simply 'left' and she could not distinguish the difference in usage at this stage of the interview. The interviewer no longer proceeded with that line of questioning. Had the interpreter been less diligent, the suspect's answer might have been taken as an incorrect indication of guilt.

3.5 'Support persons', lawyers, and vulnerable suspects

At least one independent adult person was present during 31% of sample 1 and 24% of sample 2 ERISPS. Occasionally (three ERISPs in each sample), two such adults were present.[13] As Table 3.10 illustrates, half (50%) of adult independent persons present during both sample 1 and sample 2 ERISPs were family members, with mothers appearing most frequently.

The status of 11 independent persons in sample 1 remained unknown, primarily for two reasons. Most of the people in this category were introduced by the interviewer by name only. In a few instances even though the independent person did introduce him/herself by name and relationship to the suspect, what that person said could not be heard on the ERISP as he or she was seated away from the interview table and the ERISP equipment.

---

[13]   In addition, babies were present during two ERISPS: one was the son, the other the sister of the suspect.

Table 3.10   The status of independent persons

Status	Sample 1 (N=58) %	Sample 2 (N=24) %*
Family	50	50
Private lawyer	0	8
Flatmate/ friend	3	12
Interpreter	5	8
Youth or residential care worker	5	0
Custodial officer	2	4
Aboriginal legal or other representative	5	4
Salvation Army/ person with religious affiliation	7	4
Ambulance staff	2	0
Fire fighter	0	4
Sexual assault counsellor	0	4
Unknown	21	0

*   Figures do not total 100 because of rounding.

With the exception of the prison officers,[14] interpreters[15] and (very rare) lawyers whose role will be discussed below, these 'third parties' attend interviews in the role of what NSW legislation terms 'support persons'. As part of the statutory scheme introduced in 1998, detailed

---

[14]   It is worth noting that a defendant in our court sample had agreed to be interviewed by police only on the understanding that the prison officer's presence would protect him: 'If he was *not* there, they might try something. I've had them in the past trying to use the phone book or fist on me. They didn't break anything. I don't want to tangle with the young fellows any more.'

[15]   The custody manager's responsibility to arrange for an interpreter to attend an interview (or to contribute via telephone) is detailed in the Law Enforcement (Powers and Responsibilities) Act 2002 (NSW) s128(1).

regulations require some and permit other vulnerable suspects to be accompanied at interview by a 'support person'.[16]

We found that these 'support persons' play a marginal role in interviews. This marginality is largely a product of how police involve the support person in the interview. Interviewing officers generally attempt to control the support person's involvement by arrangement of the seating. Most support persons in sample 1 (62%) were seated behind the suspect. (In another 5%, the person was out of camera view.) Clearly, support for (or indeed any interaction with) a suspect is difficult when seating is arranged in this way. It was usually only when police interests were served by active third-party involvement (notably when he or she was an interpreter) that the person was seated at the table and able to interact with the suspect.

After introducing themselves at the investigators' request, most independent persons (62% in sample 1) said nothing. Seated out of the suspect's vision and away from the exchanges at the interview table, they simply observed and listened. Some may have been able to do no more than observe: in 095, the support person's answer to the interviewer's inquiry about his understanding of English was 'A little bit'. (Even this overstates the role of some: in 155, the support person appeared to be either asleep or trying to sleep throughout the interview.) Those who did contribute did so in various ways (see Table 3.11).

The CRIME Code requires the officer adopting an interview with a child to 'ask the support person whether the statement has been recorded accurately and whether it was made voluntary' (sic) (NSW Police 1998:33). This was not done in any sample 2 ERISPs. The nearest came in 203, when the interviewer, at the end of the interview, turned to the support person and said, 'Is there anything you want to ask?' The mother commented that her son 'looks drugged out to me now, from his eyes'. After the mother spoke, the interviewer continued with other matters and did not comment on or follow-up her remark.

---

[16] Vulnerable suspects are defined by the Law Enforcement (Powers and Responsibilities) Regulation 2005 cl24 as: children; persons who have impaired intellectual or physical functioning; Aboriginal people or Torres Strait Islanders; and people of non-English speaking background. Children may not waive the right to have a support person present (cl29).

Table 3.11 **The frequency of verbal communication type used by adult independent persons who spoke during the recording of sample 1 ERISPs**

Most frequent
Answers a question asked by the interviewer to the independent person
Inaudible comment
Somewhat frequent
Interprets for the suspect
Attempts to clarify for the suspect what the interviewer said
Asks the interviewer a procedural question
Assists the suspect in answering a mundane question when the suspect hesitates
Adds further information to the suspect's answer
Asks the interviewer's permission to answer a question on behalf of the suspect
Provides information
Tells the interviewer that the suspect has lied
Least frequent
Interjects a comment after asking the interviewer permission to do so
Answers a question asked of the suspect
Tells the suspect what to do
Informs the interviewer about the suspect's usual behaviour
Tells the interviewer how she felt at the time of the suspect's arrest
Initiates a question and asks the suspect this question
Asks the interviewer to confirm what the suspect is to be charged with

Some support persons assisted suspects by providing basic social or emotional support (e.g. 020, 074, 087, and 129). Simply being present in a situation dominated by police has potential significance. Their presence may help to assure a court that a suspect was treated fairly.[17] However, as the list above suggests, the minority of support persons who do take an active part in interviews go considerably further than the regulatory definition of the role as assisting the suspect, ensuring fairness, and identifying communication problems would suggest.

In general, officers appear to regard the role of support persons as being limited to witnessing the interview. The ERISP itself generally suffices for this purpose, but the support person may be of use to police when, for example, there is a break in recording. An illustrative example is 208:

> *The support person (SP) present during this ERISP was introduced as a 'friend' of the suspect. The woman was the mother of a former girlfriend of the suspect. During the recording of the interview there was no interaction between the SP (seated towards the back wall) and the suspect. After the audio tapes were changed and the suspect had verified that this procedure had occurred, the interviewer addressed the SP on the second and final occasion during the interview (the first occasion being her introduction). The interviewer asked the SP if his account of what happened during an interview break was accurate. The SP agreed that this was the case.*

Support persons may be able to facilitate communication between suspect and police. In 225, the 'associate' of the accused took a substantial part in the interview, answering questions and volunteering information about the suspect's business. The presence of support persons can assist police by facilitating communication with suspects (030, 083, and 055).

In some cases, they themselves provide or are asked to provide information (056, 093).

> *During the ERISP the interviewer himself asked the SP a question. After the suspect said he could not remember what the girl complainant had been wearing the day of the alleged sexual assault, the interviewer then asked the SP if she remembered what the girl had been wearing. The SP offered a description of the outfit as she remembered it. (093)*

---

[17] However, the inactivity of 'appropriate adults' has been criticised in some English cases (Zander 2003:265–269).

In 212, it appeared that the support person had been responsible for bringing the alleged offence to the attention of police. She was the suspect's sexual assault counsellor, and the suspect's confession had originally been made during therapy with this counsellor concerning his own victimisation. During one break in the interview, the counsellor told the interviewer that she wanted to say something to her. The interviewer asked her to leave the room with her. At the end of the break, the interviewer acknowledged that the two women had left the room to talk to one another, but the content of their conversation was not mentioned. This suspect attended a special school for children with learning difficulties, and also reported that he suffered from incontinence. It was not clear that the suspect's sexual assault counsellor was an appropriate support person. Similarly, in 208, the suspect lived on a disability pension as a result of a manic depressive condition: his support person was the mother of a former girlfriend, rather than anyone with expertise in counselling mentally ill people.

Some support persons may be disadvantageous to suspects: for example, support persons who had some apparent friendship (036) or affiliation (157) with police were not helpful to suspects. As Hodgson suggests, if the SP is ineffective, his or her presence may harm a suspect who 'may believe that she is being assisted and protected during police custody and interrogation when she is not' (Hodgson 1997:795). More worryingly, some support persons pressured the suspect to 'tell the truth' (156) or to make a statement to police, or told police that the suspect had lied (065). In 020, the suspect initially did not respond to police questioning about a robbery. His elder brother then intervened:

> SP: Does he have to say or can he write it down?
> Police: (to suspect) You don't want to say anything?
> SP: Write it down.
> Suspect: I'll write it down.

In others, the suspect was asked to provide information which was difficult to state in the presence of a family member (120, 044, and 103). In one particularly inappropriate case, the SP was also the complainant (056). Some interventions threatened the fairness of the interview. One support person challenged the suspect's account. In 216, the SP countered the suspect's assertion that he was drug-free by asking why he had been picking up clean needles. Some parents are harsher than the police. In 229, the mother of the youth who was present during the taping of this interview proved to be a controversial presence, ordering her son to name a person:

> *Q: The guy you spoke to, sitting in the passenger seat [of the stolen car], who is he? You've told me prior to the interview a nickname. What was that nickname you told me?*
> *The suspect went to speak, then paused.*
> *SP: You tell the truth.*
> *Q: All right. I told you before the interview you don't have to answer any questions. If you don't want to answer the question, just say, 'I don't want to answer that question.' Don't feel you have to answer any or all questions.*
> *SP: As a matter of fact, you do. And you tell the truth. Don't be a fool.*
> *The suspect told the interviewer the name of the person in the vehicle.*

This 15 year old's mother pressured him to 'name the name' of the youth in the car, regardless of his 'rights'. It was the mother whom the boy would be seeing every day at home and it was the mother who was adamant that he provide the name of the other youths. For her, telling the truth entailed answering all questions posed by the interviewer. The interviewer, in turn, did remind the youth that he could remain silent. However, the interviewer did not speak to the mother directly about any of her interjections. Similarly, in 103, the suspect's mother acting as SP intervened throughout the interview, putting police questions into everyday language, correcting his misunderstanding of the caution, answering questions (about co-offenders) herself, asking her son questions, and commenting critically on his behaviour. Finally, she guided him through during the adoption procedure:

> *The suspect did not state there was any problem. However, the adoption procedure was questionable as his mother at one stage shook her head to indicate to her son how he should answer ('No'). Also, the mother answered another question (Adopting Officer: 'Do you have any complaints to make?') at the same time her son did. Had this suspect had a problem with the interview, he would have needed to have been very assertive to state this in front of his mother who was answering on his behalf.*

However, the helpfulness to police of interventionist support persons should not be overstated. The officers in 103 were clearly uneasy and annoyed about the mother's interjections. Investigators may have to control support persons who seek to pressure suspects into answering in a way that could prejudice the admissibility of any subsequent confession. In addition, the presence of family members may make it difficult for some suspects to speak freely: for example, in 063, the suspect's reluctance to account for stolen money may have been due to unwillingness to admit to a drug habit in the presence of his father. In 257, the suspect's aunt was acting as support person. It appears that, at the end of the interview, she questioned his mens rea in relation to the offence: the interview was then recommenced with further questions in an attempt to resolve this. It is difficult to say who benefited from this intervention. In 225, the support person (identified only as the suspect's business associate) helped communication between police and suspect, directed police to documents in the suspect's possession, but then went on to answer some questions for the suspect, asking at one stage 'Can I barge in here?' Her presence provided both benefits and problems in a difficult interview.

Case 103 illustrates the problem in the context of a parent's role:

Initially the suspect (a 10 year old male) said he 'was not really happy' to have his mother present during the interview. The interviewer was forceful and told the suspect 'We have got to have a parent present'. During the remainder of the interview, the mother participated in various capacities (answering questions for her son, asking questions of her son, stating what charge he was guilty of, asking the interviewer for advice as to how she could stop him from hanging around other kids and how she could keep him home at night). Eventually, the interviewer interjected to stop the mother from speaking. (103)

In 120, the SP was involved: his son had stolen keys from him which he used to get access to a house belonging to the SP's friend, and to steal from it. This example also raises the issue of using an independent person to whom the suspect objects. In the English case of *DPP v Blake*, a confession was excluded because the suspect had objected to her father attending as appropriate adult.[18] An adult must

---

[18]   (1989) 1 WLR 432. Code C, note 1C now provides that 'If a parent of a juvenile is estranged from the juvenile, he should not be asked to act as the appropriate adult if the juvenile expressly and specifically objects to his presence.'

not just be present, but must be capable of carrying out the role of appropriate adult or support person.

Interviewing officers should be prepared to look for another support person if the suspect objects. When this occurs, the support person must be able to carry out the role. In 272, a juvenile was interviewed about an offence in which his parents were the victims. Consequently, a fire fighter from the local fire station was called in. He simply acted as an observer. Apart from responding to an invitation to introduce himself by name, his contribution was limited to this:

> *The interviewer turned to the support person.*
>
> *Q: That will be the end of it, mate.*
>
> *SP: Righto, mate.*
>
> *After the interviewer had left the room and they were alone, the suspect spoke to the SP for the only time during the ERISP. While he spoke (with a sound of disgust in his voice as he said the word 'this',) the suspect looked down at his hands.*
>
> *A: Did they get you from the Fire Station to come and see this?*
>
> *SP: Yeah.*

The use of such people may have been justified before the introduction of ERISP when they could usefully witness proceedings. That function is now provided by the ERISP. If support persons are expected to do more than simply observe, then people with no training or skills, or who have a relationship with the suspect should not be used in the role.

To anyone with knowledge of the criminal process in England and Wales, the most surprising aspect of third party attendance in NSW (apart from the virtual absence of lawyers) is how few social workers attend interviews. While PACE Code C defines 'appropriate adult' for children as including social workers (s1.7), there is no equivalent in the NSW regulation (cl.4). This is unfortunate, as the PACE provisions have encouraged the development of 24 hour social work teams in some areas of England who are able to provide experienced support for suspects and, indeed, assistance to investigating officers (Dixon 1990).

Interviewers responded to verbal comments or interjections by the support persons in sample 1 in a variety of ways. Nine interviewers simply ignored the comments made by the SP. One interviewer explained the interview procedure to the SP. Another interviewer in response to a verbal comment explained the role of the SP to the suspect, but did not address the SP herself. Four interviewers asked the

SP questions during the interview. One interviewer explained the nature of the allegation and investigation. Three interviewers maintained cordial professional interactions with interpreters during the interviews. Two interviewers asked the SP to refrain from commenting or getting involved in the interview.

These problems in the contribution of support persons to interviews are, in considerable part, due to failure to make clear to them at the beginning of the interview what their role should be. According to the Law Enforcement (Powers and Responsibilities) Regulation 2005 cl30, the custody manager

> is to inform any support person for the detained person that the support person is not restricted to acting merely as an observer during an interview of the detained person and may, among other things: (a) assist and support the detained person, and (b) observe whether or not the interview is being conducted properly and fairly, and (c) identify communication problems with the detained person.

This is based on a provision for 'appropriate adults' in PACE Code C Section 11.16, with two significant modifications. First, while PACE invites the appropriate adult 'to advise the person being questioned', the NSW regulation indicates a more passive role of assistance and support. Secondly, the support person in NSW is to be informed of their role by custody managers, while 'appropriate adults' under PACE are to be informed by the officer conducting the interview. The latter is surely preferable (so long as compliance is auditable via ERISP), as doing so is both more immediate and directly effective upon the relationship between support person and investigating officers. This approach adopted in NSW has attracted judicial criticism, with judges insisting that provisions designed to protect vulnerable suspects must be taken seriously by investigating officers, that the support person should play a significant role in an interview (preventing misconduct and assisting the suspect, as well as simply being a witness to what happens) and that police should advise support persons about their role in the interview.[19]

More generally, issues raised by support persons' attendance at interviews have been inadequately addressed in NSW. It is worth, therefore, considering Hodgson's overview of the issue in England and Wales (Hodgson 1997). As Hodgson argues, 'suspects require

---

[19] See *Phung and Huynh* [2001] NSWSC 115; *Tang* [2001] NSWCCA 210; Hunter et al. 2005:584.

safeguards for both the protection of their own interests and those of the court in securing reliable evidence' (1997:786). One key finding of the research on PACE is that it is blinkered to see rights for suspects as inevitably contrary to police interests (Brown 1997; Dixon 1997). If suspects' rights lead to issues being clarified and reliable evidence being collected, there are clear benefits to police.

There are three systemic problems in arrangements for support persons. The first comes in identifying a suspect as vulnerable: police are not trained to identify mental illness or learning disability, and consequently miss most (between 75% and 90%) suspects whom a professional would regard as vulnerable (Hodgson 1997:787–788). Secondly, 'once a suspect has been identified as vulnerable, an appropriate adult must be found' (Hodgson 1997:788). As noted above, calling in a fire fighter or a Salvation Army officer is no longer adequate. However, if police are to call appropriate support persons, the Government must make them available, and this seems inevitably to lead to the recommendation of social work support teams which was made above. Thirdly, 'there is a great deal of evidence to demonstrate that most … do not appreciate the nature of their role' (Hodgson 1997:789). Social workers and others with expertise in dealing with mentally ill and intellectually disabled suspects should have access to 'a broad training programme … covering the range of suspect vulnerabilities, in order to provide a core of "authorized" appropriate adults' (Hodgson 1997:795).

Courts need to be aware of the important role that support persons should be expected to play in police interviews. In England, Hodgson detects a trend in PACE case law away from strictness about rules on appropriate adults (Hodgson 1997:792–794). In the NSW case of *Helmhout*,[20] the custody manager did not carry out his legal duty to contact the Aboriginal Legal Service for an Aboriginal suspect. The NSW Court of Criminal Appeal ruled that, in exercising the statutory discretion to admit or exclude evidence obtained following such a breach, a trial judge should 'take into account the "gravity" of the contravention concerned' by considering 'the consequences of the contravention on the individual concerned'.[21] In principle, this seems commonsensical: a contravention might affect various individuals very differently, so the consequences should not be identical. However, in practice, the individual focus is soon blurred by assumptions and stereotypes:

---

[20] [2001] NSWCCA 372.
[21] Ibid., Ipp AJA at 12.

A contravention ... involving an Aboriginal youth, who does not have a good command of English, who has had no dealings with police, who has lived his entire life in, say, desert surroundings ... could well be severe. On the other hand, the consequences if the Aboriginal person is of mature years, has had many dealings with police and is not intimidated by the idea of being questioned by them and who, generally, may be regarded as a well educated, sophisticated and worldly wise person, are likely to be minimal.[22]

Unintentionally no doubt, the appellate judge invokes a distinction (which has caused such problems in Australian race relations) between 'real' rural Aborigines and culturally and racially diverse urban Aboriginal people. More generally, courts have to be very careful not to talk of considering individual characteristics while really distinguishing between groups which do and do not need the protection of legal rights. An unfortunate example was set by the English decision in *Alladice*[23] in which a suspect's knowledge of rights (from previous dealings with police) was found to be a reason for not excluding evidence after breach of legal advice provisions. Such decisions exemplify 'a proclivity towards announcing a healthy principle while, at the same time, proceeding to disregard it under a camouflage of legal niceties' (Zuckerman 1991:499).

Lawyers are marginal figures in the crucial early stages of the criminal justice process in NSW. When police power to detain suspects for investigative purposes was put into statutory form in 1997, a formal right of access to legal advice was provided. The custody manager must inform a suspect who is detained in custody that he or she may 'communicate, or attempt to communicate with a legal practitioner of the person's choice'. If a lawyer attends the station, he or she must be allowed to consult the suspect privately, attend any investigative procedure, and offer the suspect advice.[24] However, such rights are of little more than presentational value if no substance is provided in the form of legal aid and duty solicitor schemes. Neither is available in NSW police stations. Even if a suspect could afford a lawyer, the

---

[22] Ibid.
[23] (1988) 87 Cr App R 380. For a similar Australian decision (by the Victorian Court of Criminal Appeal), see *Percerep* (1993) 65 A Crim R 419.
[24] Crimes Amendment (Detention after Arrest) Act 1997 s356N, now Law Enforcement (Powers & Responsibilities) Act 2002 s123. See also CRIME Code, pp15–17.

profession is not organised to provide in-station advice at all hours. Offering the Yellow Pages to a suspect who asks for a lawyer is an empty gesture. The legislation simply gives statutory form to the common law 'right' to legal advice which, as the NSW Law Reform Commission reported 'lacks meaning in practice, translating into something like "if you have your own private lawyer, the police should not unreasonably deny you access to him or her"' (1990:124–125). If safeguards are not given the substance which would make them 'meaningful, realisable, and enforceable' (NSW LRC 1990:29; see also ALRC 1975:49–49), accusations of hypocrisy are hard to avoid.

As might be expected, the lack of funding and duty solicitors results in very, very few suspects having a lawyer with them during interrogation. A private lawyer was identified as being present in just two of the 262 interviews in our samples of recorded interviews.[25] In four others, there was a representative of an Aboriginal legal organisation: such bodies must be informed when an Aboriginal person is detained.[26] It is possible that some others may have spoken to a lawyer on the telephone before being interviewed. English research on advice provided by telephone suggests that it is of very limited assistance to suspects except in the most straightforward matters (Sanders & Young 2000:232).

In England and Wales, lawyers have become commonplace in custody suites and interview rooms: about one-third of detained suspects see a legal advisor (Bucke & Brown 1997:ch3; Phillips & Brown 1998:ch4). Despite much ill-informed concern about their effect on use of the right to silence, legal advisors have not made police investigations impossible. On the contrary, our earlier research found that police officers often welcomed the involvement of lawyers who facilitated interaction with suspects (Dixon 1997:ch6). To a researcher with experience of the English system, the surprising aspect of the NSW scene is the lack of pressure from the legal profession and civil liberties groups for public funding of legal advice at police stations. Given the constraints on legal aid budgets and the lack of sympathy for suspects in an arena dominated by law and order populism, championing such a scheme may well be regarded as quixotic. NSW, like other states, relies on audio-visual recording as the panacea for all ills. The research reported here indicates that such faith is excessive.

---

[25] Research on police interviews in Queensland reports a similar proportion: see CMC 2004:18–19.

[26] Law Enforcement (Powers and Responsibilities) Regulation 2005 s33.

3.6   Adopting Officers

A conventional method by which police in NSW have sought to authenticate and secure admissibility of confessions is the involvement of the Adopting Officer (AO). At the end of an interview, an officer who is not involved in the investigation of the suspect's alleged offence is introduced to the suspect by the investigating officers, who then leave the room. The AO asks a series of set questions: the interviewee's name is checked, then he or she is asked

> Have you made this recorded interview of your own free will? Has any threat, promise or inducement (or offer of advantage) been held out to you to give the answer recorded in this interview? Have you any complaints to make about the manner in which you were interviewed here today?

In non-electronically recorded interviews, such questions and any answers are recorded manually. In ERISPs, recording of the adoption is a routine conclusion to the proceedings.

The vast majority of sample 1 ERISPs (160 or 91%) were adopted formally by a designated AO. In 13 ERISPs (7%) in sample 1, incomplete or faulty recording meant that it was not possible to tell whether or not this group of interviews was adopted. Two ERISPs (1%) were *not* adopted formally. One concerned a credit card application (allegedly in a false name). No reason for the lack of adoption was apparent. The second involved the case discussed above of a suspect who came to be treated as a victim. In the circumstances (i.e. his answers were not to be used against the man), it was apparently considered unnecessary to have the interview formally adopted.

The AO is normally the person in charge of the station at the time. With one exception, all AOs either were introduced to the suspect at the beginning of the adoption procedure by the interviewer or these persons identified themselves by rank and surname to the suspect when they entered the interview room. Almost two thirds (64%) of known sample 1 AOs were Sergeants. Only three (2%) Adopting Officers were women. One person was neither introduced nor did he identify himself. He simply proceeded with adoption questions. Another five persons were not referred to by rank, but were called 'Detective'. The sound quality at the beginning of another ERISP was too poor to allow for rank to be discerned.

Table 3.12   The rank of sample 1 Adopting Officers

Police rank	Officers N=160 %
Constable	4
Senior Constable	26
Sergeant	64
Senior Sergeant	1
Inspector	1
Unknown	4

Adoption requires a series of set questions to be put. It is not surprising, therefore, that the pace of questioning during adoption was often faster than that during the interview proper: Almost 40% of Adopting Officers asked questions more quickly than the interviewers.

Table 3.13   The Adopting Officer's pacing of questions compared to the interviewer's pacing of questions in the substantive interview in sample 1

Comparative pace	Officers (N=160) %*
Much faster	6
Somewhat faster	33
About the same	44
Somewhat slower	12
Much slower	0
Unknown	4

*   Figures do not total 100 because of rounding.

The comparative manner of the Adopting Officer and the interviewer in each relevant sample 1 ERISP also was examined. Many AOs appeared hurried in comparison with the interviewer at the completion of his/her questioning.

The AO was brisk in his manner. His introduction and questions were completed in one minute. (031)

Such officers apparently see no need to establish any rapport with the suspect, and are simply conducting a routine procedure. Some Adopting Officers appeared older and more formal than the corresponding interviewer for that ERISP.

The AO maybe is 20 years older than the interviewer, is in uniform and is male. He spoke more slowly than the interviewer and asked, 'Do you understand what I mean?' at the end of one question. He elicited a 'Yes, sir' from the suspect, who had not spoken as respectfully to the interviewer. (024)

Similarly, in 046,

The AO was older and in uniform which contrasted with the T-shirts and shorts worn by the detectives. He also was introduced as the most senior officer at the station. Perhaps for this reason the suspect added 'Sir' to all his answers during the adoption of the interview. (046)

Occasionally, the emphasis on brisk formality slipped into rudeness, as in 157:

This AO ignored the suspect, speaking to the interviewer about her rather than addressing her. The AO asked, 'How old is he?' The interviewer replied, 'She. 15.' '15?' the AO echoed. (157)

In another ERISP,

His manner seems abrupt. He does not introduce himself by name and rank. He does not explain his role. And, when verifying with the SP that he had no problem he asked the SP the leading question, 'You have no complaints about this interview?' (119)

If AOs' attitude towards suspects is understandable, there is no justification for this rudeness extending to third parties. However, AOs routinely ignored support persons, sometimes pointedly, as in 064 when the AO stood with his back to the SP. In 118, the AO's brusque ignoring of the suspect's mother and a mental health worker contrasted sharply with the approach of the interviewer, who had earlier asked both if they had any questions about the interview. Far from seeing the SP as a resource with which to do their job of supervising interviews with suspects, AOs demonstrate in their treatment of SPs that their role, as argued above, is presentational. A rare exception — and example of what is possible with minimal effort — was the Adopting Officer in 080 who explained his role informally ('to see if you've had any problems and been treated ok'), and did not need to refer to the pro forma list of questions, and instead asking them in a relaxed, conversational style, verified that the suspect understood the substance of each question, and asked for comments from those present.

Seven suspects asked the AO a question; two suspects simply asked for a question to be repeated; three asked for clarification of the question being asked which led to the paraphrasing of the question as well as some discussion of the meaning of the question; and one sought to help the officer by asking if he had turned the ERISP video on. Only one (075) raised a matter of substance, asking how he was supposed to know that the AO was not connected to the investigation.

It was rare for suspects to raise complaints about the way in which they had been interviewed. In 078, the suspect claimed that the interviewer had, before ERISP, offered bail in exchange for a confession. Unfortunately, the tape then ran out. By the time it was replaced and restarted, eight minutes had passed and the suspect's complaint had gone away. While some suspects treat the appearance of the AO as an opportunity to raise concerns and complaints about the manner in which they were arrested and brought to the station, AOs insist on the narrow focus of their concern. They are prepared to deal only with the conduct of the interview, insisting that complaints about other matters should be made elsewhere. For example, in 146, the Adopting Officer had obviously been informed about a head injury sustained by the suspect en route to the police station.

AO: I notice there is an injury to the top of your head there.

Suspect: That is correct.

AO: Was that injury caused during the course of this interview?

Suspect: No. It was caused being transported here.

AO: It hasn't taken part during the course of this interview?

Suspect: No.

AO: OK.

The adoption was completed at that point. (146)

He did not follow up the answer given to him by the suspect about how the injury occurred as it did not occur during the course of this interview. While technically correct, such responses signal an unfortunate lack of interest and concern.

Similarly, in 075, the AO insisted on the narrow focus of his concern and responsibility. The suspect made a series of allegations about mistreatment during his arrest. The AO simply ignored these, focusing on the interview:

AO: Have you made this interview of your own free will?

Suspect: No.

AO: What was done that wasn't of your own free will?

Suspect: Everything.

AO: Everything, eh?

Suspect: Everything from the start, from the arrest to the interview. This all shouldn't have happened. It was an illegal search warrant. Everything was illegally done ...

AO: What I am asking you about is this interview.

The AO responded to these complaints by insisting that he was there to ask about the interview specifically. He told the suspect that if he had a complaint about the arresting officer, the suspect could see a senior officer once he was on bail and then he could make a complaint about the arrest. The issue of how this arrest behaviour may have impacted on the suspect's willingness to participate in the present ERISP was glossed over. The AO's refusal to deal with complaints about the arrest apparently made the suspect regard complaining about the conduct of the interview as pointless: by the time the AO progressed to questions about threats and complaints specifically, the suspect had become mute, uncooperative, and was not answering questions or making comment.

ERISP 213 provided a notable example of police who were unused and unprepared to deal with a suspect who said that the interview had not been made of his own free will. The interviewer became upset at his intransigence, while the AO belied his supposedly independent position by seeking to persuade the suspect to cooperate. The suspect claimed that police had told him that, if he did not answer questions including identifying a co-offender, 'all the evidence will be turned against' him and he would be refused bail.

Three suspects initially stated they did not give the interview voluntarily, but by the end of the adoption procedure said they had. In two instances the interviewer signalled an 'incorrect' response by repeating the original question in a re-worded format.

> *The AO broke the longer question (Has any threat, promise, etc.) into three shorter questions. ('Has any threat been made?' 'Has any promise ...?') These questions were asked again. This suspect said, 'No' to this second version. (014)*

Another AO acted in a similar way when he faced a suspect who said there had been some difficulty with the interview.

> *The AO asked the suspect if he understood what he was saying. Then the AO re-worded the question. ('Did you answer these questions because you wanted to?') The suspect answered the re-worded question 'appropriately'. (052)*

In both of these ERISPs, it was unclear whether the original adoption question had not been understood by the suspect (and therefore was answered differently when clarified) or whether the suspect did, in fact, experience a change of mind after the AO signalled a problematic response by repeating the question in a re-worded version. This important aspect of the adoption was left unclear. In the third case (092), the suspect complained that officers had not believed what he told them.

> *When asked if any threat, etc, had been made, the suspect replied,*
>
> > *No, only that the officers did not believe me to start with. And I was only telling the truth all along. I just told the truth and that was it and they still didn't believe me.*
>
> *The AO then asked the suspect if they had threatened him to give his answer and he said no. The AO continued to ask if they persuaded the suspect in any way to give the answers that he had given.*
>
> > *Suspect: They said ... we know you're a better bloke than that. Come on, tell us the truth.*
> >
> > *Adopting Officer: And was what you told us today the truth?*
> >
> > *Suspect: Yes.*

Then, when asked if he had any complaint to make, the suspect replied no, he did not. (092)

The direct issue of voluntariness was skirted by the AO's attempt to confirm that, for whatever reason, the suspect's answers had been truthful.

Similarly, in 010, the AO responded to the suspect's complaint that the interviewers 'kept trying to put words in my mouth' by inquiring about the effect of the alleged impropriety.

AO: Are you happy with the answers you gave police?

Suspect: I am satisfied with it. I think I stood my ground.

In a case from sample 2 (282), the suspect complained to the AO that the interviewers 'were being a bit hard'. The AO's response was not to ask any further question about how the interviewers were being 'a bit hard'. Instead, he simply asked again whether there had been any threat or promise, which the suspect denied. Not surprisingly, the suspect then stated he did not have any complaint with the way in which he was interviewed. Such cases exemplify the fact that the AO's concern is the admissibility and reliability of the suspect's statement: otherwise, the propriety of the investigators' actions before or during the interview is treated as being irrelevant.

One adoption in sample 1 was particularly problematic. The suspect said that he wanted to make a complaint, claiming that the investigator had offered a familiar inducement:

Suspect: All the Detective said was if you tell them ... you have more of a chance of making bail. (078)

Soon afterwards, the adoption procedure was suspended in order to change the ERISP tapes. After an eight minute break, the suspect said he did *not* have a complaint to make about the interview, but he did have 'other matters' to raise later. It appeared that the suspect and AO had discussed the initial alleged complaints during the suspension period, although this was not acknowledged on the record. The incident illustrates the problems caused by allowing unrecorded interaction between police and suspect. Ironically, a break in the substantive interview had been recorded. In this, it was the suspect rather than the interviewer who raised the issue of bail: the interviewer's response was simply to say that granting bail was not a matter for him to decide.

In sum, most AOs in sample 1 conducted the adoption procedure in brisk or matter-of-fact manner. The few adoptions that were problematic in sample 1 raised questions about the role of AOs as independent, neutral parties. Complaints appeared to fall into three categories: those that could be resolved by repeating the question and bringing the 'inappropriateness' of the response to the suspect's attention; those that may have occurred during the recording period of the ERISP; and those that may have occurred at the time of the arrest. The 'arrest' complaints were dismissed as not the business of the AO, but were 'other matters' that were the subject for another senior officer at another time. Issues that may have been problematic during the interview itself (the issue of voluntariness, for example) were sometimes glossed over by the AOs in these few cases in which the suspect did maintain that there had been a problem with the interview. Similarly, in 278a, the suspect's mother said that she had wanted him to have legal advice: the Adopting Officer simply ignored her. Adopting Officers in these few cases appeared interested to have the suspect state the 'appropriate' answer to adoption questions. Treating the experience of arrest as irrelevant artificially suggested that issues of voluntariness or free will were not influenced by earlier police-suspect interactions.

Several defendants interviewed in our District Court study said that they did have complaints about the way in which their ERISPs had been conducted, but they had rarely voiced those concerns during the adoption procedure. Their explanation was that such complaints to someone who was just another police officer would have been pointless at best, and possibly counterproductive. These problems have long been on record: the Beach Report in Victoria described the process as 'worthless in practice and [it] may well cause grave injustice to an accused person at his [sic] trial' (Beach 1978 vol. 1:103; see also Stevenson nd:71). The Royal Commission into the NSW Police Service was scathing about the adoption procedures, describing them as 'a solemn farce' (Wood 1997:466). This is surely an appropriate assessment. It is simply unrealistic to expect suspects to regard another police officer as sufficiently independent to respond to a suspect's complaints. The awkward phrasing of the inquiry about voluntariness invites acquiescence. While the AO is instructed by the CRIME Code to conduct 'a through [sic] and professional check of the person's treatment by police' (NSW Police 1998:53), the demeanour of AOs in our samples indicated that most regarded their role as perfunctory. Adoption is a presentational device which attempts, unconvincingly, to put a stamp of propriety on the proceedings.

The Wood Commission recommended 'the abandonment of the pro forma and meaningless current procedure for the "adoption" of records of interview, and its replacement by a thorough and professional check by a duty inspector, or custody officer, of the regularity of the arrest and interview' (Wood 1997:429). The experience of PACE suggests that the supervisory capacity of custody officers should not be overestimated (Dixon et al. 1991). Nonetheless, they provide some basis for a more realistic approach to supervising investigators. NSW Police are currently considering abandoning the use of Adopting Officers. This is to be welcomed. They should be replaced by effective means of supervising the conduct of interviews with suspects.

CHAPTER 4

THE INTERVIEWING PROCESS

In this chapter, the focus shifts from the participants to the way in which police officers question suspects in ERISPs.

4.1 Cautions and introductions

The beginning of an interview with a suspect is a laborious business. Baldwin described the introductory formalities in England as 'a somewhat protracted and cumbersome process' which 'many officers regard ... as tedious, discordant, and counter-productive ... [A]nxious to move on to the real business of the day', they conduct procedures 'hurriedly and perfunctorily' (1993:336). He found 'many cautions were delivered in a very casual manner, often so garbled as to be devoid of all meaning ... the form of an empty ritual or an unthinking recitation' (1993:337). Alternatively, officers used the opening exchanges as an opportunity to try to achieve rapport, but did so in such a gauche manner that suspects were upset rather than put at ease. Baldwin wondered whether this was sometimes a deliberate tactic (1993:337–338). The introduction is a significant phase of the interview:

> Even the early explanation of the taping procedures often reveals officers as uncertain and lacking in confidence. The way that the caution is delivered also provides an early clue as to the officers' attitude and professionalism (Baldwin 1992a:15).

Practices observed in NSW were less overtly problematic. Nonetheless, the introductory phase had characteristics which affected, often adversely, the subsequent course of the interview. These were: the use of unfamiliar terminology; the tendency for routinised functions to lose their meaning for police officers; repetition of questions which made interaction unnatural and stilted; and a tendency for procedures to condition the suspect to acquiescence (notably as in the repeated questions, 'Do you agree that ...? or 'Do you understand that?' to which the 'natural' answer is 'Yes').

An interviewing officer has two main duties in introducing an interview: first, cautioning the suspect, explaining the procedure and gaining his or her consent to participate; second, explaining to the suspect what is the allegation against him or her. Procedural explanations are left to formality: officers ask a series of routinised questions before the ERISP recorder is activated, and then repeat them on tape, securing the suspect's willingness to participate and cautioning him/her.[1] As Baldwin found, such requirements are often 'regarded by officers as minor preliminaries to be dealt with in a perfunctory manner' (1992a:12). In NSW, a pro forma guide to 'Conversation with offender [sic] prior to interview' directs officers on pre-ERISP procedure. First, officers are expected to introduce themselves. They should then specify the allegation to be investigated, caution the suspect, explain that the interview will be electronically recorded, and inform the suspect that he or she will be given one of the audio tapes at the end of the interview and that the suspect and his or her lawyer will be able to view the video tape. The suspect should be asked if he or she understands each of these pieces of information. When the ERISP begins, the lead officer names himself or herself, his or her partner, the suspect (again inappropriately described as the 'offender' in the notes of guidance), and any third party attending. The suspect is asked to confirm that there is no-one else in the room. The time is stated.

In our samples, one suspect (106) agreed to be interviewed but refused to be electronically recorded. No reason was given. Another (117) refused to take part in an ERISP, but had already been interviewed, with a record made in the officer's notebook, which the suspect had signed. There was no significant evidence in our research of suspects being concerned about the ERISP recording process.[2]

The suspect is then informed of the allegation, cautioned, and asked 'Do you understand that?' This question is an unfortunate starting point: it breaks a basic rule of interviewing that questions should not be ambiguous. The question appears (and is taken by some suspects) to be inquiring about understanding of both the allegation and the caution. It would be better to make clear that the question relates to the caution, and to follow it up by appropriate probing of the suspect's understanding, particularly as so very few suspects are able to receive legal advice before being interviewed. Hasty, monotonic recitation of formulaic questions sends a clear message: these matters

---

[1]   The caution is a prerequisite of a confession being admissible at trial: Evidence Act 2002 (NSW) s139(1).

[2]   See also 3.3.6, above.

are insignificant, and the suspect's role is merely to agree. Whether this is deliberate is hard to tell. American research suggests that such tactics are studied techniques of avoiding *Miranda* (Leo 1996a, 1996b). This may be the case in NSW. But it may simply be that officers are performing a routinised function which they genuinely consider to be insignificant. It is hardly surprising that they should do so, as so few suspects remain silent or attempt to exercise such right as they have to legal advice.

The problems of routinised compliance are notable in cases involving suspects who are affected by alcohol or illegal drugs.

> *As part of the introduction of the ERISP, the interviewer did not clarify if the suspect was drug affected. He rushed through the preliminary (caution) questions in a manner that would be difficult for most persons to understand, and especially a suspect who appeared to be heroin affected. (222)*

The suspect is then asked four 'Do you agree ...?' questions in which he or she is asked to confirm that, before the ERISP began, the officer stated that he/she intended to ask questions about the matter, the interview would be electronically recorded, the suspect would be given a copy, and subsequent viewing of the video could be arranged. The confirming questions are presumably mandated in a legal 'belt and braces' approach to admissibility. However, this hardly justifies the cost, which is a flat, often hasty, and routinised introduction to the interview which has potential costs for both suspects and police in setting an inappropriate tone for what follows. Suspects often appear bemused at being asked such repetitive questions. Those who are used to the procedure appear bored and disinterested. All, almost inevitably, adopt a compliant role, agreeing and cooperating with the officer whose dominance is emphasised by the required response from the suspect. From a police perspective, the opportunity to establish good communication is jeopardised as officers trudge through the formalities. On the other hand, some might regard this pedantic procedure as useful if it habituates the suspect to answering police questions compliantly. However, it surely would be preferable for all concerned if the substantive questions were asked at the beginning of the ERISP and the 'Do you agree?' questions were dropped. A separate procedure could be provided for the rare suspect who refuses to cooperate in electronic recording.

The suspect is then asked, 'for the purpose of this interview', to provide his or her full name, spelling the surname. Again, this appears in some interviews to be an obstructive repetitive, formality: why not do this during the introductions at the beginning of the tape? He or she is then asked to provide date of birth, address, marital status, and employment details. As noted in the previous chapter, information about income is sometimes used directly in investigations when questions are asked about the suspect's ability to afford items such as drugs.

The caution was given at the beginning of every sample 1 ERISP that was fully recorded, with one exception in which the interviewer's partner reminded him after a few substantive questions that he had forgotten to caution the suspect. For the majority of interviewers, the delivery of cautionary questions at the beginning of the ERISP was straightforward. Interviewers did differ in their manner of delivery, however. While the caution was paced about the same as other interview questions in most (59%) sample 1 ERISPs, in more than one quarter of interviews (29%), this caution was worded somewhat faster or much faster than other questions.

The introduction and caution are often followed by another series of 'DYAs' about substantive matters which occurred before the ERISP, including earlier admissions. As will be discussed in more detail below, an important function of the ERISP is to incorporate accounts of police-suspect interaction into the formal record. The relevant issue here is the impact that a lengthy series of DYA questions has on the interview. First, it complements the introductory exchanges in making the interview formal and conversationally unnatural. Second, it emphasises police dominance of the interaction: suspects who want to tell their side of the story learn that they have to wait. Third, it habituates some suspects to answering: suspects who may wish not to answer questions about alleged offences may well find themselves drawn into an exchange with officers who begin by asking, not about the allegation, but about pre-ERISP activity. Fourth, and consequently, the DYA questions may reinforce the impact of the caution in habituating some suspects to compliance.

Table 4.1   **How quickly or how slowly did Sample I interviewers pace preliminary cautionary questions compared to the pace for most other questions?**

Comparative pace	Interviews (N=175) %
Much faster	4
Somewhat faster	25
About the same	59
Somewhat slower	3
Much slower	2
Unknown/not applicable*	8

*   Unknown/not applicable: in this and subsequent tables, unless otherwise indicated, this category include ERISPs with technical quality problems and "right to silence" interviews that were terminated immediately.

4.2   Introductory accounts

As the analysis in Chapter 5 will suggest, a key objective of the currently approved approach to investigative interviewing is that the suspect should be invited to present his or her account of the alleged incident before police interviewers ask specific questions. Against this background, it was initially unexpected (as these interviewers had not received training in investigative interviewing) to find that so many suspects in sample 1 were asked to give their version of events. Almost three quarters (74%) of sample 1 suspects were asked in an open question to tell their version of events for all allegations raised.

However, as discussion in Chapter 5 will elaborate, there was a significant difference between requests for accounts in samples 1 and 2. Normally in sample 1, the request for an account followed a statement by the interviewer about the allegation against the suspect and about police knowledge of the circumstances. By contrast in sample 2, interviewers often sought the suspect's account without the possibly contaminating effect of providing information from witnesses or other evidence about the alleged offence. In the investigative interviewing approach, the suspect should give his or her account, not respond to what he or she is told by interviewers. It should then be followed up by a structured dissection of what has been said, including challenges based on witness statements, and physical evidence.

Table 4.2   Were sample 1 suspects asked to give an account at the beginning of the interview?

Request to give account	Suspects (N=167) %
Yes, for all allegations	74
Yes, for some allegations	5
No	9
Undecided	1
Unknown/ not applicable	12

Table 4.3   The stage during the ERISP that Sample I suspects (who had been asked an open question about what happened for all allegations during the ERISP) gave their account

When during the ERISP the suspect gave his/her account	Suspects (N=123) %
Immediately	3
At the beginning	38
In the middle	14
Towards the end	3
During the course of the interview	24
Never	15
Unknown	2

As Table 4.3 illustrates, many suspects (41%) who were asked to tell the interviewer their version of what had happened in an open question did so at the start of the interview or following a series of introductory

DYA questions about earlier police-suspect interaction. Another 24% told their version of events later in the ERISP, while 15% (18 suspects) never told their story of what happened in full as a response to an open question.

Some potential benefits of inviting an account rather than asking questions were suggested in 004, in which a drunken suspect's initial truculence was mollified by the interviewer's approach. The suspect contrasted his treatment by the interviewers with that by the 'plastic copper' (a private security guard) who had arrested him.

It was rare for these accounts to be interrupted by interviewers. In almost one third of cases, the suspect's account was so brief that interruption was not an issue. These suspects either chose not to tell their story in full or responded in such a brief way that did not allow for interruption. Answers such as those below were typical of the responses offered by this group:

We were fighting. (054)

I don't know. (051)

Nope. (057)

I lit the one on Monday night. (080)

Yeah, I took it. (120)

I was just bored and that's about it. (156)

Some of these suspects who initially were brief in response to the invitation to give an account of what happened did go on to tell a fuller version of events. They did not tell their story in one neat segment, but rather their version of events emerged as the ERISP progressed. Another suspect gave his account only after the third time the interviewer asked him about what had happened (109). Some suspects found it difficult to respond to open questions: for example, when asked such a question, the suspect in 095 replied

What do you want to know? You've got to ask me questions.

Of the very small minority who were interrupted, one of the three interruptions came not from police but from the suspect's mother.

Table 4.4   Interruptions to suspects' accounts

Was the suspect interrupted?	Suspects (N=123) %
No	63
Yes	2
N/A: story brief	32
N/A: chose to do a hand-written statement	2
Unknown: sound poor	2

We also analysed the frequency of interruptions other than those during the suspect's introductory account. Most interviewers recognised the importance of not interrupting the suspect. However, some interrupted in attempts to keep a suspect's answers relevant to the question being asked:

> *The interviewer interrupted this suspect several times during the interview when he gave confused, apparently irrelevant, answers. An example occurred when the interviewer asked the suspect about his occupation.*
>
> *Q: What is your occupation?*
>
> *A: I take tablets in the morning and night and I see the doctors and that — sitting on the lounge ...*
>
> *Q: [interrupting] Hang on. Hang on. Do you work?*
>
> *A: No. (027)*

Other interruptions showed the interviewer's understandable frustration:

> *At one point, the interviewer interrupted the suspect to say 'Whether the poetry was good or not is irrelevant to me. What can you tell me about this card?' (082)*

Other interruptions seemed to reflect an interviewer's lack of competence. In one ERISP concerning a visibly heroin-affected 29 year old man facing allegations of receiving and making out a false cheque, the interviewer sometimes interrupted the suspect, interjecting another question before the suspect had an opportunity to answer the first (114).

However, the vast majority of sample 1 suspects were not interrupted while answering questions. In 138 sample 1 ERISPs (79%), the suspect was never interrupted. In an additional 22 ERISPs (13%), the suspect was interrupted sometimes. (In the remaining 15 ERISPs (9%), the frequency of interruption was unknown, primarily due to sound and other recording problems.)

4.3 Challenges

Having given his or her account, the suspect was almost always (95%) asked a question about some part of it. Often these sought clarification or expansion. Many also involved some challenge to the suspect's account. In 48% of sample 1 ERISPs, the suspect was asked at least one challenging question. However, in another 70 ERISPs (40%), no challenging question was asked. In 21 ERISPs (12%), the number of challenges was unknown due to sound or recording problems or the issue was not applicable, for example, due to the suspect remaining silent (although some suspects who attempted to remain silent were challenged: see below).

The manner used by interviewers to challenge suspects ranged from mild subtlety to sarcasm and direct confrontation. There were a number of methods of challenge. The most common was reference to a statement by the victim or a witness of the alleged offence.

> *After the suspect told the interviewer that M was 17 years old, the interviewer said 'I have been informed she told you she was 15. Would that be correct?'[3] Subsequently, the interviewer used the statements of four girls about what had happened. He asked the suspect questions stemming from those statements. 'What can you tell me about that?' In general, the statements challenged in part the details of what the suspect had said happened. However, they also verified some of what the suspect had said. (034)*

Occasionally, the interviewer used other evidence in order to make a challenge.

---

[3] This question was (at least) ambiguous: was she 15, or had the suspect been told that she was 15?

In the pre-ERISP interview, officers had asked the suspect to write the words 'five thousand dollars' and the numbers '$5,000' on a blank piece of paper. This writing exercise was used during the ERISP to challenge the suspect. He was asked to explain how the word 'dollar' was written 'doller' on both this piece of paper and on the fraudulent withdrawal slip used at the bank. Similarly, he was asked to explain the idiosyncratic use of capital letters in both cases. (143)

Another approach was to raise inconsistencies between the suspect's account and what he or she had said pre-ERISP or during a previous answer in the ERISP:

A second challenge was made after the suspect said that she didn't know until later that the taxi driver had been stabbed. The interviewer interjected, 'You said earlier they jabbed him with the knife'. (078)

The most common type of challenge was to the logic or simple credibility of what the suspect said.

Why didn't you take the most direct route home if you took the vehicle basically to get home? (132)

The suspect had stated that he did not think that anyone was living in the unit (where the break and enter had occurred). The interviewer challenged him, 'Didn't you think it was strange they would leave a good doona, TV and toiletry equipment?' (158)

Some interviewers repeated questions (or repeated answers offered by the suspect in question form) to challenge what the suspect had said.

When asked about the knife he carried, the suspect said he used the knife to peel fruit. Subsequently, the interviewer twice asked the suspect what he used the knife for. (078)

In 069, the suspect had denied each allegation of (domestic) threat and assault. Then he mentioned that his partner left the van in which they had been travelling: 'She grabbed the baby and ran'. The interviewer asked a challenging question, following it by another question repeating the suspect's answer.

Q: Why do you think she took off on you?

A: Mate, no idea.

Q: No idea?

> *A: I had a few beers, but I never hurt her. I'd never in the world hurt them. (069)*

On one occasion, interviewers disbelieved the suspect's account, so they asked him to demonstrate physically what he claimed had happened when a car was damaged:

> *The officer asked the suspect to stand and demonstrate how he held the dog's leash and suggest how the height of the leash, as it was held, could have interfered with the vehicle. (009)*

Finally, some interviewers made a direct challenge to the suspect's credibility. For example, when a suspect offered a thoroughly unconvincing account of how he had come to be in possession of some stolen alcohol, the interviewer responded:

> *Do you believe in the beer fairy? ... Did the beer fairy drop it there? (014)*

However, this sarcasm was unusual: most challenges were made in a cool, detached manner.

> *It was a very serious assault against this young lady. You were there at the time and I believe you were involved in it. What have you got to say about that? (032)*

We did not find any recorded examples of the kind of persistent, aggressive questioning which has been the subject of criticism in England. What happens off-camera may, of course, be a different matter.

On the other hand, challenges were quite frequently not made when it seemed that they would have been appropriate. For example, in 073, an unemployed man who lived in a boarding house was interviewed about a set of golf clubs that he had pawned. A man whose clubs had been stolen from his car at a golf club had identified the clubs as his. The suspect simply insisted that the clubs had been given to him 'a number of years ago' by his family. An obvious challenge would have been to ask the suspect about when, where, and with whom he played golf. However, the officers simply collected his account. Perhaps the officers thought it was not worth the effort: the suspect's account was unconvincing.

However, the lack of challenge in some other cases was more surprising: for example, in 115, a sawn-off shotgun, cartridges, and a balaclava were found in a man's car. His story (that he knew nothing, and that they belonged to a friend) begged challenge, but none was made. Lack of attention and poor listening skills were partly responsible for such faults. Some officers seemed to be so preoccupied with forming their next question that they were unable to pay critical attention to what the suspect was saying.

Fifty-one (30%) of the 167 suspects in sample 1 made inconsistent statements within the interview. (We could not, of course, assess inconsistency with anything said before the ERISP, unless an officer pointed it out on tape.) In the case of eight suspects who made an inconsistent statement (8 of 51 suspects, 16% of this group), it was not clear that the interviewer recognised the inconsistency. These interviewers continued to ask questions that were unrelated to either the inconsistent statement or the subject matter of the inconsistency. In the case of two additional suspects, the interviewer did not ask clarification questions, further questions about the subject at issue, or challenging questions, but the interviewer did appear to acknowledge that an inconsistency had emerged.

> *The interviewers told the suspect 12 minutes after the interview started that she was speaking irrationally. (She was very upset, crying.) They suggested that the interview be suspended in order for the suspect to get herself 'together in a more calm state of mind'. (133)*

In another ERISP,

> *When the inconsistent statement was made, both interviewers turned their heads and stared at the suspect simultaneously. Then the interview was continued with the asking of further (unrelated) questions. (108)*

The interviewer's response to the remaining 41 suspects who made inconsistent statements varied. A portion were asked further questions about the subject matter of the inconsistency, but were not challenged directly.

> *The interviewer did not make a point of overtly challenging the suspect. Rather, when the inconsistency emerged, he asked further follow-up questions on the issue at hand. (043)*

> *The suspect made a statement about him telling the driver of the stolen car to 'floor it'. The interviewer asked a few other questions, then returned to what the suspect had told the driver.*

The suspect's statement about what he had said changed. The interviewer asked further questions about what was said to the driver. None of these questions was confrontational or challenging. (065)

Other interviewers brought attention to inconsistencies and asked for further clarification by doing so.

The interviewer said to the suspect at one stage in the interview, 'You have got me confused as you said they went for a walk at 1 am and you also said they did at 3.30'. (128)

Another example of the interviewer seeking clarification of an inconsistency arose in 121.

Q: Do you agree you then told me your car was at the hospital?

A: Yes.

Q: Do you agree that prior you told me your car was at a friend's place?

A: Yes.

The partner also pointed out an inconsistency:

Q: You said you found it [a bullet] in your car?

A: Yes.

Q: Do you agree earlier you said you found it in the toolbox?

Other examples of challenges to inconsistencies included these:

The partner challenged the suspect, 'Before, you said you went to speak with JB and GE ...'. (134)

The interviewer asked questions that began with 'A moment ago you just mentioned ...' and 'Earlier you mentioned ...'. (017)

In sum, only a portion of interviewers responded to the suspect's inconsistent statement through use of confrontational, challenging questions. Other interviewers ignored (either intentionally or not) the inconsistency; asked further questions about the matter (perhaps having realised the inconsistency, perhaps not); or recognised that inconsistency and, by drawing attention to it, asked for further clarification or confirmation of what had been said.

4.4 Interview practices and props

This section considers a variety of interview practices and props which are used by interviewers. First, engaging the interviewee by eye contact is usually a basic requirement of good interviewing.[4] Almost four in five sample 1 interviewers (79%) attempted to have eye contact with suspects for all or most of the time during their questioning of those persons. For partners who asked questions, the figure was even higher (91%).

Interviewers relied on notes or papers to form questions of substance some or most of the time in 82% of sample 1 ERISPs. As Chapter 5 will discuss, notes can be used appropriately to structure an interview: however excessive reference to witness and other statements indicates poor preparation.

In half (87) of the sample 1 ERISPs, the suspect was shown at least one exhibit during the interview. Some officers (16% of cases involving exhibits) made a point of displaying the articles to the ERISP camera. Such displays were inconsistent: the size of exhibit and its corresponding visibility in the interview room generally did not appear to be the decisive factor. For example, in 058, the interviewer asked the suspect to help her lift a lawn mower onto the interview table so it could be viewed by the camera (058). Meanwhile in 013, a set of mag wheels were exhibited to the camera. Other items (pliers, mag wheel covers, wheel nuts) were not shown to the camera, but nevertheless they could be seen on the interview table. The use of such displays in drug cases was illustrated in 075,

> One exhibit was displayed to the camera. The suspect said he could not see any white powder in the foil. The interviewer then attempted to show the foil to the camera. The suspect then said he could see something in the foil. Ironically, even though the foil was shown to the camera, the white powder was not visible on camera.

In 67 ERISPs (77% of those for which an exhibit was shown to the suspect), no exhibit was shown to the ERISP monitor camera. However, for some of this group, the interviewer identified the

---

[4] However, it may be culturally inappropriate on some occasions. For example, in 109, the interviewer appeared sensitively not to make continuous eye contact with an Aboriginal suspect.

exhibit(s) or some of the exhibits in other ways rather than making use of the visual recorder. For example, various interviewers asked the suspect to sign and date an exhibit, described an item in detail (or asked the suspect to do so), read a document aloud, and quoted a police notebook number, a cheque number, a receipt number, a serial number or a licence number.

Police notebooks are an important tool in the interview process. As might be expected, officers frequently consult them for information entries, for example, details such as the registration number of a stolen vehicle, names, dates and times. However, in interviews, their primary use was as a source of the material which the suspect was asked to confirm or adopt in a series of DYA questions, either by the suspect reading the notebook and agreeing generally to its accuracy, or by the interviewing officer reading the entries aloud and getting the suspect to accept them. This was sometimes a second adoption, because some suspects had been asked to read and initial the notebook entries at the time that they were made.

Most importantly, notebooks are used to record interviews made in the field (or indeed in a police station, but not electronically recorded). As will be shown below, such interviews are 'adopted' by police asking and the suspect answering questions about them In sample 1, notebook interviews with 25 suspects (15%) were partially or fully adopted electronically on ERISP. (A statement was adopted in four more, but problems with picture quality meant that it was not clear whether notebooks had been used.)

4.5   Interview breaks

Concern about informal police-suspect interaction is primarily related to what happens before the ERISP. However, there is also the possibility of such interaction during ERISP breaks[5] or after the interview.[6] There were 198 breaks in the 157 sample 1 interviews for which relevant data were available. The most common type of break is when an interviewer leaves the room to locate an Adopting Officer. Although these come at the end of the interview, they should be considered along with other breaks because some significant

---

[5]   See the High Court's consideration of this issue in *Nicholls v The Queen* [2005] HCA 1.

[6]   See *Kelly v The Queen* [2004] HCA 12.

exchanges can occur between the suspect and those remaining in the room. The second most common type of break was caused by technological malfunction, usually involving tapes popping out of the ERISP machine unexpectedly. The third was to replace tapes which had ended.

Table 4.5   Reasons stated by the interviewer for breaks taken during Sample I ERISPs

Stated reason	Breaks (N=198) %
To locate an Adopting Officer	77
To locate an interpreter	1
To change audio tapes	5
To change video tapes	2
Audio/video tapes ejected	8
To confer with partner	3
To allow the suspect to make a hand-written statement	1
To locate an exhibit	1
To locate paperwork/map	1
To obtain a drink for the suspect	2
To show the suspect a CCTV tape	1
To respond to a knock on the door	1
To allow the suspect to calm down	1

Sample 1 breaks varied in duration from less than one minute to 2 hours and 43 minutes. However, about one quarter (24%) of breaks were less than two minutes long, and 69% were less than five minutes. During breaks, normal procedure is for the audio tapes to be stopped (to facilitate subsequent transcription) but for the video to continue recording (both vision and sound). However, this was not followed in one third of cases.

Table 4.6   Were breaks in sample 1 recorded on ERISP video?

Break recorded on ERISP video	Breaks (N=209) %
Yes	63
Partially recorded	3
No	33
Not applicable*	1

*   One break was used to transfer participants from one interview room in the station to another due to a faulty ERISP machine.

The issue of whether or not the suspect was aware that the break period was being recorded on video tape was examined. While the suspect may have noticed that the interviewer turned off the audio tapes during a break, he or she may well not have been aware that sound as well as picture was still being recorded during the break, unless an officer provided this information.

Table 4.7   Were suspects told that the break was being recorded on video tape?

Were suspects told the break was recorded?	Breaks (N=131) %
Yes, at the beginning of the break	62
Yes, during the break	4
No	33
Unknown	1

Warnings during the break that the video was active came in response to comments or questions by the suspect. For example, in 150, the suspect pointed to a document on the table and asked:

SUSPECT: Is that my record there?

PARTNER: The tape is running so keep quiet for a little while.

In one sample 1 ERISP, it was an interpreter who informed the suspect (without instructions from the interviewer) that the break was being video taped. In one third (33%) of all breaks recorded in full on video, it appeared that the suspect did not know that the break was being recorded on video tape. In situations of multiple breaks in one interview, it appeared to be haphazard whether or not the suspect would be informed about the continued recording.

Breaks while waiting for Adopting Officers are often socially awkward periods. The remaining officer busies him or herself with paperwork, not least, it appears, to signal a lack of interest in interacting with the suspect:

> *There is no conversation between the suspect and the interview partner. The suspect sits with her arms folded across her lap. The only noise emitted by her is a single cough. The partner meanwhile does paperwork, stares at the table and stares at the monitor. He does not look in the direction of the suspect. (085)*

> *For the duration of the two minute break three persons (suspect, partner, support person) sit silently, each staring in a different direction. (067)*

In contrast, another break offered an example of an emotional suspect who barely waited for the interviewer to leave the room before her aggressive outburst. The suspect asked the partner,

> *So what is going to happen? What am I going to get charged with? Fuck this shit ... It's a fucking load of shit.*

The partner did not respond (079).

In another interview break, a volatile suspect offered to be an informant, then made a series of allegations that police had stolen money, insulted him, and set him up:

> *You set me up with the heroin. You fucking pinched me money. You've done this. You've done that. Fuck this. (078)*

The interviewer responded by getting up and leaving the room.

Officers appeared to be aware of the potential allegations about questioning suspects during breaks. At the end of breaks (other than those for the purpose of finding an Adopting Officer), the suspect was asked to verify the reason for the break in three quarters of cases (34 of 46). Typically, officers would ask the suspect to confirm that they had not discussed the alleged offence during the break. Other questions included asking the suspect to verify: that no one had come into the interview room during the break; that two other detectives in the tea room where the suspect had obtained a cup of tea did not talk to him; that no threat had been made to the suspect to continue the interview; and that during the break no one had asked him questions.

4.6 Three interviewing modes

Through analysis of question-type sequences, police interviews can be categorised into three general interviewing modes. In the first, police ask a series of closed questions, inviting specific responses. In the second, police tell the suspect what is alleged against him or her, invite a response, and follow up with more detailed questions. In the third, suspects are asked 'Do you agree?' questions, to which the appropriate, invited answer is simply 'yes'. These modes are not entirely distinct: as might be expected, some overlap in sequences is found in most interviews. Nonetheless, dominant modes can be identified in each interview. Doing so proved to be a difficult task because of the length of some interviews (up to 3 hours and 33 minutes) and the variation and complexity of some questions. However, we were able to identify recurrent patterns in question-types and the over-representation of certain police-favoured phrases in questions used by interviewers.

In this section, these three interviewing modes will be illustrated by selecting typical interviews of each mode, and analysing all questions which police asked the suspect between the formal caution at the beginning of the interview and the formal closing questions (which addressed issues of voluntariness, the possible making of a hand-written statement, and the formal adoption of the interview).

4.6.1 Mode one: closed questions

This mode involves interviewers asking specific questions, rather than inviting the suspect to give an account as he or she wishes. In case 123, the interviewer told the 49 year old suspect that he was making inquiries into the theft of rolls of material. He asked the suspect about his possession of some such rolls. The suspect had made a pre-ERISP admission in relation to possession. However, he denied during the first half of the interview that he had had any suspicion when he bought the material that it had been stolen. During the second half of questioning, he admitted that he had had suspicions that the material had been stolen. Interviewers' questions were as follows.

Do you agree [police officers] attended your premises today at [address]?

Do you agree at your premises we had a conversation?

Do you agree that conversation was in relation to rolls of material that are in your possession?

Do you agree that you located five rolls of material that you indicated to us?

Can you tell me where you got this material?

How do you know R?

How long have you known R?

Do you have much contact with him?

How did you get the material from R?

Is that in [location]?

Can you recall when that was?

What month was that?

Was it on a mid-week day?

What time was it?

Who was there?

Did you see their rolls of material?

How many rolls were there?

Where was the material when you saw it?

Can you describe the vehicle to me?

Had you ever seen that vehicle before?

What happened to the material in the van?

How did you happen to be there at that time?

Who did you make arrangements with?

What was the conversation?

When the rolls were in the garage, was there conversation in relation to the price?

What was your reaction to this?

Did you come to an agreement about this?

Can you describe the materials in these rolls?

Can you tell me what happened then, did you leave?

Was there anything else there?

Was the object covered?

What was it covered with?

What would you say it was?

What happened then?

The next time you saw the material was in P's garage?

What happened then?

What rolls were that?

Did you take that in your vehicle?

What happened to the rest of the rolls that were left?

Have you seen them since?

The rolls of material you took to your work, in your opinion, what was the cost to buy them in normal market price?

If you had to guess a combined price, what would you say it was?

How much did you pay?

When you spoke to R did you ask where it was from?

Did he tell you where it was from?

Did you have any suspicions about the origin of the material?

Is there any reason why you purchased the stuff for half the value without knowing its origin?

Did you think that was a good price?

Do you normally expect to get that price?

Was it too good to be true?

When I spoke to you earlier do you agree I asked you if you knew it was stolen and you said, I had a sneaking suspicion it may have been?

Do you agree I cautioned you about that?

Can you now tell me what suspicions you had about the materials?

You said you paid $1300. Was that all your money?

How much did you actually pay for the material you took?

Earlier you told us you paid $900 and $600 for someone else. Is that correct?

$600 was for the canvas. What did you do?

What is his name?

What did he pay you for the canvas?

Where does he live?

Where does he work?

Did he ask you where it came from?

Did you tell him where it came from?

How did you get the $1300 to R?

Was there any conversation in relation to the money?

What happened to the upholstery material?

When you got it, what happened after that?

Where did you take it to?

What is the name of the man you sold it to?

When was that?

How was payment supposed to be made?

Was there any agreement with R about the money you received for these other materials?

Do you have anything else to say?

Have you gone through these notes of Investigator [W]?

They go from page 5–12. You read that?

Is that a correct version?

Is that your signature?

This notebook is Number [x] and belongs to Investigator W. (123)

In this and similar cases, the interviewer did not ask a general open question. He already knew, from the pre-ERISP questioning, what the suspect's account was, so he therefore proceeded to more detailed, closed questions which invited the specifics of this account in a convenient, ordered sequence. 'Can you tell me where you got this material?' preceded a number of follow-up questions that requested detailed information (presumably in part for the purpose of further investigation or charges against other suspects) about people, locations, time periods and possibly other stolen materials. However, the pre-ERISP interview had not produced a sufficiently incriminating answer regarding mens rea. Consequently, questions focused on the suspect's claim that he did not have any suspicion the material he had bought may have been stolen. Questions included a challenge: 'When I spoke to you earlier do you agree I asked you if you knew it was stolen and you said, "I had a sneaking suspicion it may have been"?' This illustrates the need not to assume that the occurrence of pre-ERISP questioning makes the ERISP a mere formality. As suggested in Chapter 2, an officer's purpose in questioning a suspect informally may be primarily to find out what he/she is going to say in the ERISP rather than to conduct a full rehearsal interview.

This ERISP also began with the standard series of DYAs that attempted to establish, from the police perspective, pre-ERISP activity in relation to this allegation. In this case, in the middle of the interview, there was a request for verification ('Do you agree I cautioned you about that?') that proper pre-ERISP procedure had been followed. The pre-ERISP notebook admission was adopted at the end of the interview. This interviewer tended to use formal phrases for these questions. While this suspect could understand what the interviewer meant by 'attending your premises' and 'you indicated to us', other suspects did have difficulty with such police phrases. 'Do you have anything else to say?' was the standard closing question.

This example illustrates the need to distinguish between closed and leading questions, and the difficulty of doing so. A closed question is an appropriate interviewing tool which asks for specific information. A leading question is one which pushes the suspect towards an answer. This would be improper if it steered the suspect towards self-incrimination, rendering the product potentially inadmissible. DYAs are leading questions. Usually, this characteristic is insignificant. But this may not be the case, as in the example cited above in which the officer uses a DYA to introduce an earlier admission of mens rea regarding suspicion about the origins of the cloth. More straightforward and blatantly leading questions were rare. When they occurred significantly, there was sometimes an excuse, as in 064 in which the suspect's brief, monosyllabic answers pushed the interviewer into asking questions such as

Did he run out of the bank?

Was he holding any money?

Was someone getting served?

Leading questions were found more often among procedural than substantive questions. For example:

Q: Was any threat, promise or any offer held out to you to participate in this record of interview?

A: I was told that I wasn't the one that they wanted, they being the police. And, if I helped them in every way I could, they would help me in every way I [sic] could.

Q: So do you consider that a promise for you to participate in this interview or would you have done that anyway?

The suspect answered that he would have done that anyway. This use of the leading question by the interviewer appeared to be an attempt to 'gloss over' an inducement offered by another officer.

In order to ask closed questions effectively, the interviewer has to have prepared for the interview and be capable of reacting intelligently to the suspect's answers. Emphasising preparatory and reactive skills is central to the investigative interviewing style discussed in Chapter 5. The need for such skills was illustrated by numerous interviews in sample 1 in which hesitant, unprepared interviewers made very heavy weather of what should have been straightforward inquiries. One example of many is 064, the case of the stolen remover's trolley mentioned in Chapter 2. The suspect was obviously guilty, and his denials were so incredible that, as suggested above, they would have been more useful to the prosecution than the defence. Nonetheless, the suspect was given confidence to persist with denial by the interviewer's clumsiness. The fact that the latter had to read the file must have encouraged the suspect, as must weak 'challenges' such as 'What if I said to you there was a trolley in the truck?' and questions such as

Is there any reason that you can give that the trolley identical to the one that was in the truck you hired a few days before has been sold to Cash Converters?

Not surprisingly, the suspect replied

What do you mean? Can you repeat that again?

4.6.2 Mode two: allegation, response, challenge

The second question-type sequence involves police presenting the suspect with an allegation (often in some detail), asking for a comment, and then asking further questions in response. An example of this involved the questioning of a 21 year old male allegedly involved in a robbery outside a restaurant late one evening (122). The suspect made unswerving denials. He did admit that his friend 'A' and the complainant had a verbal and physical dispute, but he denied personal involvement in the fight or in the alleged robbery. Questions were as follows:

Do you agree police first spoke to you with A at about 12.15 am on [date], near a block of units at [location]?

Do you agree prior to speaking with police you were with A?

I received information you are responsible or partially responsible for a robbery or theft at [location]. Can you tell me what occurred at about 12 am, just prior to you being spoken to by police?

I will take you back to the start of the incident. You said A and the other guy had an argument. Where did that occur?

You don't know what that was about?

Do you know the person who ran off to get security?

Do you remember what he looked like?

Did anything occur to that person prior to him running off to get security?

This person said you approached him and said, 'What have you done to my friend?' He said you lunged forward and grabbed his mobile phone. What can you tell me about that?

Did you at any time while you were near him then take anything from him?

What were you carrying with you at that stage?

Where were all of those?

So your hands were free?

I also received information that the person involved with A, he saw you walk around the front of his vehicle. He saw you grab hold of his wallet. What can you tell me about that?

When you left [restaurant] would you agree you turned left into [street]?

How far down [x] Street did you walk?

I have been told security spoke to you on [x] Street.

Why did you go to that block of flats?

He tells me he spoke to you as well as the security guard. He asked you to give back his wallet. Is that correct?

He said he saw you pass his wallet to A, who was behind you. Can you tell me anything about that?

Where were you sitting when police spoke to you?

I have been shown a section of flats on a corner...

Was that where you were sitting?

Do you recall at the Police Station you provided Constable T a written statement?

The day following this incident the person who had an altercation with A returned to the flats. Behind the brick wall he found an Ericson mobile phone. Can you tell me anything about this?

He said it was the phone taken from him.

Do you play basketball?

What year did you leave school?

You don't remember what year you left school?

How old are you now?

How old were you when you played basketball at school?

Do you remember ripping your shirt?

Had you and A been anywhere else that day?

Was that the first time you spoke with A that day?

Do you recall when I spoke with you at the Police Station I said I would obtain some police statements and speak with you again?

About an hour ago I spoke with you at your premises?

Do you have anything further to say? (122)

This is an example of the most common type of interview, in which officers structure the interview around an initial allegation, followed by an invitation to the suspect to provide his or her account, then more specific, often closed questions which ask for more detail and challenge the suspect's account by referring to victim or witness statements or other evidence.

After two introductory DYA questions, police told the suspect that the complainant claimed that he was involved in an assault and the taking of a mobile phone and then asked for his account of what happened. As reported above, almost three quarters (74%) of sample 1 suspects were asked in an open question to tell their version of events: 38% of suspects gave their account at the beginning of the interview, while almost one quarter of suspects (24%) did so, usually in response to more specific questions, later in the interview. The suspect's account was then checked and challenged by follow-up questions exploring his answers and drawing on statements from victims or witnesses. In this case, as so often, the open question was somewhat disingenuous: the interviewer's later questions revealed that he had already seen a written statement and had earlier spoken to the suspect at his premises and at the police station. The objective of the interview is not so much to discover the suspect's account as to have it (and the officer's checking and challenging of it) in an ordered, recorded, legalised format. This emphasis on legalisation rather than investigation is even more dominant in mode three, below.

In eliciting accounts, officers often ask 'What happened next?' This can be a useful tool, but it can also become an automatic, inappropriate question, indicating that the officer cannot think of anything more specific to ask. For example, in 206, after the suspect finished giving his account, the interviewer, who appeared not to have been listening, asked 'What happened next?' The bemused suspect simply repeated the account which he had just given.

Asking the horribly worn question 'What can you tell me about that?' (WCYTMAT, as it commonly appears in police notebooks) is an even more problematic practice. The frequency of this question meant that some interviewers asked this repeated question at a faster pace than other, more spontaneously worded questions. At times, WCYTMAT becomes a verbal blur. An example of a more productive approach was 086, in which the interviewer avoided stock phrases, instead inviting the suspect to 'Tell me your side of the story.'

Simply collecting the suspect's account and then contrasting it to information provided by victims or witnesses provides an easy and economical approach to interviewing: the officer can read through a witness statement and ask the suspect to comment on discrepancies between it and his/her account. However, the effectiveness of this approach is questionable. It is all too easy for a suspect to answer that he/she has nothing to say about it, that he/she has said what happened. A standard police response in such circumstances was a hypothetical concerning a victim or witness statement, such as 'Why would she say that if it isn't true?'

> *The interviewer asked questions such as: 'Why would a number of witnesses tell me you kicked R?' (032)*

The frequency of such questions in NSW is an indication of how rarely legal advisers attend interviews in NSW. In England, solicitors routinely intervene to tell the interviewer that his/her client has no way of knowing why someone else would say something and that, therefore, the question is inappropriate and should not be answered. Moreover, such questions infer a reversal of the burden of proof, as if it is the suspect's responsibility to disprove allegations rather than that of the police and prosecution to prove them. Putting pressure on a suspect in this way could be regarded as constituting unfairness and consequently could lead to the exclusion from evidence of any resulting answers (Hunter et al. 2005:1214–1216).

Occasionally, the suspect used the tactic of asking hypothetical questions against the interviewer:

> *During questioning about a stolen Mitsubishi van, the suspect asked the interviewer, 'Plus, why would I want to steal a van for?' Similarly, he later asked in relation to another allegation, 'What would I want a video for?' And when the interviewer challenged the suspect, the suspect, in turn, challenged the interviewer in relation to an allegation that the suspect had stolen a Toyota Landcruiser.*
>
> *Q: Why did R say that you did?*
>
> *A: R's up himself. He doesn't know what he's talking about. How would he know I stole a Toyota Landcruiser ...? (160)*

In both cases, such hypothetical questions are probably better considered as rhetorical devices than genuine requests for information.

Unskilful use of WCYTMAT can signal to the suspect that the interviewer is unprepared. In 209, in which the interviewer had to read a statement during the interview to familiarise herself with it, she asked:

Q: What can you tell me about that?

A: In relation to what? 'Is that right?' — is that what you are asking me?

On occasions, WCYTMAT emerged as a leading question: in 245, the interviewer asked 'What can you tell me about the sexual assault on [A] at [place B]?' As the suspect claimed that the sex had been consensual, it was inappropriate to ask the question in this form. A variant is to precede the WCYTMAT with the statement 'I have been informed that …' (e.g. 233). This distances the interviewer from the allegation, perhaps making it easier to deny.

More effective checking and challenging of the suspect's account would require officers to have spent more time preparing for the interview so that they do not need to look at the victim or witness statement during the interview and are able to construct more probing questions based on knowledge of such statements. Whether it is realistic to expect officers to have time for such preparation is a critical question which will be addressed in Chapter 5.

The point at which thorough checking of detail slips into pedantry is not certain. However, some interviewers seek what appears to be unnecessary detail in checking suspects' accounts. For example, in 251, one might have thought that there would be few questions to ask about a blue and pink ceramic bowl in which cannabis seeds had been found. However, following the suspect's remark that she did not know how the seeds got there, the detective continued to ask detailed questions about the bowl, how long the suspect had owned it, where she kept it in her house, how often she looked at it, who else had access to it, and so on. The detail of questions and the depth of questioning at times brought a slight smile of amusement or disbelief to the suspect's lips. The suspect's perception that these questions were absurd appeared to give her confidence in denying the offence. Similarly, in 269, a cooperative suspect became increasingly irritated by the interviewer's follow-up questions. The way that this was done gave the impression that he was not listening to answers provided. Antagonising suspects may have uses, but it also has costs.

Meanwhile, in 266, detail seemed to provide a substitute for substance: the interviewer had considerable difficulty communicating via an interpreter with a man suspected of transporting heroin from Sydney to Melbourne:

The two interviewers struggled to get the suspect to give relevant, specific answers. He repeatedly seemed to answer questions other than those asked of him. This misunderstanding or avoidance, coupled with the suspect's insistence that he did not know or could not remember, made the interviewers became increasingly interested in obtaining specific answers that they could verify through further investigation. Finally, the interviewer did find out the name of the motel in which the suspect slept for a few hours during his drive from Sydney to Melbourne. Even though the interviewer was pleased to have this specific information, its usefulness was dubious. How did knowing that the suspect had stayed in a specific motel to sleep briefly contribute to the investigation? It was as though this interviewer had lost sight of the task at hand, but was pleased to have something to latch on to that would somehow allow further investigation.

Meanwhile, in some other cases, inadequate detail was collected. For example, in 272:

The interviewer did not gather sufficient detail and as a result important issues remained unresolved. For example, he asked which police officers had allegedly assaulted the suspect upon arrest. He did not ask what each individual had done, however. Similarly, the interviewer was told that the suspect had been tackled twice by either one or two friends, in a successful attempt to remove a rake and a knife from him. The interviewer recognised that the suspect had visible injuries (including blood on his cheek, a swollen eye and redness at his wrists). Lack of detail in questioning meant that, at the end of the ERISP, it was not clear how the suspect had been tackled by the friends and whether his injuries could have been sustained during the tackles rather than during arrest. Perhaps the interviewer decided that clarifying the source of the injuries might be problematic in that

it might have elicited the 'wrong' answers, leading to criticism of
the arresting officers.

There was a marked contrast between the mass of apparently inconsequential detail collected in some cases and the seemingly obvious information gaps in others.

In our example, the questioning began with two DYAs about pre-ERISP police contact. Unusually, the interviewer returns to two further DYAs at the end of the interview before, as usual, questioning ended with the standard, 'Do you have anything further to say?' These are examples of the third mode of questioning, to be considered below.

The success of interviewing by means of allegation, response, and challenge depends, not surprisingly, on the skill and commitment of the interviewer. In the hands of a good investigator, it can provide a useful structure and, indeed, is similar in key respects to the strategy of investigative interviewing discussed in Chapter 5. However, without the elaboration provided by investigative interview training, allegation, response, and challenge can and often does slip into two problems. First, in outlining the allegation, too much information may be given to the suspect, making it difficult to know whether any subsequent confession is reliable or whether he/she is simply restating information provided by the interviewer. Secondly, if the interviewer is not willing and able to check the suspect's account actively, then the interview can be little more than an exchange of statements.

4.6.3 Mode three: legalising previous activity

One of the many myths about policing which media representations continue to feed is the belief that interviews are the primary site where investigative activity occurs (Reiner 2000:ch5). By contrast, many interviews in our samples were concerned not with investigation and discovery, but rather with the legal packaging of previous interaction between police and suspect into legal categories and terminology which can then be processed through later stages of the criminal justice process.[7]

Such 'legalisation' in police interviews with suspects comes in two forms. First, closed questions of the type discussed in mode 2 are used to ensure that the legal requirements to prosecute successfully are satisfied. In particular, this means proof of intention is supplied when

---

[7] More generally on legalisation, see Dixon 1997:268–274.

this is a component of an offence. An example of this is the officers' questions in 123 (discussed above) about the suspect's suspicion that the cloth had been stolen.

Secondly, police use interviews in order to construct an accepted, recorded account of events and police-suspect interaction (including interviews) before the ERISP. As Baldwin stresses, the priority is to 'limit, close-down, or pre-empt the future options available to the suspect' (1993:351). A key to doing this is to use the interview as an opportunity not just to ask the suspect about the alleged offence, but also about his or her treatment by police. The aim is to lock the suspect into an account which will prevent him or her from subsequently challenging police accounts of or raising complaints about police activities.

In this sense, interviewing practice corresponds closely with the concern (discussed in Chapter 1) to use electronic recording as a means of preventing disputes in court and allegations of police misconduct. Large sections of the interviews in our samples were concerned, not with the alleged offence, but with the interaction between police and suspect before the ERISP began. Legalisation involves the suspect being asked, in a series of questions beginning with the phrase 'Do you agree …?', to confirm the police account of matters such as initial contact, search, seizure of evidence, arrest, transport to station, weighing and packaging of illegal drugs. In one extreme example (246), a suspect was asked 96 'Do you agree?' questions in 15 minutes. Most importantly and potentially problematically,[8] 'DYA' is used to incorporate into the electronic record an account of questions and answers in earlier interviews.

The following example of a series of questions in one of our sample 1 interviews illustrates the use of DYA questions:

> *Do you agree (DYA) that at about 2.40 pm this afternoon you were stopped by Detectives X and Y in the vicinity of the car park at [Restaurant M]?*
>
> *DYA you were then taken by those Detectives to the (Station H) Detectives' Office?*
>
> *DYA upon arrival at the (Station H) Detectives' Office you were seated in an interview room?*

---

[8]   On the problems of 'quoted speech', see 2.4.3, above.

DYA at about 3.15 pm Detective K and I first spoke with you in that interview room?

DYA I told you I was making enquiries in relation to a B&E with intent to steal on 21 October 1996?

DYA I told you I had received information that you were involved in this matter?

DYA I (cautioned you)?

DYA you told me in fact you were involved in this matter?

DYA I also spoke to you in relation to an attempted fraud committed at the (P Bank), (Kville), on (date)?

DYA I was speaking to you in relation to that matter and you admitted being involved in that offence?

DYA when speaking to you I showed you two black and white photographs?

DYA those photographs depicted yourself?

DYA during our conversation Detective P asked you to write certain words on a white, blank A-4 piece of paper?

DYA those words were 'five thousand dollars'?

DYA you wrote those words as best you could on a white piece of paper?

DYA he also asked you to write 'five thousand dollars' in numbers?

DYA that you wrote that?

DYA that I told you I intended to conduct an interview on this matter?

DYA that you agreed to be interviewed electronically in relation to this matter?

DYA you were conveyed to the (Z) Police Station?

DYA you were then brought to this interview room?

I now intend to ask you further questions about this matter. Do you understand that? (143)

DYA questions in ERISPs are used extensively to produce a record of what happened when police arrested a suspect and/or searched his or her person, vehicle or premises. If the suspect agrees with the police account, he or she will find it difficult subsequently to dispute the police account or to make allegations of wrongdoing against police. As might be expected, DYAs are particularly useful in dealing with alleged drug offences. Legalisation of pre-ERISP interviewer-suspect conversation is also illustrated by ERISPs in which pre-ERISP police notebook interviews are adopted or mentioned.

The range of uses of DYA questions is illustrated by 148, the questioning of an 18 year old suspect who had been stopped by police while driving a van. The interviewer divided the ERISP into three areas: the suspect's alleged possession of two bags of cannabis leaf (9.81 gm and 1.17 gm); his alleged self-administration of cannabis on a specified day; and his alleged possession of a drug-related implement (a pipe used for smoking cannabis). The suspect made a straight confession from the outset in relation to all three allegations. Questions asked were:

> *Do you agree that I first spoke to you at about 9.05 pm on [date]?*
>
> *Do you agree (DYA) this was the result of stopping you in your vehicle, a white VW Combi-van?*
>
> *You were stopped at [location]. DYA it was adjacent to the off-ramp at [location]?*
>
> *DYA the registration of your vehicle is (registration number)?*
>
> *DYA I submitted you to a roadside breath test?*
>
> *DYA you were the only person in your vehicle at the time?*
>
> *I will show you the official police notebook number [#]. For the purposes of transcription, this official police notebook is issued to me.*
>
> *DYA I made these notes as they appear on pages 2–7 inclusively?*
>
> *DYA I made these notes in your presence at the [X] Hospital?*
>
> *DYA that these notes are a true and accurate record of our conversations?*
>
> *DYA that these notes are a true and accurate record of our movements?*
>
> *DYA you signed each page to verify the correctness of these notes?*

DYA that on page 7 you wrote, 'This is a true and accurate record of what has happened and been said'?

DYA that you signed the notebook at [X] Hospital?

DYA you signed these notes at about 10.35?

I will now show you a bag containing certain items.

What can you tell me about these items?

Can you tell me how many items are in this bag?

And you call it marijuana?

DYA these bags containing marijuana were weighed in your presence at [X] Police Station?

DYA the piece of paper inside the bag is a photocopy of the weight docket?

Is that the same weight docket that was weighed in your presence, or a photocopy of it?

DYA — is this your signature on that docket?

Are there two signatures on that docket?

And are there two separate weights?

And can you tell me what those weights are? Thank you.

Was any threat, promise or offer of advantage held out to you to sign the docket?

Was the contents of this bag as they were, when Senior Constable [X] located them in your vehicle?

Is it true that I was present when they were located?

DYA I conducted a further search of your vehicle?

DYA I located this smaller clear re-sealable bag?

Can you tell me what they were doing in your vehicle?

Where did you get the cannabis?

Can you tell me the name of that friend?

What is D's last name?

Can you tell me where D resides?

How old is D?

Can you describe D for me?

How much did you pay for the cannabis?

For which bag?

You just said that you did not know the other bag was in there, is that correct?

DYA that was, in fact, located in your presence?

Are you in any way, shape or form insinuating that the police planted that drug in your vehicle?

Is it possible the police planted that in your vehicle?

And what quantity was in the larger bag when you paid $200 for it?

Why have you got the cannabis?

Have you ever sold cannabis?

Is there anything else you wish to tell me about the cannabis?

I now intend asking you questions in relation to your allegedly administering cannabis to yourself on [date] at [location]. [Caution].

DYA at your vehicle I said, 'When did you last smoke it?'

DYA you clearly understood I was referring to the cannabis?

DYA you said, 'Just then, after —'

Can you tell me how long prior to police stopping you that you had smoked it?

Where exactly did you smoke the cannabis?

Who did you smoke it with?

What is your friend's name?

Do you know R's last name?

How did you smoking the cannabis make you feel?

Did it make you feel any other way?

For how long now have you been smoking cannabis?

Having smoked cannabis for three years, would it be fair to say your knowledge of cannabis is quite good?

Did you know whilst at the [X] car park, just prior to us stopping you, that you were smoking cannabis?

How did you know you were smoking cannabis?

Can you tell me how you knew it was cannabis?

Does cannabis give you certain effects?

How did you smoke the cannabis?

That's the pipe you are referring to here?

(The suspect was shown a pipe.)

I am now going to ask you questions in relation to this implement. [Caution].

DYA while searching your vehicle I located this pipe in the glove box?

What can you tell me about that pipe?

The piece you made ... and the other two pieces you referred to, what would you call those two pieces?

Did you intend using the pipe in the future?

When did you intend using the pipe next?

What were you going to use it for?

Is there anything further you wish to tell me about your possession of this implement?

Is there anything further you wish to tell me about any of these matters? (148)

This interview is an example of a mode of interviewing that is almost entirely concerned with obtaining a legalised record of earlier police interaction with the suspect. The question-type sequence used in this interview was exhibit focused. Largely by nature of the alleged offences, there was neither a complainant statement nor a witness statement. At the end of the series of DYAs, the suspect was shown an exhibit, a bag containing prohibited drugs and a drug 'implement'. In each case, he was asked an open question about this exhibit, 'What can you tell me about these items/that pipe?', followed by a series of closed questions.

The suspect was asked, via DYA questions, to confirm the police account of: how his vehicle was stopped and searched; how he was questioned; what was found in his possession and his knowledge of them; the weighing of the drugs found; and his dismissal of any suggestion of impropriety by the police. A series of closed questions about the suspect's experience of using cannabis serve to cover the element of knowledge needed to prove an offence of possession. The interviewers only step outside this legalising mode into anything approaching an investigative mode when they ask questions about supply: who supplied the drugs to the suspect, and did he intend to sell them. Unusually, the suspect provided information about his supplier. Like all drug possession suspects, his priority is to deflect officers from thinking of him or charging him as a supplier. This section of the interview ended with the standard question whether the suspect wished to say anything further about any of these matters discussed.

In another example, 239, the suspect was arrested while carrying bottles of liquor from a shop which had been robbed. The primary purpose of the interview appeared to be to produce a legalised account linking the suspect to the robbery: the interviewer got the suspect to recognise the bottles and the clothes which he was wearing, and to answer DYAs about the arrest. In such cases, the interview is a secondary complement to the primary investigative tools of physical evidence and witness statements.

4.6.4 Comparing modes of interviewing

As the discussion above has shown, these modes are not exclusive: some interviews, for example, include substantial investigative questioning as well as extensive legalisation of pre-ERISP interaction. However, it is useful to distinguish these three broad modes of questioning. They present a considerable challenge to the popular belief that police interviewing is exclusively or even predominantly an investigative function.

CHAPTER 5

'PEACE' AND INVESTIGATIVE INTERVIEWING SKILLS

5.1   The origins of investigative interviewing

Traditionally, learning to interview suspects has been regarded as a matter of absorbing a craft skill. A Victorian police inspector advised young officers in the following terms:

> Most outstanding interrogators will be able to help you with certain advice, but rarely are they able to define themselves just what makes them so successful in this field. It is an ability developed over the years, coupled with experience of all types of criminals, which enables them to sum up the suspect and ask the right questions at the appropriate time (Crowley 1972:419–420).

This concept of interviewing as a skill which had to be learnt, not taught, has come under increasing criticism. In England and Wales, concerns about investigative weaknesses and miscarriages of justice led to scrutiny of the quality of police interviewing. The Royal Commission on Criminal Procedure recommended reform of interview training (1981:10.14), but this was 'the neglected recommendation and little was done for nearly ten years to implement' it (Williamson 1993b:92).

In this vacuum, police officers who were interested in improving their interviewing skills almost inevitably looked to the United States. American interview training manuals — notably Inbau and Reid's — were a significant influence in some areas, encouraging officers both to use persuasive interrogation techniques and to attempt to recognise deception by suspects (Williamson 1993b:92; Milne & Bull 1999:156; Mortimer & Shepherd 1999:299, 300). American material was used in training materials and strongly influenced the first British police interview manual, Walkley's *Police Interrogation* (1987). In turn, such material was promoted in Australia. Notably, extracts from Walkley's book were reproduced in police magazines. When such approaches to interrogation began to be officially frowned upon, nothing was provided to replace them, and so they continued to form a significant part of an informal curriculum of material distributed amongst police officers.

When research on how English police interrogated suspects began in earnest, significant problems were discovered:

> Questioning practice could be characterized as bland information gathering ... The level of questioning skill was quite low, with Officers (sic) capitulating at the slightest obstacle ... Many interviews appeared chaotic and unstructured. In a significant number the allegation was never put to the suspect. In others the questioning appeared to lack basic preparation and planning. Many of the Officers seemed more nervous than the suspect (Williamson 1993b:97–98).

Similar assessments were made by Baldwin (1993) and Moston and colleagues (Moston & Engelberg 1993; Moston & Stephenson 1993b).

Such research had a major impact, directly influencing a new National Investigative Training Course which was launched in 1993 (Home Office 1993), complemented by Home Office circular 22/1992 on 'Principles of investigative interviewing' (NCF 1998:157) and the Central Planning and Training Unit's *A Guide to Interviewing* and *The Interviewer's Rule Book*. The accredited approach was 'investigative interviewing', which was constructed around the seemingly inevitable police use of a mnemonic acronym, PEACE.[1] The new approach was positively appraised by the Home Office (McGurk et al. 1993) and, with more qualification, by Clarke and Milne (2002). The episode is a significant example of academic research influencing police policy: other than Baldwin (a criminologist), the principal contributors were psychologists, and psychology's status as a 'scientific' discipline undoubtedly facilitated this (Williamson 1993b:98).

By the mid-1990s, there was already interest in PEACE in New South Wales. Watching ERISP tapes had led some police supervisors and judges to be concerned about interview quality. The standard process of policy transfer then began. International literature was consulted, and NSW officers went on study tours to the UK. The result was that the NSW Police adopted a version of PEACE which began to be used in interview training.

The concern generated by ERISP images also prompted this facet of our research, in which we focus on what ERISP tells us about the quality of interviewing practice. This chapter assesses the quality of interview practice in NSW by presenting the results of research on a

---

[1]   PEACE = Preparation and planning; Engage and explain; Account, clarification and challenge; Closure; Evaluation.

randomly chosen sample of 75 officers who had received the new interview training (sample 2). Comparisons are made both with interviews conducted by such officers before training and with the broader group of officers in sample 1. Quantitative data are collected in an appendix at the end of this chapter.

5.2   Identifying good interviewing

How does one identify good interviewing of suspects? The traditional criterion was obtaining a confession from a suspect who would not otherwise have confessed. The problem with using such a criterion is that, as noted above, a simple shift from denial to confession is very rare. We are left with 'what if?' speculation about interviews ending in denials and silence. Even if a confession was made, perhaps better interviewing would have produced a fuller account. Furthermore, it is now widely accepted that undue concentration on obtaining a confession can be harmful. At worst, officers may single-mindedly focus on proving that their case theory was right, leading them to ignore evidence to the contrary. Such interviewing has been associated with numerous miscarriages of justice (Gudjonsson 2003:ch7). More generally, confession-focused interviewing may lead officers to gather information inefficiently.

Consequently, other criteria for evaluation are needed. While an interview with a suspect undoubtedly has special characteristics, in general, it is appropriate, as Baldwin suggests, to apply 'standards of good interviewing practice adopted in other situations to the tapes of police interviews'. This approach entails

> allowing suspects an unhurried and uninterrupted opportunity to state their position; listening to their responses; avoiding harrying, coercive, or authoritarian tactics; and testing a suspect's account with fairness and integrity. It is evident that a competent interviewer in any situation requires a variety of communicative and social skills, including a calm disposition and temperament, patience, subtlety, imagination, an ability to respond quickly and flexibly, and legal knowledge (Baldwin 1993:329; see also id 1992a:9).

It is against this background that the PEACE interviewing method was developed.

In analysing our sample of interviews, we adapted criteria which were used in McGurk et al.'s evaluation of PEACE training in England

and Wales (1993) and in the discussion of PEACE in the National Crime Faculty's *A Practical Guide to Investigative Interviewing* (1998). Quantitative measures of performance were developed by classifying 14 elements of the interviewing process as excellent, acceptable, less than acceptable, or unacceptable (see Table 5.4, below page 218). These elements were: planning/structuring the interview; using notes, witness statements etc; covering legal issues; introducing the interview; establishing relationship with suspect; adopting appropriate style for offence/suspect; communication skills; listening skills; inviting suspect's account; checking suspect's account; adopting open-minded approach; using questioning techniques; participants' understanding of interview and outcome; and planning closure (for details see Table 5.4, below page 218). Nine of these criteria broadly conform to McGurk et al.'s indicators, allowing some comparative assessment. In retrospect, it might have been better for both studies to choose five rather than four categories. 'Acceptable' became effectively a default category, thereby producing quantitative results which appear a little more favourable than our qualitative analysis.

Between 3% and 26% of interviews are categorised 'not applicable'. The reason for this varied. For example, suspects who refused to answer questions did not present an account that could be checked. On the other hand, if a suspect confessed from the start, the officers could usually do little to indicate that they remained open-minded. More straightforwardly, sections of some interview were not recorded.

5.3   Preparation and planning

5.3.1 Value of preparation

Commentators on interviewing frequently stress the importance of preparation and planning. In the policing context, this has two major elements. First, officers should interview only after other investigative work has been carried out (except, for example, when officers are dealing with a case requiring immediate arrest and detention, such as a brawl which they break up). This marks a shift from older styles of investigation, in which post-arrest interrogation was often the first investigative step. Such tactics have been held responsible for inefficient investigations, some of which degenerated into substantial miscarriages of justice.

Secondly, there is the specific preparation required in order to interview: 'it is a prerequisite of good interviewing that officers know the relevant law, have studied the available evidence in the case, and have given thought about how best to structure the interview' (Baldwin 1992a:12). Almost half the interviews in sample 2 were regarded as acceptable in this respect. One quarter were excellent, but 18% were unacceptable to some degree. The extent to which an officer has prepared is not always evident. There are, however, some clear indications of both good and inadequate preparation. Planning can be inferred when interviews feature a logical, systematic development of questions. It is most clearly indicated when the interviewer has on hand exhibits, such as illicit drugs or stolen goods, which are used as the focal point of the interview and with which he/she is evidently familiar. Many sample 2 interviews involved reference to exhibits or, more commonly, statements (from witnesses, victims, or arresting officers). The interviewing officers' familiarity with such documents was an important indication both of good preparation and successful interviewing. Similarly, in 202, the interviewer began by playing four selected excerpts from telephone intercepts which incriminated the suspect in cocaine dealing. The suspect was quietly told 'We have about 60 calls of the same nature.' The selection of appropriate intercepts was a vital preparatory activity.

We broaden the concept of good planning to include the completion of necessary pre-interview investigation, and the interviewer's consideration of how to introduce the products of such activity into the interview. A good example of an officer doing so is 238:

> A search at the suspect's residence of the suspect had been conducted. Personal items and the suspect's mobile phone were collected. The interviewer had visited the complainant's house and had seen the hole in the ceiling and other evidence of the reported break-in. A telephone company enquiry had been made and a list of phone calls to the complainant's house during the relevant period had been obtained. The interviewer appeared to have prepared and thought about how she would proceed with questioning.

By contrast, lack of planning was evident in a number of interviews in which officers shuffled through notes and witness statements which they had apparently not consulted beforehand. It was common to see officers looking at material with which they were either unfamiliar or which they had forgotten, and framing questions on the run. For example, in 241, the interviewers were unprepared, lacked confidence and made a mountain out of what should have been a simple matter. In 230, the officers did not know the location at which the offence occurred, and had to go to find a map in the middle of the interview in order to make sense of the suspect's answers. When the primary interviewer ran out of questions, he turned to the partner in apparent desperation, asking if he had any questions. Occasionally (e.g. 036), this sort of disorganised process proceeded until the end of the audio tape put the interview out of its misery.

However, regarding such practices as always deserving criticism may be harsh. We have to be realistic about the need for extensive preparation in everyday cases, and about officers' opportunity to prepare. First, many interviews involving straightforward interviews with cooperative suspects do not require extensive planning. The interviewer follows the basic structure of putting the allegation, asking for a response, and then checking it against available information, usually from witnesses (see Chapter 4, above). Indeed, the PEACE formula reduces the need for active planning by providing a standard format for such interviews. Secondly, officers argue that, in a busy Local Area Command, they may well not have time to prepare extensively for standard, uncontentious interviews. While champions of investigative interviewing may dismiss such claims, it would be unfair and unrealistic to criticise officers as if their interviewing style was unaffected by contextual conditions and demands.
Researchers in England have emphasised that

> interviewers often have to work to short deadlines and have high case loads. Managers and supervisors want quick 'clear-ups' ... 'Lack of time' is often referred to by police officers as being an important factor which affects the quality of their interviews (Milne & Bull 1999:160).

> There are still too many pressures posed by managers and supervisors which cumulatively preclude sensible prior investigation and force the officer to interview prematurely, without sufficient information, information processing, and forethought (Shepherd 1993a:10–11).

Consequently, we were generous in our assessments: interview planning and structuring were treated as less than acceptable or unacceptable only in clear cases.

Nonetheless, there were some such cases in which preparation would have been helpful, and indeed its absence was surprising. Such examples show how necessary and important preparation can be in appropriate cases. In 230, an assault suspect was re-interviewed some seven months after the original interview. The second interview was apparently intended as an opportunity for the officers to confront the suspect with incriminating evidence in witness statements. However, they showed no familiarity with these statements, and fumbled their way through the interview. The officers had found witnesses to the alleged assault, but their lack of preparation meant that their questions had no impact on the suspect. The principal effect of this interview appeared to be to strengthen the suspect's commitment to denial.

We also categorised as unacceptable interviews for which the preparation for the interview included pressurising the suspect inappropriately, as in 213 when the suspect reported that the interviewer had told him that he would be remanded in custody if he did not name another person involved in the alleged offence. Similarly, discouraging access to a solicitor (224), failing to act on the clear need for an interpreter (215), and inappropriate pre-ERISP interviewing (216, 251, 261) were regarded as unacceptable. Proceeding with interviews with evidently intoxicated or drug-affected suspects were other examples of poor preparation (260). Fifteen per cent of interviews in sample 2 involved suspects who were clearly affected by drink or illicit drugs, despite the CRIME Code's clear instruction to '[d]efer questioning suspects affected by alcohol or drugs until they are no longer affected' (NSW Police 1998:23; this problem was addressed in Chapter 3, above). By contrast, 254 concerned a suspect who had been too intoxicated for interview when arrested, and so had been released without charge and had returned voluntarily for interview six days later. In this case, the officers had followed procedure, and their investigation did not suffer.

5.3.2 Use of notes, witness statements and physical evidence

An officer's appropriate level of familiarity with strong evidential material must facilitate the suspect's cooperation. In several cases, officers showed suspects physical evidence, such as stolen property.

As in the case involving taped intercepts noted in Chapter 3 above, confident, well-organised use of such material strengthens the interviewer's hand.

Fifty-seven per cent of interviews in sample 2 included excellent or acceptable use of notes and statements, while in 14% use was less than acceptable or unacceptable. The use of documents again raises issues of lack of preparation. Officers who flick through witness statements, extracting material apparently at random and asking for the suspect's comments often appear unprepared. Focusing on unfamiliar paperwork prevents some from interviewing effectively. Suspects faced with unprepared officers may gain more from the interview than the investigators. Evident unfamiliarity may breed contempt.

More prosaically, there were several examples of poor interviewing practice in sample 2. For example, in 230, various statements were available, but their use was not optimised. For example, one witness statement was read in detail and after each section the suspect was asked, 'Do you understand that?' Then, at the *end* of the document he was asked if he had any comment to make in relation to the document as a whole. This approach asked for a general response to the witness statement and did not encourage the detailed information that might have been collected had information-gathering questions been more specifically focused on smaller sections of the statement. In other cases, there were references to pre-ERISP interviews of which there were no contemporaneous record (251) and to unspecified witness/victim statements (254).

The potential benefits of using statements were illustrated by their absence in 243. This interview concerned an alleged robbery. If witness or victim statements were available, they were not used. The suspect simply denied any involvement and claimed that he could not remember various matters, such as where he was at the time of the robbery. The result was a rather pointless interview. The interviewer should have been able to ask specific questions stemming from a witness or victim statement, thereby attracting a more precise and detailed denial which could be investigated and challenged if necessary.

5.3.3 Coverage of legal issues and points to prove

As discussed in 4.6.3 (above), the prime purpose of many interviews with suspects is to 'legalise' the account by securing their adoption of what has gone before. In general, sample 2 interviewers spent less time than those in sample 1 on lengthy incorporation of material previously recorded in police notebooks. For example, in 273, the suspect's pre-ERISP claim that he had owned an allegedly stolen Nintendo 'for years' was dealt with in a simple (albeit double-barrelled) question:

> *Q: Do you agree you told me you owned the Nintendo for years and you brought it for your daughter from Melbourne?*

In sample 1, such matters would have been dealt with by lengthy adoption of written questions and answers. Reducing the stilted DYAs certainly improved interaction in sample 2 interviews.

Here, we are concerned with the more specific issues of whether the interviewing officers cover the points needed to prove an offence and whether procedures are followed appropriately. Sixty-eight per cent of interviews were rated as acceptable or excellent, while 20% were unacceptable or less than acceptable.

Usually, the reason why the suspect is being interviewed requires no legal elaboration: they have been arrested for a straightforward offence. However, legal issues can be more complex. There may, for example, be numerous legal elements of an offence to be covered. Similarly, there can be difficulty when the suspect's account is a denial of primary responsibility for the alleged offence, but amounts to an admission to complicity, or to a lesser or other offence. Such cases disrupt the neat division of confess/deny/silence. Officers tended not to explore the potentially complex elements of offences included in such admissions, understandably preferring to concentrate upon the simpler issues of primary responsibility.

In other more legally complex cases, some suspects deny committing the offence, but what they say amounts to an unintentional admission. For example, in 091, the suspect considered that he had done nothing wrong in pushing the victim during an altercation in a soccer game: however, what he described constituted at least a common assault.

Occasionally, officers appear not to have considered what offence category would fit the suspect's action. In 105, police had apparently given no thought to this before the interview. A young man had fired an arrow up in the air. On its descent, it hit a neighbour. There was no reference in the interview to what the offence was: it was apparently taken for granted that an offence had been committed, and that the categorisation could come later. Sometimes, failure to specify a suspected offence was deliberate: as we will suggest at the end of this section, in some cases, officers appeared to treat a person as a suspect in order to put pressure on them to provide information about another person.

Failure to deal with certain issues may be problematic as when, for example, defences or potential limits on responsibility are not raised. As noted above, some officers failed to acknowledge the potential problems of interviewing suspects who were affected by alcohol or other drugs. Similarly, the responsibility of suspects displaying intellectual disability received inadequate attention, at least in the interview setting.

Comprehensive legal coverage need not require technicality. 204 provided an example of an excellent interview:

> The interviewer proceeded through a step-by-step re-enactment of the incidents alleged and asked the suspect firstly to tell what had happened and then to respond to allegations. At the end of the interview, there was detailed information about what the suspect admitted and denied for each aspect of the alleged incidents. (204)

Here, the points to be proved were skilfully elicited by the interviewer's probing of the suspect's factual account.

In some cases, it may be inappropriate for the interviewer to ask legally focused questions. If the suspect denies an allegation, the legal issues contract: it would, for example, be obviously inappropriate to ask if the suspect had an owner's permission to take an item if the former denies having taken it.

Sometimes, the suspect cooperates in covering the legal issues. For example, in 239 the suspect faced a series of allegations about fraud:

> By the third set of questions about the suspect's attempt to obtain money unlawfully, the suspect himself was versed in what he would be asked about legal issues. In response to the open question of what he had done, he followed his cue by stating,
>
> A: I didn't know the people and I had no right to do it.

After being shown an exhibit (a letter used to obtain money), he stated

> A: I wrote that letter with the intention of fraudulently withdrawing this money from the account of [J].

Some officers showed a good understanding of law and procedure. For example, in 241 the suspect was attending the station for interview voluntarily, but when he admitted to an offence, the officers suspended the interview while he was arrested, and taken to the custody manager to be booked in and advised of his rights. Similarly, in 248 when this suspect said that he did 'not really' want to participate in an ERISP, the interviewer clarified the suspect's desire to remain silent and ended the interview immediately.

On the other hand, significant procedural shortcomings included failure to record pre-ERISP questioning, which led to an unproductive dispute about what the suspect had said in 251. In 253, the suspect's attempts to rely on the right to silence were countered by the interviewer trying to talk through a refusal to answer questions:

> At the beginning of the interview, in response to the preliminary caution, the suspect stated that he did not want to participate in an interview. Soon afterwards, he said to the interviewer: 'I have been told, guilty or not guilty, I shouldn't answer any questions'. The interviewer responded: 'I will just clarify some circumstances of you being here.' He then went on to ask several 'Do you agree ...?' questions outlining the circumstance of the suspect coming to the police station. After confirming this information, the interviewer returned to the issue of the suspect's initial statement that he wanted to remain silent.
>
> Q: So what you're now saying is you don't wish to participate in any form of interview, is that correct?
>
> A: Yeah. From what I have been told I should —
>
> Q: I want it to be your decision, you know. Forget about what you've been told. Do you wish to be interviewed?
>
> A: No.
>
> Q: OK.

Despite this clear answer, the interviewer then proceeded, saying that he wanted 'to show you a couple of items for the transcript'. The first was a pack of cigarettes. The interviewer asked where the suspect had bought them. The second was a knife that the interviewer said was found in the police vehicle in which the suspect had been transported to the police station. In relation to this knife, the interviewer asked if the suspect could tell him anything about it.

When the suspect said, 'No', the interviewer asked, 'Nothing at all?' Questioning then continued. Had the suspect ever been to a particular news agency? The interviewer's partner asked the time, location and day that the cigarettes had been purchased, telling the suspect, 'We'll check the cameras to see if you were in there at that time.' The interviewer told the suspect that he wanted to specify the allegations. Having done so, he asked,

Q: Can you tell me anything about that?

A: What do you want me to say?

Q: I am asking you. Can you tell me anything about that?

A: I've got nothing to say. I don't know anything.

Q: So is there anything further you wish to tell me about any of the matters I've raised this morning?

A: When do we all go home?

After mentioning the adoption procedure, the interviewer again asked,

Q: So, is there anything further you can tell me?

A: No.

In short, this interviewer did not accept the suspect's decision to remain silent. He became slightly aggressive in manner and repeatedly asked the suspect to answer questions despite the suspect's clear indication that he was not prepared to do so.

Similarly, in 279, the interviewer established that the suspect intended to remain silent. He then stated that he wanted to show the suspect the items brought from his house that day in order to ensure that these were correctly recorded. But, rather than simply showing the suspect the items and asking for confirmation, the interviewer asked further questions about the items, despite the suspect's stated desire to remain silent. The interviewer asked, for example,

Q: What can you tell me about this shirt?

He then pointed to one section of the shirt and asked,

Q: Can you tell me what that is there?

The suspect identified the spot as blood that had come from his nose. The interviewer asked further,

Q: What can you tell me about this jacket?

Q: This was the jacket you were wearing on Saturday night, was it?

Again, in 286a, the interviewer at one stage counted notes that were found in the suspect's wallet at the time of arrest.

Q: Where did you get this $480 in $20 notes from?

A: I don't wish to answer that.

Q: Pardon?

A: I don't wish to answer that.

Q: Why don't you wish to answer that?

A: You told me that I don't have to.

Q: Did you get this money from supplying heroin?

A: No. I don't supply heroin. I use heroin.

Q: Did you get this $480 in $20 notes from supplying cannabis?

A: No.

Q: You don't wish to say anything further about that money?

A: No ... When I've got a solicitor present ... When I go to court ...

While it was apparent that this interviewer recognised the suspect's right to remain silent, it was as though he could not help himself asking these further questions about the supply of heroin and cannabis. The officers in these cases displayed a clear unwillingness to accept a suspect's refusal to answer questions. Similarly, in a sample 1 case, the suspect had received legal advice before the interview not to answer questions. Having established that, the interviewer simply proceeded to detail what had been found during a search of the suspect's property and asked for her comments. He then asked a series of questions about the property, who lived there, her knowledge of it, use of the land, and many others related to the allegation that she had grown cannabis (151). In effect, her stated intention not to answer questions on legal advice was swept aside by a barrage of questions which eventually drew replies.

As has often been the case in the past, judicial discretion bears considerable responsibility for such incidents. Contrary to what may be common belief,

> There is no absolute rule that an interview conducted in the face of an
> objection by a suspect, or continued in the face of an indication that he

or she does not wish to participate any further in it, should be rejected if tendered in evidence ... Each case must be determined upon its own facts.[2]

This may appear to be the right course to a judge whose focus is on the individual case. However, it exemplifies the inadequacies of this approach to legal regulation. In effect, police are encouraged to continue interviewing despite attempts to exercise the right to silence. They can hope that the trial judge will accept the evidence. If he or she does not, nothing is lost.

What if a suspect answers, but the interviewers think he or she is lying? As in England, judges are reluctant to give specific guidance to interviewers. In a much-quoted ruling in *Heron*, Mitchell J said that police questioning can be 'persistent, searching and robust'. But an officer seeking guidance on what this means will be disappointed: 'Where the line is to be drawn between proper and robust persistence and oppressive interrogation can only be identified in general terms.'[3] A similar approach has been taken in Australia:

[T]here is a large body of case law which takes a benign attitude towards police who keep questioning their suspect about matters as to which they think they have been given a lie ... [W]hile police may not 'cross-examine' their suspect, that term is to be given a fairly extreme meaning in the context of deciding the involuntariness issue (Hunter et al. 2005:642).

The replacement of the involuntariness test by the Evidence Act's more specific grounds for exclusion has not had a significant effect in this respect:

Persistent questioning will not, of itself, create a basis for exclusion under s.85 (or s90) [of the Evidence Act 1995]. It is a matter of degree that will depend also on the qualities of the interviewee and other surrounding circumstances. Evidence will be excluded if 'there is any suggestion of intimidation, persistent importunity or sustained or undue insistence or pressure'.[4]

---

[2] Wood CJ, in *R v Vinh Ngoc Phan*, NSW CCA, 4 June 2001, unreported, paras 54, 56.

[3] Unreported, Leeds Crown Court, 1 November 1993. On the problem of reconciling what is allowed in the police interview room and the courtroom — and the way electronic recording has affected it — see Dixon 1997:174–175.

[4] Hunter et al. 2002:272, quoting *R v Clarke* (1997) 97 A Crim R 414. Hunter et al. note that 'The standard seems to be lower, however, where a suspect has taken legal

Such advice is not very helpful to a police officer seeking to ascertain just what he or she can and cannot do in questioning a suspect.

Coverage of legal issues may be a problem when officers apparently use a suspect interview for the purpose of investigating an offence by another person. Legal issues are often not clearly distinct. There may be a less serious offence of which the person is suspected: the classic use of this is the 'holding charge'. Police may genuinely not know what has happened. But if so, custodial interrogation is inappropriate. For example, in 284, the suspect was questioned about a murder. It became apparent that he was not a suspect, but that the investigating officers were using a custodial interview in order to obtain information about a third person whom they did suspect. The possibility that the interviewee had committed an offence by sheltering this third person was raised, but in a fairly perfunctory manner. Its purpose seemed to be to justify the interview: there was no indication that the police were seriously interested in pursuing the suggested complicity offence.

Similarly, in 277 a juvenile was questioned about incidents involving a shooting and vandalism at a massage centre. No clear allegation was made against the suspect apart from, at the end, asking him to confirm that he had not damaged the property. Observers were left with the impression that this vagueness was deliberate, and that the juvenile was questioned about the shooting as if he was a suspect in order to get him to give information about someone else. In 087, a man was interviewed about a sexual assault at a party by a friend. It was not clear if he was being interviewed as a witness or as a suspect and, if the latter, what the alleged offence was. Treating a person as a suspect is a powerful means of inducing cooperation from someone who might well not otherwise have spoken to police. As a use of the statutory power to detain and question, it skirts the fringes of legality.

5.4 Engage and explain

5.4.1 Introducing the interview, explaining what will happen and why

In introducing the interview, 10% of officers were excellent, 61% acceptable, and 22% less than acceptable or unacceptable. As noted in

---

advice, and told the police on the basis of that advice, he or she wants to exercise the right to remain silent' (2005:642).

Chapter 4, too often the caution is delivered in a brusque monotone, without eye contact with the suspect. For example, in 281, the interviewer's contribution to the introductory matters was very fast paced and delivered in a flat tone. Ironically, at the end of the introductory section, he asked the suspect 'Can you speak slowly and in a clear voice?'

Such problems are not inevitable, even if it is thought necessary to maintain the current cautioning format. 264 provided an example of how to introduce an interview well:

> *The interviewer asked preliminary questions in a relaxed, fresh manner. He clearly knew some of the material verbatim and did not need to refer to written material. He spoke to the suspect directly, in a more natural way than in many other interview introductions. The content of what was said covered legal issues and outlined the allegation in question.*

Second, how is the substance of the interview introduced: for example, do the officers explain what offence they are investigating and the grounds for suspecting that the suspect was involved in it? Fairness to suspects requires that they be informed of the offences alleged against them. It may well be in the investigating officers' interest to do so, for suspects who feel that they are not being treated fairly may be less willing to cooperate. This may be particularly relevant when suspects are legally represented: Dixon's study of legal advice at English police stations found that lawyers would advise clients not to answer police questions if they felt that the officers were unfairly not disclosing the nature of their investigation (1997:ch6).

Some officers performed poorly in this respect:

> *The introduction of the interview was especially weak. The interviewer stated the reason for the interview was 'an assault' that allegedly had occurred on a specified date. She also referred to 'an incident' that occurred at a service centre. While it could be assumed that this assault was against the suspect's former spouse, this was not clarified. And, in fact, as the interview progressed, the interviewer produced two complainant statements; one from the suspect's former partner and one from the suspect's mother-in-law, both claiming to have been assaulted. The purpose of the interview was not clear from the*

beginning. Who was the victim? How many victims were involved? (209)

The interviewer stated that the allegation involved 'some assaults on three young males'. A property damage allegation (which had not previously been mentioned) was raised in the middle of the interview. This did not develop from the suspect's answers. The failure to mention it initially may have contributed to the suspect's refusal to answer questions about the matter. (269)

Some of these interviews seemed premature. These interviewees had been arrested and detained by the use of powers requiring reasonable suspicion. In some cases, it was not clear that this standard had been met, and it would have been in the interest of police and suspect alike if more investigation and preparation had preceded the interview.

5.4.2 Establishment of relationship with suspect

An interview room is, of course, a very peculiar place to establish a relationship. Against a backdrop of restraint, authority, and potential personal cost, a suspect is not in a sociable situation. With this caveat, officers' attempts to establish a relationship with the suspect were graded quite highly. Twenty-four were excellent, 59% were acceptable, while only 10% were less than acceptable or unacceptable. Of course, officers and suspects had already established relationships in many cases, either during earlier stages of the investigation or in previous dealings. 284 provides an example of the benefits to police of a good relationship. In the context of a murder inquiry, the interviewee was questioned about his relationship with young male prostitutes. He was initially reluctant to answer questions concerning his sexual activity, but was persuaded to do so by the interviewer's relaxed, comfortable, non-pressured manner.

An officer's approach may not be reciprocated. Two cases provide contrasting examples of this. In 251, while the suspect appeared relaxed, suggesting a positive rapport, the interviewer was distant and cool. Meanwhile, in 252, an officer tried to be positive towards the suspect, genuinely trying to understand his side of the story, but the suspect remained defiant, sitting with arms crossed. There were a few cases in which an overtly negative relationship was evident. The attempts (e.g. 253, noted above) to use the right to silence tended to incite antagonism.

It is not always clear what a 'good relationship' is in this strange context. Sometimes, bare civility may be a considerable achievement, as in 272:

> *The interviewer-suspect relationship was civil, which was all that could be expected under the circumstance of this interview. Questioning involved the alleged assault of two police officers from the same station as the interviewer. The suspect sat at the interview table, in an intoxicated state, and used obscenities on occasion in reference to the arresting officers.*
>
> *Q: And how far away were the police?*
>
> *A: About fucking five feet.*

Other cases are more complex. For example in 268, an officer appeared to control and shift relations with the suspect as an investigatory method.

> *By the end of the 68 minute interview, the suspect had become more accusatory and irritated by the interviewer. The interviewer, in turn, had become forthright, seemingly as a calculated questioning technique rather than as an emotional outburst. This questioning technique was used at the cost of a more conventional police-suspect relationship in that the attitude of the suspect towards the interviewer did deteriorate. However, this deterioration in relationship seemed to be a calculated risk for the sake of possibly gaining more reliable evidence in a drug-related interview, in a matter without any complainant or witness.*

5.4.3 Adoption of appropriate style for offence and suspect

Closely related to establishing a relationship is adopting an appropriate style. There was an unusually clear division between good and bad in this respect. Excellence was observed in more interviews in this respect (29%) than in any other. However, more were also judged to be less than acceptable or unacceptable (31%).

The relatively high number of poor ratings is due largely to officers relying on a default or standard style which is formal and distant. In part, this results from officers not preparing adequately, and consequently having to read through statements and other papers in the interview room. But being aloof and distant may be considered appropriate by some officers in dealing with suspects against whom there is strong evidence and with whom they feel no need to establish a relationship. Similarly, it may be more effective and appropriate not to establish a relationship with some. In one notable example (209), a suspect was interviewed about an alleged assault on his ex-wife. The interviewer was a female officer. The partner was male. The suspect tried to draw the male officer into the interview, directing responses to the female interviewer's questions towards him. This appeared to be an attempt to get a more sympathetic audience. However, the partner resisted this by turning away from the suspect so that there was no eye contact. When he spoke to the suspect, he did so gruffly over his shoulder. In other situations, this would have been unacceptable and rude. Here, it seemed right.

Assessing style inevitably involves subjective judgment, particularly as we were not aware of the broader context in which the recorded interview was set. Sometimes, we found it impossible to judge interviews, when it was simply not clear what an appropriate style would be. For example, in 246,

> The interviewer relied on 'Do you agree?' questions for most of the interview. Was this a deliberate choice due to the suspect crying and appearing upset at the beginning of the interview? Was the interviewer allowing the suspect to calm down by needing only to say 'Yes' repeatedly? Was this an appropriate type of repeated question in this circumstance? Without knowing more detail of how upset the suspect was before the ERISP, it was difficult to assess how appropriate this repeated use of 'Do you agree ...?' was in this circumstance.

In other cases, this style of distant professionalism seemed more clearly inappropriate, and a potential source of problems. Three examples illustrate this:

> The style of questioning used by this interviewer (stick to the criminal allegations) seemed an inappropriate style for a suspect whose first response to a question was to disclose feelings of suicide. (201)

> The style of questioning was inappropriate for a woman who wanted to 'pour her heart out' to the detective. She wanted to talk about her problems. The interviewer decided to restrict his questions to the allegations at hand, with follow-up questions

relating to possible additional, more serious charges of supplying drugs. The interviewer did not appear to want to talk to this suspect about her life's problems. He appeared disrespectful when he smirked at his partner, who, in turn, was rolling his eyes. This woman was upset. She did make numerous inconsistent statements which understandably caused suspicion and frustration. This was no excuse for smirking and overtly unprofessional behaviour in front of this suspect. (256)

The interviewer spoke quickly and asked very direct questions about the suspect's involvement in two robberies. Questions did not attempt to gather detailed information ... The suspect appeared shocked and this abrupt, official ('What-can-you-tell-me-about-that?') style did not create an atmosphere in which the suspect may have been more willing to discuss the allegations. (218)

Other problems stemmed from mistakes or problems at the beginning of the interview. The failure to get an interpreter caused many problems in 250. More commonly, officers' failure to deal with apparently drug-affected suspects caused problems in cases 256, 260, and 272. The worst case was 267:

This suspect was visibly and audibly intoxicated. His speech was slurred. He was interviewed electronically at 10.33 pm. He stated that around the time of the alleged armed robbery of a petrol station, at around 8.50 pm, he was 'pretty pissed'. The suspect claimed that he had consumed four litres of Moselle wine and was headed back to his hostel when arrested. As the interviewer questioned this suspect less than two hours later, he was still very intoxicated. It was inappropriate to interview a suspect in this condition.

It also was inappropriate that the interviewer did not clarify this suspect's state of intoxication at the beginning of the interview. Rather, at 11.11 pm, the interviewer asked the suspect a leading question. (Earlier, the interviewer had asked about how much alcohol the suspect had consumed before being arrested, but had not asked about his present state of intoxication.)

Q: You totally comprehend what's being asked of you, do you?

A: Yes.

While the suspect responded compliantly to the leading question, the audio-visual record showed that his fitness for interview was very doubtful.

By contrast, other examples showed that officers could combine sympathy with effective questioning:

While the alleged offences (assault, abduction) were serious, the interviewer showed that he also recognised that these incidents involved family members and required perhaps a more sensitive approach than if the complainants had been strangers to the suspect. In turn, the interviewer adopted a sensitive, open, non-judgmental approach that nevertheless showed persistence in fully addressing the allegations. (204)

This is one of several interviews in which a relaxed but thorough and persistent style was effective.

The best illustration of good interviewing style came in interviews where a direct contrast with poor style was available in the same interview. In two cases (031, 096), interviewers attempted to conduct an interview in a formal, distant style, reading from statements. No attempt was made to make eye contact with the suspect, who sat slumped at the end of the oblong table, giving monosyllabic answers. When the interviewers were demonstrably getting nowhere, their partners stepped in. They adopted a quite different style, turning their body towards the suspects, making eye contact, and speaking in a way that expressed interest in what the suspects had to say. In both cases, the suspects responded and went on to cooperate. Interviewing style was crucial to success here. Nothing more was required than interest, some intelligence, and basic social skills.

5.4.4 Communication and listening skills

As in respect of interview style, success in communication and listening does not require sophisticated skills. Good interviewers speak clearly, in a manner appropriate to the suspect, listen to the suspect, and demonstrate that they are listening by providing appropriate responses (including corollary questions). This is not merely politeness (although that has its instrumental value too) but a matter of efficient interviewing. Baldwin warns that officers 'who are hell-bent on securing a confession very often do not listen to what is said and so fail to respond appropriately when the interview takes an unexpected turn' (Baldwin 1992a:12).

These examples illustrate how straightforward social skills can assist interviewing:

> *The interviewer was thorough in the questions asked, but was calm and non-judgmental in his approach. He was patient and at times requested a suspect (who had a speech impediment) to repeat an answer so that the interviewer could 'be sure' he had understood correctly. The interviewer explained that he needed to fully understand and avoided any implication that the suspect had any problem or might have been lying. (204)*

> *The interviewer maintained eye contact with the suspect throughout the interview. She spoke fluently, using straightforward vocabulary that the suspect appeared to understand without difficulty. (238)*

> *The interviewer appeared to be understood well by both the suspect and his mother. He spoke clearly and used vocabulary and a question structure that were appropriate for a youthful suspect. (247)*

> *From time to time, the interviewer reviewed and re-stated the suspect's version of events in order to clarify understanding. The detective listened to the suspect as he spoke, uninterrupted. She allowed him to answer open questions in full. She wrote notes as he spoke and appeared to use the details of those notes to form further follow-up questions. (277)*

By contrast, simple failures in listening can produce difficulties:

> *A few times, the interviewer asked questions that suggested poor listening skills. For example, just after the suspect replied that he did not know who had given him the CD player in question, the interviewer asked if his girlfriend had bought it for him. Similarly, the interviewer asked a challenging question based on incorrect information. Although these errors by the interviewer were few, they did appear to reflect inadequate listening skills. (283)*

In 225, the interviewer asked about the suspect's association with a person:

A: She's been a good friend of mine for 10 years.

Q: How long have you been involved with her?

A: More than 10 years. (225)

A familiar problem in police interviewing is the stultifying effect of 'police-speak'. This may consist of merely using jargon, or attempting to provide legal precision, or seeking to present formality and gravitas.[5]

The interviewer occasionally used vocabulary that was not suitable for the education level of this suspect.

Q: Who resides at the house?

A: Who lives there?

Q: Yes, who lives there? (208)

Similarly, various interviewers asked questions such as 'How were you conveyed to the police station?' (208) and 'Can you tell me what your clothes comprised of?' (206) which caused the suspect unnecessary difficulty and hampered the interviewer's attempt to build rapport. In 226, the interviewing officer again used inappropriate terminology which the suspect did not understand.

Q: What can you tell me about how these transactions transpired?

A: How did I get it?

Q: Yes.

Convoluted speech patterns may make the suspect reply inappropriately:

Q: Would it be fair to say that at the time you deposited this cheque you knew certain things about the cheque that would not be apparent to the bank?

A: Er ... yeah.

Q: What's that?

A: Sorry can you repeat the question?

---

[5]   See Fox 1993; Gibbons 2003:85–87. For early criticism of police-speak, see Dovey (1954:16), where a police officer conceded that what he had really said to a colleague was not 'We will make inquiries around King's Cross', but 'We will have to go around the pubs and see if we can find out what happened to the bastard'.

Certain police terminology may be unknown to the suspect: for example, in 201, the interviewer asked if the suspect agreed that the interview should be 'ERISPed'. The suspect said yes, without indicating he knew what this meant.

Occasionally, suspects responded in kind, although this could be for very different reasons. When the suspect in 004 referred to 'the alleged insultee', this reflected his initial mocking truculence. When the suspect in 057 aped police talk by telling the interviewer that he received a cheque from 'person or persons unknown', it was one of several expressions of his disrespect for police. However, others stressed their cooperation with police by speaking in 'official' language, as in 021 where the suspect responded to a question about the police search of his home: 'They made enquiries about a camera that I acquired off some young person. I then went and got the camera in question'.

Basic listening skills involve showing that you are listening by responding and prompting, asking appropriate follow-up questions, and offering summaries of the suspect's account in order to check that you understand and that he/she has said what was intended. The objective is both to understand fully what the suspect says and to encourage and facilitate communication.

> *After the suspect gave an uninterrupted account of the attempted robbery, the interviewer used notes to repeat what the suspect had said, to verify his comprehension of the account given. He offered a detailed and accurate précis. (232)*

> *The interviewer never interrupted the suspect as he spoke. On occasion he summarised what the suspect had said to verify that what he, the interviewer, had understood was correct. In each instance the suspect agreed that the interviewer's version of what he had said was correct. (208)*

Poor listening is indicated by apparent inattention and inappropriate responses. However, categorising responses in this way is not always straightforward. What may appear to be a product of poor listening may equally be regarded as a challenge to the suspect's account or a persuasive tactic.

> *After the suspect offered his version (that is, his denial of taking money from the couple in question), the interviewer asked, 'Where did you go after you took this money from the man and*

the woman?' While it could be argued that the interviewer had poor listening skills, such a question could simply reflect investigative 'tunnel vision', or it could be a tactic designed to challenge the suspect's denials. (216)

Towards the end of the interview, after the suspect had stated that the complainant had offered him money, the interviewer still referred to the suspect having asked for money from the complainant. Was this a listening skill issue or was the interviewer verifying the suspect's account in this manner? (258)

5.5 Account, clarification and challenge

5.5.1 Inviting suspect's account

As explained in Chapter 4, a notable contrast between our first and second samples was the tendency of officers in the first sample to present a detailed allegation or to make a series of statements, seeking the suspect's agreement with each, while in the second sample, officers tended to ask the suspect to provide his or her version of events before asking exploratory questions. This shift suggests the influence of PEACE training, which emphasises the need to structure the interview around the suspect's account. Among the benefits of this approach is that it helps to ensure that information comes from the suspect. If the suspect merely confirms what officers already believe, or elaborates on information about an offence provided by the interviewer in detailing the allegation, the results may be unreliable. In some cases, serious miscarriages of justice have resulted from this type of interviewing. A notable British example is the case of Stefan Kiszko, who spent almost 16 years in gaol for a murder which medical evidence eventually proved that he could not have committed. His conviction was based upon a confession which contained information only police and the real killer could have known. As Kiszko was innocent, the information 'must have been communicated to Mr Kiszko by the police ... either deliberately or inadvertently' (Gudjonsson 2003:529). In the light of our knowledge about cases like that of Stefan Kiszko, the shift in interviewing practice reported in our research is an important one. In sample 2, a quarter of interviews (25%) were excellent in this respect, and half were acceptable (51%).

Inviting the account often depends upon other interview skills: while a bald request to 'say what happened' may be unsuccessful, establishing a relationship with the suspect by talking about contextual matters and adopting an appropriate style using good communication and listening skills can all help to draw out a useful account from the suspect. An example of an excellent interview was 223:

> *The interviewer encouraged the suspect to give his account at several stages of the interview. At one point he told him, 'Take your time and give it a bit of thought.'*

The benefits of inviting an account were evident in a case involving suspected drug offences:

> *Having seen many cultivation/supply interviews in sample 1, this sample 2 interview questioning on the same charges does stand out. Sample 1 interviewers tended to present the results of the search to the suspect and asked them to agree with what had been found as a result of a search. This interviewer, however, asked the suspect to describe the search of his house in contrast to sample 1 interviewers who tended to describe to the suspect what was done and what had been found. In this interview the suspect was asked to take a more active role rather than the more common (sample 1) agree/disagree less active role. This more active involvement of the suspect (in comparison to sample 1 suspects facing the same drug allegations) would have increased the reliability of the information offered. (224)*

The benefits can also be seen by contrasting atypical cases which were problematic in this respect:

> *It was the style used by this interviewer to question this suspect that was most problematic for this interview ... Repeated questions were asked about material extracted from witness statements: 'Do you understand that?' 'Is there anything you care to say about that?' This approach relied on the interviewer providing the statement and the suspect answering, mostly in a monosyllabic 'Yes', he had understood or 'No', there was nothing he could say about that. Most sample 2 detectives have been successful in getting the suspect to discuss the allegation in detail (by asking about activities on the day, relationships with the persons involved, etc) which this interviewer did not. It would have been more appropriate for the interviewer to have done less talking and for the suspect to have done more. (230)*

The interviewer used 27 'Do you agree ...?' questions at the beginning of the interview to establish a denial (that the suspect was in possession of illegal drugs) and later a change to an admission (that he had drugs on his person, in his underwear). Mostly closed questions were asked. In short, this interviewer did not seem interested in obtaining a detailed account from this suspect of his version of events. (278)

The interviewer largely framed the suspect's account through the use of a lengthy series of closed questions. The suspect's admissions and denials were clear at the end of the interview. However, those admissions/denials and the suspect's version were known almost exclusively through the interviewer's asking of closed questions.(246)

These were apparently successful interviews. However, while the investigators' suspicions were confirmed, their knowledge was no wider than it was before. Recent cases of confirmed miscarriages of justice (see Chapter 1) have emphasised the dangers of this approach.

Sometimes, of course, a suspect refuses to cooperate, either by resorting to silence or by providing a limited account (see Chapter 3, above). Other suspects are, for a variety of reasons, unable to provide an extended account. In such cases, other techniques are needed.

Although the interviewer did ask the suspect to 'tell me about that robbery', when she said little, he was not creative in getting her to give her account. Unlike other interviewers who have had suspects go back and describe the events of their day, for example, he reverted to a series of closed questions that continued to focus on the allegation exclusively. (222)

The tendency of some officers to fall back on the accustomed statement/request confirmation tactic suggests that more needs to be done to equip them with interviewing skills.

One case suggested that the success of PEACE interviewing could be reduced if more suspects gain access to legal advice before charge. (It should be noted there is no reason to expect that this will happen in NSW or Australia generally in the foreseeable future.) In 232, a juvenile suspected of involvement in a series of serious offences was interviewed in the presence of his solicitor. The solicitor insisted to the investigators that the suspect would provide a full account of what happened, but that he would not answer subsequent questions. (This was said to be because he had already been interviewed about the alleged offences by police in two other states, Queensland and Victoria.) If this tactic were to become standard, the suspect would be able to have what he or she likes put into the record without fear of challenge. As will be shown in Chapter 6, some defence lawyers already regard ERISP as a vital opportunity for the suspect to give an account without having to face cross-examination from the prosecution in court. For the rare, well-informed, articulate suspect, such an account, followed by refusal to answer questions or give evidence could take the place of the much maligned, and now impermissible, dock statement.[6]

The benefits to some suspects of giving an account in the ERISP were illustrated by 091. The suspect was an articulate, middle-class male who was able to give his lengthy, detailed account of an alleged assault during a soccer game. This contrasted with the brief, unfocused accounts given by many suspects. Similarly, in 093, the suspect had initiated the interview: in response to rumours that he had sexually assaulted a child, he had rung the police and arranged to be interviewed. The interview simply consisted of DYAs about photographs taken by police at the suspect's house and his statement denying the allegation. There was no challenge to the suspect's account, presumably because the usual order had been reversed, so that here the police were interviewing the suspect before the victim. Some are much more able than others to use an opportunity to put their side of the case: inevitably, this variation is structured by divisions of class and race.

5.5.2 Checking accounts

Checking the suspect's account is another important part of the interview, which again is dependent on other skills, particularly of listening to the suspect. An interviewer has to process the information provided, assess its strength, and formulate questions in order to test this and to fill gaps. Again, one quarter of interviews (25%) were excellent, while 42% were acceptable. However, 20% were less than acceptable or unacceptable in this respect.

---

[6]　A defendant's right to make an unsworn dock statement on which he or she could not be cross-examined was abolished in NSW in 1994.

The best interviewers clearly displayed the skills taught in PEACE training, particularly the deconstruction of the suspect's account into sections for detailed analysis.

This interviewer wrote notes as the suspect made his confession. Then, at the end of the uninterrupted confession he used his notes to break the confession into subsections. He then reviewed each subsection, asking follow-up questions and further information. The outcome of each review of each subsection then was repeated by the interviewer ('Just so it's clear in my mind ...') to verify that the information understood by the interviewer was correct. (208)

The interviewer was most thorough in the way in which he checked the suspect's account. He checked and re-checked information. He asked her to draw a diagram to further illustrate her description of events. He then used the complainant statement to further ask the suspect to comment on the alleged assault. By the end of the interview the suspect's version of what happened was clear. (217)

The interviewer used several approaches to check the suspect's account. She read a notebook entry and asked the suspect to verify the admissions made pre-ERISP. She asked him further clarification questions about what he had said had happened. She asked him to illustrate the location of events by the use of a drawing that showed the properties involved. And she read the complainant statement and asked the suspect to respond to its contents. (245)

The suspect's version of events and denials were checked thoroughly in this ERISP. This was the result of a combined effort that involved both interviewers. While the main interviewer asked numerous follow-up questions and incorporated the complainant's statement into questioning, the partner in particular asked a series of challenging questions. Perhaps due to the rigour of this checking of his account, the suspect told the Adopting Officer during the adoption procedure, 'They were being a bit hard ...'' (282)

A murder inquiry, 284, demonstrated the investigative power of PEACE interviewing:

Perhaps the strongest aspect of this interview was the questioning technique used by this interviewer. Although the suspect denied any knowledge of the murder, the interviewer used a variety of approaches to obtain information. He asked the suspect about his movements on the day of the murder. As the suspect could not recall his activity on a day that passed seven months previously, the interviewer attempted to find a 'target date' (which happened to be Christmas Day) and then used the memory of that day to try to get the suspect to recall what he had been doing on 27 December. As the suspect still could not remember his movements on the day in question, the interviewer then asked if he knew the victim by name and further whether he had read about his death in the newspaper. Places that the suspect may have frequented were raised, including a hotel mentioned by name. The suspect's knowledge of a specific halfway house was explored. The suspect then was questioned about whether he knew the victim and their common relationship with X. Similar questions were asked about two other young associates of X. The suspect then was asked about what he did on a day-to-day basis. Questions continued in this manner, with numerous follow-up probes. In short, while many interviewers in sample 1 accepted the suspect's denial, usually with few follow-up questions, this interviewer explored a range of issues in his attempt to obtain the suspect's version of events in relation to this murder.

The interviewer needs to be well-prepared in order to check the suspect's account in detail. This was illustrated by an interview in which such preparation seemed to be lacking.

This interview suffered from lack of detailed follow-up questions by this detective. Did he have statements from the other two persons who were with the complainant on the night in question? Were there inconsistencies between what the four persons claimed? How could the suspect account for those inconsistencies? An insufficient number of challenging questions were asked of this suspect to check his account in detail. (254)

Checking normally consisted of contrasting the suspect's account with information in witness or victim statements. Such checking requires skilful adaptability if it is to be done to optimal effect. Typically, an interviewer refers to a witness statement by saying 'I have been informed that ...', and then invites a comment by asking a question such as 'What can you tell me about that?' (see Chapter 3, above). This mode distances the interviewer from the accusation. In some cases, this may make it easier for the suspect to speak about the offence: the interviewer is not personally involved, not a victim. Similarly, distancing may be adopted by the suspect. In an example discussed in Chapter 3 (263), a late middle-aged male professional was interviewed about various frauds. He discussed these as if he were talking with his bank manager about legitimate transactions, analysing material in dispassionate detail, but making substantial admissions in so doing. On the other hand, such distancing of interviewer and accusation may have the opposite effect: if the allegation is regarded by the suspect as 'merely' the victim's, and the investigator appears to have no stake in it, it may be easier for the suspect to deny. This appeared to be the outcome in 233, in which an allegation of child sexual assault was denied by a suspect. If such cases can be identified, it would be better for interviewers to check the suspect's account without distancing themselves from their source.

If the suspect does not respond to the witness statement, officers often resort to posing a hypothetical question — 'Why would he/she say this if it wasn't true?' As noted above in Chapter 3, such an accusation may work against a naïve suspect, but an experienced suspect (particularly the rare one assisted by a competent lawyer) would say that he/she has no way of knowing why someone would say something.

Another problematic aspect of reading from witness statements is that doing so may indicate to the suspect how much (or how little) evidence the police have against him/her. If a suspect has been uncommunicative in giving his/her own account, then the checking may do little more than indicate that the police case is weak and that continued non-cooperation is appropriate.

What of challenging, rather than merely checking the suspect's account? Some feel that PEACE encourages an excessively passive, reactive approach to questioning suspects. For example, Pearse and Gudjonsson identified

> a number of instances where officers chose not to scrutinise a suspect's account despite possible discrepancies ... Perhaps the 'C' in PEACE might also represent 'Challenge' so that before an interview is brought

to a conclusion officers will be encouraged to test the substance of a suspect's account (Pearse & Gudjonsson 1996:71–72).

In general, officers appeared content to allow a contrast to be seen between the suspect's account and the witness statements and other evidence, and to rely on the suspect's inability to explain discrepancies. However, there were a number of challenges to credibility.

> *The interviewer balanced the request for the suspect's account with some challenging questions. For example, 'How could your former partner have dragged you from the vehicle when she is much smaller in size than you are?' (209)*

> *The interviewer asked open and closed questions, and did challenge the suspect's suggestion that the 463 gms of cannabis were for personal use and that the 25 cms long knife was in his back pack simply because he had forgotten it was there. (211)*

> *The suspect did admit when challenged that if the bank realised that he had no money that he would not have been eligible for loans totalling $625,000. (225)*

The nearest sample 2 interviewers came to a confrontational challenge was in 268.

> *The interviewer was forthright in his doubt about the truthfulness of the explanation offered.*

> *Q: Your story to me, at best, is unrealistic.*

> *The suspect objected,*

> *A: Mate, I'm telling you the truth right down the line here.*

What distinguished this challenge from similar cases in sample 1 was the controlled manner in which the interviewer expressed his disbelief in the suspect's account. There was no expression of anger or frustration, simply a forthright, professional statement. While the interviewer looked calm, the suspect was shaken, making impassioned claims of innocence. This style of challenge provided a creative questioning technique in a difficult interview.

There was a surprising lack of challenge on some occasions.

> *A few statements made by the suspect begged to be challenged and were not. For example, the suspect alleged that he paid $95 for a motel room and when he and others (including the*

complainant) entered the room, the room was in disarray. The suspect suggested that the motel room was not in disarray due to the sexual assault that had allegedly occurred, but because the condition of the room was messy from the time it was rented. A challenging question was needed at this stage of the interview: why did he accept a room in this condition? (271)

Perhaps such discrepancies would be evident to a court, making it unnecessary for officers to challenge accounts. As noted above, some suspects, notably those who were found in possession of drugs or stolen property, gave thoroughly implausible accounts. So long as there is other evidence on which prosecution could proceed (as in these cases, the finding of drugs or stolen property), the court would be able to make its own assessment of credibility (if the defendant chose to plead not guilty).

5.5.3 Adopting an open-minded approach

A common problem in many of the investigations which led to miscarriages of justice in the later twentieth century was the premature commitment of officers to belief in a suspect's guilt (Dixon 2006). Such 'case theories' turned investigations into campaigns to prove guilt.[7] Interviewers suspect that the interviewee committed the offence: this is, of course, a prerequisite of their detention. However, officers have to be open to the possibility that their suspicion will be allayed rather than confirmed by the interview. Indeed, 236 provided an example of an interviewer becoming convinced of the suspect's innocence.

In sample 2, 14% of interviewers were judged to be excellent in adopting an open-minded approach. Being calm and non-judgmental proved to be a successful approach in several interviews. For example,

The interviewer seemed interested in the suspect's account and in a relaxed, neutral manner checked points that were not clear initially. He also asked follow-up questions about the suspect's allegation that prior to this alleged assault the complainant had threatened her. (217)

Being open-minded does not imply being 'soft'. It can also be an accusatory method, if it invites the suspect to provide an explanation

---

[7]   In NSW, the Blackburn case is particularly good example: see Lee 1990 and discussion in Dixon 2006.

inconsistent with guilt and he/she is unable to do so. For example, in 240 the suspect's fingerprint was found at the scene of a break and enter. In a neutral manner the interviewer checked all possible reasons for the suspect's fingerprint having been located at the crime site, an exploration that indicated an open-minded approach. The interviewer was prepared to listen to a credible explanation, but the suspect was unable to provide one.

Open-mindedness was found to be an irrelevant criterion in 19% of interviews. In many of these cases, the weight of inculpatory evidence and the unproblematic nature of the confession provided (i.e. from non-vulnerable suspects without any suggestion of coercion by the interviewers) left little room for an officer to express his or her open-mindedness.

This was one in a group of interviews concerning cocaine supply. As police had over 60 intercepted telephone conversations between this suspect and her supplier, there was little need at this stage of the investigation for the interviewer to adopt an open-minded approach. (202)

More problematic are cases in which the officer has become convinced of guilt in pre-ERISP interviewing:

If the suspect was to be believed, the interviewer told him before the ERISP began that he would be charged with the second offence and that he would not receive bail. (213)

A poor interview, almost a caricature of a closed mind interviewer. This interviewer told the suspect he would be charged with possession of prohibited drugs before the ERISP was conducted. (278)

5.5.4   Use of questioning techniques

Good interviewers displayed flexibility, adapting to suit their suspect by, for example, employing a variety of techniques (open and closed questions; use of exhibit documents that needed comment; presenting a statement previously made by the suspect; and checking questions). Thirteen per cent of interviews were regarded as excellent, 57% were acceptable, and 19% were less than acceptable or unacceptable.

Our sample provided varied examples of excellent questioning technique:

Questions asked avoided the standard police phrases. Most were closed questions, which appeared appropriate for this suspect. Questions asked were successful in changing a 'No response' to a confession. (202)

The interviewer, knowing that the suspect intended to deny allegations, encouraged the suspect to talk in general about work, finances and his activity on the day in question. This questioning approach then was used to challenge the suspect's alibi, when the suspect's co-offender did not back up the suspect's story. This suspicion led to further investigation. (205)

The interviewer used three different approaches in obtaining the suspect's confession. First, he asked the suspect the standard open question, 'Tell me in your own words what happened'. Then he asked closed questions as follow-up questions for each subsection of the confession. Finally he stated the suspect's position on each subsection and asked the suspect to agree or disagree that these summaries were correct. (208)

A variety of question types were used (open and closed questions). Challenging questions were included, but asked in a non-confrontational manner. The interviewer had available substantial other evidence that he used throughout this interview to check the suspect's full denial. The interviewer also seemed to make a deliberate decision about how he would structure the interview. This structure meant that he used the most incriminating piece of evidence (the set of finger prints on the note found at the crime scene that matched finger prints from the suspect) at the end of the interview, after other exhibits had been shown and reviewed. This created a crescendo in questioning. It did not bring a confession from the suspect, but it was apparent that he was upset. He did say, 'I used to do these things when I was young'. When questioned further about the meaning of this statement, the suspect closed up again. In short, the interviewer used gathered evidence and questioning technique and structure to the benefit of this interview, in spite of never obtaining a confession. (275)

Poorer interviews included those in which the interview was dominated by familiar, standard format questions such as 'Do you agree …?' and 'What can you tell me about that?'

> *The interviewer read from the witness statement and repeatedly asked the suspect if he understood. Then at the end of the statement, he asked if the suspect cared to comment on the statement. This questioning technique did not encourage the detailed information that was needed in this second (denial) interview about the suspect's alleged involvement in a serious assault. Additionally, the repetition of the same few questions (Do you understand that? Is there anything you care to say about that?) brought a monotony both to questions and to the subsequent monosyllabic responses of 'Yes' and 'No'. More open ended questions would have been helpful in gaining more detailed information. (230)*

If DYA prompts 'Yes', then 'Is there anything you care to say about that?' often prompts 'No'.

There were a few examples of leading questions:

> *In the closure, the interviewer asked the suspect the standard question concerning inducements to participate in the interview.*
>
> *Q: Was any threat, promise or any offer held out to you to participate in this record of interview?*
>
> *A: I was told that I wasn't the one that they wanted, they being the police. And, if I helped them in every way I could, they would help me in every way I {sic} could.*
>
> *Q: So do you consider that a promise for you to participate in this interview or would you have done that anyway?*
>
> *The suspect answered that he would have done that anyway. (229)*
>
> *Two leading questions were used to clarify whether an inducement had been used by the interviewer to encourage this suspect to participate in the ERISP. Additionally, the interviewer used a series of 'Do you agree …?' questions at the beginning of the interview to try (unsuccessfully) to have the suspect agree to a pre-ERISP admission. That no contemporaneous notes appeared to have been taken of this alleged pre-ERISP admission made the interviewer appear more manipulative in his*

questioning technique than most other interviewers in sample 2. (261)

The interviewer asked the suspect (who was visibly and audibly drunk) how he was feeling. He then asked a leading question that encouraged a 'proper' response from the suspect that in turn would assist in the admissibility of the interview.

> *Q: You totally comprehend what's being asked of you, do you?*
>
> *A: Yes.*

As the suspect had told the interviewer earlier in the interview that that afternoon/ evening he had consumed four litres of Moselle wine, this leading question appeared to be an attempt to manipulate a proper response. (267)

Another problem of technique was the occasional use of questions which combined more than one issue and to which a single response could be misleading.

There were problems with the questioning technique used in this interview. There was frequent use of double-barrelled questions. For example,

> *Q: Can you tell me who that person is (whose name was on the document) and why these items were in your possession? (263)*

Good interviewing combines open and closed questions, but the former should come first. Some closed questions were asked before open questions.

In another instance the interviewer asked a closed question.

> *Q: Is it correct you presented these documents to the X bank with the purpose of opening an account?*

He asked this before he asked an open question about what happened. For yet another set of documents, one of the interviewer's initial sets of questions was one that assumed guilt prior to asking what had happened.

> *Q: Upon opening that account, you received a cheque book to access that account? (263)*

A significant problem noted above is some officers' tendency to continue questioning suspects who have said that they do not want to answer questions.

5.6 Closure

5.6.1 Planned closure

Few interviews gave any real indication that their closure was planned. More often, they run their course: the interviewer finishes his/her questions, asks the partner if he or she has anything to add, then the interview concludes. In some, typically poorly organised, interviews, closure is rushed as officers realise the tapes are running out and the interview is concluded quickly.

In almost three quarters of interviews (72%), the closure was judged to be acceptable. This usually consisted of a formulaic run through the adoption procedure. There were a few minor problems in handling this procedure: for example, some officers turned the video off while obtaining an adopter. But the real issue here is the lack of value in the process, which has been discussed above in 3.6.

5.6.2 Participants' understanding of what has happened in the interview and what will result

Before the ERISPs in Sample 1 ended, one fifth of suspects were told something about what would happen next. However, more than two thirds were not.

Although ERISPs themselves do not reveal whether suspects were charged as an outcome of police questioning, ERISP System Return forms[8] do usually contain this information. It was available for 154 of 167 suspects in sample 1. As Table 5.2 shows, 82% (127) of sample 1 suspects for whom System Return entries were made were charged after questioning. Two suspects who had been interviewed on different occasions for multiple offences were each charged with one offence only. Only 16% of suspects (25 persons) were not charged following their police interviews.

---

[8]   Local Area Commands reported statistics relating to their use of ERISP on these forms to the central ERISP Unit.

Table 5.1   Whether in sample 1 ERISPs the suspect was told what would happen in relation to the offence allegation(s)

Whether the suspect was told what would happen	Interviews N=175 %*
Yes, told he/she would be charged	14
Yes, told the matter was still under investigation	7
Yes, other	1
No, nothing said	68
Unknown/ not applicable	11

*   Figures do not total 100 because of rounding.

Table 5.2   Charges resulting from sample 1 interviews

Was the suspect charged?	Suspects N=154 %
Yes	82
Yes, charged for one offence, but not for another	1
No	16

Most suspects appear to understand what has happened: in almost three quarters of cases in sample 2 (72%), suspects' understanding of what had happened appeared to be excellent or acceptable. However, in only 15 (20%) cases, officers explained what would result (either charge or further investigation).

In substance, a planned closure should leave participants with understanding of what has happened and of what will result. If this suggests an explanatory summary, no such conclusions were observed. Few interviews concluded with a clear statement about what would happen next, notably relating to charge. Sometimes (e.g. 214) officers ignored requests for information about what was to happen, or deflected them:

At the end of the interview the suspect appeared unsettled. He asked both the interviewer and the Adopting Officer about the charges he would face. He was told, 'We'll talk about that after the interview'. (206)

Some suspects are left with little idea of what is to happen to them:

It was unclear at the end of the interview whether the interviewer intended to ask the suspect for fingerprints (to test forensically whether they matched fingerprints on the stolen liquor bottles found); whether the suspect would be questioned further about being a passenger in a stolen car; or whether he would be charged with the break and enter. (201)

As regards charging, there are contradictory pressures: while the PEACE approach expects interviewing officers to inform the suspect about the result, officers may wish to take time to consult with colleagues or (as in 252) with the NSW Police Legal Services section about appropriate charges. More significantly, the decision to charge is formally that of the custody manager, not of the investigators. The CRIME Code provides that 'When an investigating officer considers there is sufficient evidence to prosecute a detained person ..., the officer will without delay ... take them to the custody manager who will consider whether action should be taken and by which method (cautioned, charged, summonsed or issued with a court attendance notice)' (NSW Police 1998:21).

There are good reasons for not requiring officers to make an immediate decision on charging. Indeed, expecting them to do so suggests an outdated overstatement of the significance of the interview in the process of investigation. However, suspects may well not appreciate these reasons, and interviewing officers should perhaps explain (for example) that further inquiries are to follow, or that the decision will be made after consultation.

5.7 Comparisons

5.7.1 Comparing samples 1 and 2

We attempted an inevitably subjective judgment about whether the standard of interviewing in sample 2 was good, average, or poor according to expectations set by better interviews in sample 1. The result was an even spread: 28 (32%) good, 27 (31%) average, and 27

(31%) poor (with 5 (6%) unclassifiable because of machine failure or the suspect's silence).

Many sample 2 interviews were indistinguishable in style from those in sample 1, with similar problems of poor preparation and excessive reliance on 'DYA ...?' and 'I have been informed that ...' questions. However, a third showed some clear effects of interview training. The most common contrast between sample 1 and sample 2 came in the tendency of numerous sample 2 interviewers to ask a wider range of questions about the suspect's background and activities, and to be less offence-focused. While 'DYA ...?' was still employed, several sample 2 interviewers preferred to ask suspects to provide their account of preceding events. For example, in 270

> *The interviewer did not follow the standard series of 'DYA ...?' questions at the beginning of the interview. After the initial, 'Do you agree earlier tonight you were arrested by police ...?', the interviewer then asked the suspect what time the arrest had occurred and the reason for the arrest. This approach meant that the suspect was invited to participate actively in the interview, rather than merely agreeing with a police account. Another example of good questioning technique was that the interviewer on occasion had the suspect explain his understanding of a question. In addition, on another occasion he used a reflective statement to raise an allegation, 'Just so I can fully understand ...'*

In general, the manner of the better sample 2 interviewers was more relaxed, neutral, and 'professional' than that of many interviewers in sample 1. For example, 282 was the type of case in which officers might have been expected to be confrontational: a 22 year old unemployed male of Arabic background was suspected of involvement in a mugging and drug sales. His account was not credible: he did not know who was in the car with him, where it went, or anything about drug sales. The suspect was questioned thoroughly, but in a relaxed, non-confrontational manner. He did not 'crack' (although he shifted to saying that he might have touched an empty plastic bag in the car when the interviewer told him that the exhibits would be tested for fingerprints). This is an example of a case in which an incredible account offered by a suspect is more useful to police and prosecutors than a dubiously obtained confession. It is impossible to say whether the skill displayed in this case was due to training or to personal characteristics: most likely it was a combination.

5.7.2 Sample 2 interviewers before and after training

As a pilot project, we obtained interviews conducted by a sub-sample of 10 sample 2 interviewers before they had received PEACE training and compared these with their post-training performance in the first interview which they conducted on their return from training. This was a modest attempt: it became clear that, if it were possible at all, it was beyond our resources to find pre-training interviews which provided a controlling match for key dimensions such as suspect characteristics, suspect response to allegations, and offence type. In other words, it would be unrealistic to claim with confidence that specific differences between pre- and post-training interviews were due to the training received by interviewers. However, our general assessment was that there was more similarity than difference in performance. Not surprisingly, training did not radically change these officers: it is unlikely that much if any training has such effects. This was just one of many courses that officers do, and just part of a more general attempt to shift policing styles. In this respect, experience in NSW is similar to that reported by Clarke and Milne (2001) in England and Wales.

5.7.3 NSW and England and Wales

Some comparison is possible between our sample 2 and the interviews studied by McGurk et al. for the Home Office. Several of their performance indicators are the same as, or very similar to, ours. McGurk et al. allocated a score by taking the numbers 4, 3, 2 and 1 to represent grades A (the best), B, C and D respectively, and then calculating an average score. The table below presents the scores for McGurk et al.'s trained students and our sample 2 officers. For the latter, we have allocated the numbers 4, 3, 2 and 1 to excellent, acceptable, less than acceptable and unacceptable respectively. (As noted previously, a five- would have been preferable to a four-part scale.)

Table 5.3:   Comparing evaluations of interviewing in England and NSW

	McGurk et al.	Dixon
Introducing interview	2.9	2.8
Obtaining suspect's account	3.5	3.1
Questioning technique	3.4	2.9
Communication skills	3.7	3.0
Having an open mind	3.6	2.9
Structuring the interview	3.1	2.9
Listening skills	3.5	3.0
Closure	1.5	2.8
Covering points to prove	3.6	2.8

5.8   Conclusion

Assessing interview performance is difficult. It is clear that the same approach will not be appropriate in every case. Skilful flexibility is important: good interviewers 'adapted their interview styles to the suspect and the particular circumstances of the case' (Baldwin 1993:336). How can one say that the rather cold, distant interviewing of a suspect accused of child sexual assault was a mistake (other than by amassing experience of many such suspects)?

What clearly emerges from this study is that good interviewers are people with intelligence, commitment, capacity for empathy, and social skills. This may sound too much like stating the obvious, but it emphasises the point that interviewing in everyday cases need not be complicated. Our findings confirm Baldwin's suggestion that 'very many recorded interviews are such simple and straightforward exchanges that no special interrogatory skills are required' (1993:335). As we have seen, many suspects admit from the start, 'and in most of these cases the interviewer needed to do little more than ask suspects what happened, keep quiet while they answered, and then follow up with a few sensible, straightforward questions to clarify basic details' (Baldwin 1993:335).

PEACE and investigative interviewing are based on this approach and, as such, it appears to offer a valuable model for interview training development. As has been suggested above, PEACE and investigative interviewing are as important for what they are not as much as for what they are. Perhaps their greatest achievement is providing police officers with an effective alternative to the traditional craft skills and role models which were associated with the problems outlined in Chapter 1. As noted above, too much should not be expected of training per se, but it can contribute to a broader process of cultural and professional development.

Appendix — Table 5.4 Variable results — Sample 2

	n/a (%)	Excellent (%)	Acceptable (%)	Less than Acceptable (%)	Unacceptable (%)
Planning/ structuring the interview	9	22	51	8	10
Using notes, witness statements etc	26	9	48	14	2
Covering legal issues	11	11	57	14	6
Introducing the interview	3	10	61	23	2
Establishing relationship with suspect	8	24	59	5	5
Adopting appropriate style for offence/ suspect	9	29	32	23	8
Communication skills	6	14	70	9	1
Listening skills	10	10	69	10	0
Inviting suspect's account	13	25	51	10	1
Checking suspect's account	13	25	42	15	5
Adopting open-minded approach	19	14	54	7	6
Using questioning techniques	11	13	57	13	6
Participants' understanding of interview and outcome	25	11	55	5	3
Planning closure	14	3	72	6	5

CHAPTER 6

PERCEPTIONS AND EXPERIENCES OF VIDEOTAPING THE QUESTIONING OF SUSPECTS

This chapter reports the results of a series of questionnaires administered by mail to key groups of criminal justice professionals — police, judges, defence lawyers and Crown Prosecutors — which aimed to explore their experiences and perceptions of ERISP. The questionnaires shared a common core, but were specified for each group. The targeted populations were: detective sergeants in operational supervisory positions at local and central levels; judges of the District and Supreme Courts; Public Defenders and private lawyers with a substantial criminal practice; and Crown Prosecutors. They were from across the state, although by nature of the professions' organisation, there was some concentration on Sydney (e.g. more than half the Crown Prosecutors were located at the Sydney head office, but the rest were from across the state, including all major regional centres). Good response rates were produced by including supporting letters from senior members of the respective professions (with the exception of the judiciary, whose superiors thought it inappropriate to endorse the research) and intensive follow-up of non-respondents. Responses were received from:

- police: 152 Detective Sergeants (response rate 89%);
- prosecutors: 71 Crown Prosecutors (response rate 91%);
- defence lawyers: 19 Public Defenders and 58 private defence lawyers (response rate 58%);
- judges: 33 District Court and 16 Supreme Court judges (response rate 69%).[1]

Some participants did not respond to all questions.[2] The omissions are reflected in the varying number of answers from participants which are reported below.

---

[1] In the case of both defence lawyers and judges, results from two component groups are combined, although any significant differences are noted. One senior judge refused to complete the questionnaire on the ground that 'it would be judicially inappropriate to do so. I, and other judges, have views about "ERISP". We have, however, more appropriate means of communication of those views rather than by means of some academic paper'. Despite this charming expression of judicial arrogance, many judges did complete the questionnaire, and I am most grateful to them, and to our other respondents.

6.1   The impact of ERISP on the criminal justice process

As noted in Chapter 1, ERISP is one of many changes to affect the criminal justice process in recent years. We asked detectives which change in the criminal justice process (including ERISP) had had most impact on their work. Among those who felt able to single out one, the most frequently nominated change was in identification procedures (23%). A smaller proportion (16%) nominated ERISP. However, a substantial group (20%) unhelpfully stated 'Evidence Act', without specifying which part of this voluminous legislation. It is likely that some of these were indirectly referring to the significant changes in identification procedures brought about by the Evidence Act.[3] Some others may have been referring to the recording of the questioning of suspects: while the NSW provision mandating electronic recording was in fact placed in the Crimes Act[4] rather than the Evidence Act, subsequent inquiries indicate that officers often use 'Evidence Act' as shorthand reference for the package of changes to criminal procedure in the mid-1990s (see Chapter 1). Thereafter came a great variety of factors nominated by between one and five officers: changes in sentencing, committals, disclosure of evidence, DPP practices, bureaucratic demands, abolition of the accused's right to make an unsworn 'dock' statement, holding prisoners in gaol rather than at police stations, evidence presentation in court, time limits for court appearances, the expansion of summary jurisdiction, and, finally, the Royal Commission into the NSW Police Service (Wood 1997).

Amongst judges, the most commonly cited factor (16 of 49, 33% judges) was the abolition of 'dock statements'. ERISP was cited by 9 of 49 (18%), and judge-only trials (disapprovingly) by 4 (8%). Three mentioned the High Court's interventions, 2 changes in sentencing laws, while one each mentioned legal aid for the accused, 'difficulties put in the way of both the police and the Crown in prosecuting offences', 'increasing legalisation', the Evidence Act, 'loss of daily transcripts and security in court rooms', 'a more up to date appraisal of all evidence', and changing public attitudes since the Royal Commission into the NSW Police Service. One asked, presumably

---

[2]   Because of an administrative error, 29 officers' answers to some questions were incomplete. In these instances, n=123.

[3]   See Evidence Act 1995 (NSW) part 3.9

[4]   Introduced as Crimes Act 1900 (NSW) s424A in 1995, the provision is now Criminal Procedure Act 1986 (NSW) s281.

sarcastically, 'Has there been a change?' The significance of these lists is that they illustrate the extent to which criminal justice was changing during the period of ERISP's implementation, and the consequential difficulty of distinguishing a separate impact of ERISP.

As noted in Chapter 1, confessional evidence has been relied upon particularly heavily in NSW criminal justice (Stevenson 1980, 1982). The introduction of ERISP has not changed this position significantly. The centrality of confessional evidence was confirmed by most participants:

Table 6.1 **'Confessional evidence usually is central to the Crown's case'***

	Police (N=123) %	Prosecutors (N=71) %	Defence (N=77) %	Judges (N=49) %
Agree/ strongly agree	67	63	79	55
Neutral/ undecided	9	24	19	28
Disagree/ strongly disagree	24	11	2	14
Don't know	0	1	1	0
No response	0	0	0	2

*   Figures do not total 100 due to rounding.

Similarly, three quarters of prosecutors (76%) stated that the ERISP was important or very important to the Crown in the last case in which they were involved, with only one quarter (24%) saying that it was not important.

As discussed in Chapter 1, ERISP was intended to provide several benefits to the justice process. In general, these were to protect suspects, to reduce demands on courts, and to protect the reputation of the police. Each group was asked whether any, and if so which, group in the criminal justice process had benefited more than others from the introduction of ERISP. Most (89% of police, 79% of Crown Prosecutors, 84% of defence lawyers, 75% of judges) were prepared to nominate a group which had benefited most from ERISP.

A significant shift in police attitudes from initially opposing ERISP to appreciating its benefits is demonstrated by the fact that almost half of police respondents thought that they had benefited most from its introduction. Significant minorities of defence lawyers and judges emphasised the benefit to suspects. A notable pattern in Table 6.2 is the identification of the assistance given to juries: no longer having to judge a swearing contest between police and defendant about what was said in the interview room, jurors have been significantly assisted by electronic recording. When respondents nominated 'others', they either referred to the 'community' or to 'everyone' or, most commonly, to a combination of other nominated groups. Two Crown Prosecutors pointedly remarked that all have benefited except defence lawyers. (However, as Table 6.2 shows, not all lawyers would agree.) One police officer nominated victims, while another mentioned psychiatrists and psychologists. A judge suggested that 'The pursuit of the elusive just result is the real beneficiary.' Another even-handedly commented: 'The only persons who have not benefited are accused who are in fact guilty and police who would otherwise fabricate records of interviews or verbals.'

Table 6.2   Who benefited most from ERISP's introduction?

	Police (N=135) %	Prosecutors (N=55) %	Defence (N=65) %	Judges (N=37) %
Police	46	22	12	14
Suspects	4	9	31	24
Prosecution	4	16	8	14
Defence	3	0	11	0
Judges	2	0	0	0
Juries	13	31	17	24
Others	27	22	21	24

Another perspective on who benefits from ERISP was sought by asking who, in the participants' most recent case involving an ERISP, asked for the ERISP to be shown in court. Forty-nine of our Crown Prosecutors reported that evidence in their most recent case included an ERISP. The Crown alone wanted it shown in 24 of these cases. There was a joint desire by defence and Crown in 16, and by defence,

Crown and judge in 7. In no case was the defence alone in wanting it shown. Reasons given by defence lawyers for not wanting the ERISP shown included 'the unkempt and hostile attitude of accused', agreement with the prosecution on adequacy of the transcript, and the fact that it was a judge-only trial. Time constraints were reported to be an insignificant factor in deciding whether an ERISP should be shown.

Publicity surrounding disputes over alleged verbals was thought to have damaged the public's evaluation of the police and court system. Consequently, participants were asked to comment on whether they thought that the introduction of ERISP had improved public confidence in the justice process.

Table 6.3 **'The introduction of ERISP has had a beneficial impact upon public confidence in the criminal justice system in NSW'**

	Police (N=123) %	Prosecutors (N=71) %	Defence (N=77) %	Judges (N=49) %
Agree/ strongly agree	53	85	62	80
Neutral/ undecided	28	8	25	14
Disagree/ strongly disagree	9	1	5	2
Don't know	9	6	8	2
No response	0	0	0	2

It is notable here that judges and prosecutors were closest in their perceptions.

Participants were asked to indicate what they considered to be the main advantage that ERISP provided to their professional group. The identified advantages are shown in Table 6.4. While several participants nominated more than one, defence lawyers provided fewer. Indicatively, one commented: 'I can't think of any. The advantages are all with police'. Of course, an advantage may have a different emphasis for certain groups: for example, defence lawyers were interested in being able to view the demeanour of police, while police were interested in that of suspects.

Table 6.4   Main advantages of ERISP to each professional group*

	Police (N=152) %	Prosecutors (N=71) %	Defence (N=77) %	Judges (N=49) %
Reduces allegations, disputes, voir dires	56	58	9	47
Integrity, reliability of record, efficiency	74	19	43	24
Shows appearance, demeanour, tone	31	42	19	33
Controls police, protects suspects	2	7	25	12

* Other advantages mentioned by:
- police: more detailed, thorough interviews (12); more guilty pleas (8); better communication; process is fairer (6); interviews conducted at crime scene can be adopted; increases pre-interview planning; increases pre-interview investigation; increased professionalism; dispels myths; easier, more accountability (1);
- Crown Prosecutors: increases guilty pleas; fairer to suspect (2); enables record of exhibits, shorter trials, more detailed questioning (1);
- defence lawyers: earlier guilty pleas; earlier exculpatory statement (2); client can put allegations of police impropriety on record; client may not have to give evidence; client can 'speak' direct to the jury without giving evidence in court (1);
- judges: increases guilty pleas (2); improves police questioning; system is fairer (1).

Selections from participants' comments on these main identified advantages are discussed below.

6.1.1   Impact on allegations, disputes, and voir dires

For police, prosecutors and judges, a major advantage of ERISP has been its role in reducing the frequency of allegations about misconduct during police interviews, and the consequential voir dires and other disputes in court. There had been particular concern that such allegations were often groundless, but had become a routine tactic of some defence lawyers. There was general agreement – including from almost two thirds of defence lawyers – that ERISP has deterred false allegations against police.

Table 6.5 **'ERISP has deterred false allegations of improper police behaviour'**

	Police (N=123) %	Prosecutors (N=71) %	Defence (N=77) %	Judges (N=49) %
Strongly agree/agree	71	85	63	84
Neutral/undecided	9	8	13	4
Strongly disagree/ disagree	19	4	17	6
Don't know	1	3	8	4
No response	0	0	0	2

Police officers stressed that ERISP prevented suspects from making false allegations about the way in which they were interviewed:

> *Allegations of 'verbals' have all but ceased, particularly at court.*

> *The allegations of police verbals and fabrication of evidence will be minimal if not eliminated altogether.*

> *It rebuts the traditional 'verbal' lie.*

Crown Prosecutors reported that the effects of ERISP had been

> *to reduce endless nasty voir dires as to what the accused did or didn't say and reduce allegations of corrupt police behaviour.*

> *Issues as to voluntariness have all but disappeared.*

The reason for this was thought to be clear:

> *The jury can see the confessions — the visual impact has a power, words do not.*

> *No one can now doubt that many accused persons make damaging admissions upon arrest.*

Similarly, judges commented that ERISP 'removes superficial and fatuous arguments based on voluntariness' and avoids 'false claims of fabrication by police'. However, less than one defence lawyer in ten regarded this as a significant advantage: one commented tersely that ERISP 'should avoid verbals (but does not)'.

6.1.2 Integrity, reliability of record, efficiency

Clearly, a reduction in disputes about confessional evidence is causally linked to the next group of advantages — ERISP was perceived by substantial numbers of participants as having enhanced the integrity and reliability of interview records and thereby increased the efficiency of the process. Notably, three quarters of police respondents reported this as a leading advantage of ERISP. These findings were echoed when participants were asked to report their response to claims about ERISP's effect. Ninety-three per cent of police, 88% of prosecutors, 78% of defence lawyers and 96% of judges agreed or strongly agreed that 'ERISP has provided an objective means of resolving disputes about the conduct of police interviews'.

Table 6.6   **'ERISP has provided an objective means of resolving disputes about the conduct of police interviews'**

	Police (N=123) %	Prosecutors (N=71) %	Defence (N=77) %	Judges (N=49) %
Strongly agree	61	62	31	51
Agree	32	28	47	45
Neutral/undecided	3	6	10	0
Disagree	2	3	6	2
Strongly disagree	2	1	1	0
Don't know	1	0	0	2
No response	0	0	4	0

Similarly impressive proportions agreed that ERISP has provided the courts with a reliable account of statements made by suspects (see Table 6.7).

From the state's perspective, an efficient system would reduce disputes about confessions, providing courts with evidential material on which they could rely. While, as will be shown below, participants identified some problems with ERISP, the perceptions reported in Tables 6.6 and 6.7 show that ERISP has very substantially achieved its primary goal of legitimising the process of interviewing suspects. One judge summed up crisply his view of ERISP evidence: 'More powerful. More detailed. More convincing'. For police officers, the benefits of 'Quicker interviews that are more accurate' were direct: 'Lengthy police statements and parrot memorisation for court is a thing of the past'. In this respect, there was substantial agreement between defence lawyers and other parties, although it should be acknowledged that defence lawyers were significantly less enthusiastic, with only one quarter strongly agreeing, compared to more than three quarters of both police and prosecutors. It would be wrong to underestimate defence lawyers' interest in a process which operates with crime control efficiency, weeding out as quickly as possible those cases which can be resolved without a trial: one commented that ERISP records 'help to crystallise a decision as to a plea more quickly and decisively because you can't challenge a live recording'. Less assiduous defence lawyers may well treat electronically recorded confessions at face value. It is only those who are prepared to dig beneath the surface who will become aware of potential problems, such as the impact of pre-ERISP interaction or the potential unreliability of confessions by vulnerable suspects.

Table 6.7   **'ERISP has provided the courts with a reliable account of statements made by suspects'**

	Police (N=123) %	**Prosecutors** (N=71) %	**Defence** (N=58) %	**Judges** (N=49 %
Strongly agree	77	79	23	53
Agree	18	18	60	45
Neutral/ undecided	4	1	5	0
Disagree	0	1	10	0
Strongly disagree	1	0	1	0
Don't know	0	0	0	2

Before its introduction, there was some concern that ERISP would reduce the number of confessions and admissions made during police interviews. A significant number of participants in the study considered that this had been the result.

Table 6.8   Effect of ERISP on the number of confessions in police interviews

	Police (N=123) %	Prosecutors (N=71) %	Defence (N=77) %	Judges (N=49 %
Increased	12	21	19	24
Decreased	41	48	25	12
Neither	37	7	31	20
Don't know	9	24	22	35
No response	0	0	3	8

A number of factors accounted for the widely perceived decrease. Notably, it was suggested that interviews had become more genuinely investigatory (rather than mere attempts to confirm a case theory). It was also suggested that questioning focused on the offence for which the suspect had been arrested and was less likely to produce confessions to other offences.

There was no concern expressed about the decline in confessions: the reduction of 'efficiency' in criminal justice to a quantitative measure was resisted. In the eyes of our respondents, if there had been some decline in quantity of confessions and admissions, this was more than offset by the increase in quality. A defence lawyer explained:

> One of the significant consequences of use of ERISP has been (that) the quality of evidence produced by police interview is dramatically enhanced. A full confession on ERISP will almost certainly result in a plea of guilty. This was not necessarily the case where a 'confession' was obtained by way of a typewritten 'record of interview'.

Nonetheless, a crucial indicator of systemic efficiency was expected to be an increased rate of guilty pleas. While it may be impossible objectively to distinguish the impact of ERISP from that of other contemporaneous changes (see above), considerable majorities of participants in each category had no subjective doubt that ERISP had increased guilty pleas.

Table 6.9   Effect of ERISP on guilty pleas

	Police (N=132) %	Prosecutors (N=71) %	Defence (N=77) %	Judges (N=49) %
Increased	62	73	49	49
Decreased	0	0	4	2
Neither	28	13	21	18
Don't know	11	14	21	20
No response	0	0	5	10

As noted in Chapter 1, concern about the cost (in terms both of resources and legitimacy) of voir dires concerning confessional evidence had been a major motivating factor in the introduction of the ERISP process. There was a widespread perception among judges and prosecution and defence lawyers that the number of voir dires had declined. However, police were more equivocal:

Table 6.10   'ERISP has reduced the frequency of voir dires (and other disputes about evidence) relating to police interviews'

	Police (N=123) %	Prosecutors (N=71) %	Defence (N=77) %	Judges (N=49) %
Agree/ strongly agree	44	90	71	75
Neutral/undecided	29	3	12	12
Disagree/ strongly disagree	20	3	5	6
Don't know	6	4	12	0
No response	0	0	0	6

We asked the judges to comment on how often in the previous two years voir dires related to police interviews in their direct experience related to various factors (see Table 6.11).

Table 6.11   Factors in voir dires related to police interviews identified by judges

	Editing of video	Should jury see video	Transcript accuracy	Visibility, audibility etc of ERISP	Volume	Admissibility re fairness	Admissibility re public policy
Never	19	24	10	19	22	11	18
Rarely	12	16	19	12	13	11	16
Sometimes	6	5	13	13	7	16	9
Often	7	0	3	1	3	5	2
Very often	1	0	0	0	0	0	0
No response	4	4	4	4	4	6	4

Most (35/49) thought that voir dires concerning confessional evidence were more likely to be resolved in favour of the prosecution since ERISP's introduction.[5] One third of judges (15/49) thought that the number of voir dires not related to the police interview had increased, with only two thinking they had decreased.

A consistent concern in the criminal justice system has been delays in bringing cases to trial. Consequently, a welcome perceived result of the reduction in challenges to confessional evidence was that the time a case took in court had been dramatically reduced:

Table 6.12   ERISP's effect on the number of days spent in court in trials

	Police (N=123) %	Prosecutors (N=71) %	Defence (N=77) %	Judges (N=49) %
Increased	8	4	21	10
Decreased	58	76	61	65
Undecided	18	13	1	0
Neither increased/ decreased	10	7	9	10
Don't know	6	0	6	8
No response	0	0	1	6

We asked police officers about the impact of ERISP on court-related aspects of police work. More than half (51%) reported that the number of his/her staff who give evidence in court had decreased somewhat or decreased greatly, with 40% saying there had been no change. However, 84% reported that the amount of time that their staff spent specifically answering questions about alleged police misconduct related to interviews had decreased. Seventy-six per cent (84) agreed or strongly agreed that the experience of being cross-examined in court

---

[5]   Two judges commented that the emphasis in the questionnaire on formal voir dires may be misleading: 'Mostly the issues are resolved by discussion in the absence of the jury rather than by conducting a voir dire.' For present purposes, the distinction is not significant. In any case, both procedures for dealing with 'preliminary questions' would be treated as a voir dire by the Evidence Act 1995 (NSW) s189.

about interviews with suspects had become easier since ERISP's introduction. More generally, 71% thought that time spent answering questions about matters other than allegations of misconduct had declined. Only a third (32%) of officers thought that their staff spent less time preparing for court appearances, with 51% saying there had been no change.

In general, these reported perceptions suggest that the ERISP system has had considerable success in reducing concerns about integrity, reliability, and efficiency in the interview process.

6.1.3 Demeanour and deception

As discussed in Chapter 1, ERISP was designed as a system in which the video tape would be held in reserve to guarantee the authenticity of transcribed and audio evidence. However, judges (and prosecutors) have insisted upon showing the video in many trials. They have done so because they believe that the visual record is itself significant as evidence. Seventy-eight per cent of judges (36 of 46 responding to this question) rejected the suggestion that trials could rely on transcripts rather than electronic evidence (with 2 neutral and 8 agreeing). Judges liked making the ERISP available to the jury: 90% (43 of 48 responding) agreed that 'the judge's instructions to the jury should include a statement advising jurors of their option to watch the ERISP video in the jury room' with 4 neutral and 1 strongly disagreeing).

Table 6.13 'A suspect's demeanour is significant as evidence'

	Prosecutors (N=71) %	Defence (N=77) %	Judges (N=49) %
Agree/ strongly agree	84	78	73
Disagree/ strongly disagree	3	8	8
Neutral/ undecided	11	14	14
Don't know	1	0	0
No response	0	0	4

It is widely believed that the visual image allows assessment of the defendant. As Table 6.13 indicates, the great majority of legal professionals think that a suspect's demeanour as depicted in the ERISP is significant as evidence.

More specifically, 64% of judges (30 of 47 responding) agreed with the proposition 'How the suspect speaks in the police interview is as important as what she/he says.' (8 disagreed, 9 were neutral.)

Assessing demeanour has various facets: does the suspect understand questions? Is he or she apparently drunk or drug-affected, or even awake? Does he or she appear to be scared or confident? However, such assessment is commonly directed to a particular end: deciding whether the suspect is telling the truth. Table 6.14 indicates participants' views of this crucial question:

Table 6.14 **'A suspect's demeanour during the interview indicates whether he/she is telling the truth'**

	Police (N=123) %	Prosecutors (N=71) %	Defence (N=77) %	Judges (N=49) %
Agree/ Strongly agree	28	56	26	57
Disagree/ strongly disagree	32	10	38	20
Neutral/undecided	36	28	35	16
Don't know	3	6	1	2
No response	1	0	0	4

It is notable that a majority of both judges and prosecutors believed that demeanour is an indicator of veracity. By contrast, more police disagreed than agreed with the statement. Direct experience of interviewing suspects and the NSW Police's discouragement of pretensions to read deception from body language are presumably responsible for this.

The capacity to assess demeanour was widely regarded as a key benefit of electronic recording. Several prosecutors stressed the evidential value of the suspect's demeanour and 'body language':

> *The film graphically shows the demeanour of the suspect. All available indications are that non-verbal communication can*

carry far more weight than verbal (or typewritten) communication.

A properly conducted ERISP discloses to the viewer the demeanour of the suspect together with non-verbal clues and cues which juries (and judges) pick up on quickly.

There was widespread judicial agreement:

You are able to judge from demeanour the genuineness (or otherwise) of the accused's statements. I have found this to be of enormous significance in 'Judge Alone' trials, so that juries must also.

It gives a better opportunity to assess credibility. Observation of the witness, his physical bearing and clothing is significant.

Opportunity to observe accused's demeanour under questioning.

You hear the tone in which the parties to the interview speak and you see their body language.

The evidence can be understood more easily due to the fact that one has the advantage of observing the body language.

As noted above, police officers were generally more sceptical about reading body language: while a substantial minority (28%) agreed that demeanour indicates veracity, their explanations usually were concerned more with the suspect's physical appearance than his or her 'body language'. This reflected a longstanding complaint from police about how drunk, unkempt suspects are transformed into polite, conventionally dressed defendants in court.

The court gets a true representation of suspect at time of interview — his demeanour, attitude and version — not the later 'painted' picture offered by many defendants and/or lawyers when challenging the evidence.

It dispels a lot of the myths associated with police interviews as well allowing the court to see the offender at time of arrest and not (as a) well dressed, respectable looking person sitting behind counsel.

While demeanour seemed usually to be examined for evidence of guilt, it could also be exculpatory: as a defence solicitor commented,

The demeanour of the accused ... may be a plus or a minus.

It might, for example, be in the defendant's interest to be able to establish from the video that he/she was emotionally disturbed or drunk or drug-affected at the time of interview. A Public Defender suggested that guilt may sometimes be indicated by demeanour, but that such cases rarely went to court:

> *Occasionally, one look at the video is enough to convince anyone of the client's guilt (but this is extremely rare and if so they'll end up pleading guilty).*

Emphasising that ERISP was intended to provide accountability as well as to act as investigative device, another defence solicitor made clear that the interviewers were also examined:

> *The way the police ask the questions (i.e. their demeanour) can be seen.*

Similarly, two judges commented on

> *the ability to judge from demeanour the genuineness of both exculpatory and confessional statements made by the accused.*

> *It provides an accurate record of the interview including tone and manner of interviewer.*

From this perspective, assessment of the suspect's demeanour may provide an indicator of how the suspect has been treated by police before recording began — a crucial possibility if police conduct significant interviews before the ERISP.

Table 6.15 **'A suspect's demeanour during ERISP allows the viewer to assess police treatment before recording began'**

	Prosecutors (N=71) %	Defence (N=77) %	Judges (N=49) %
Agree/ Strongly agree	86	45	59
Disagree/ strongly disagree	1	40	14
Neutral/ undecided	11	13	24
Don't know	1	1	0
No response	0	0	2

Prosecutors and judges were much more likely than defence lawyers to regard the ERISP as a useful indicator of the suspect's treatment by police. The prosecutors' faith in ERISP is indicated by the fact that only one disagreed that ERISP could be used in this way.

This section confirms that there are grounds for concern about the confidence of some criminal justice professionals that they can use the ERISP image to assess body language and thereby credibility and guilt or innocence. However, such confidence is more prevalent among prosecutors and judges than among police officers. This suggests the potential benefits of training criminal justice professionals to recognise the limits of their ability to read 'body language' (or perhaps shielding them from unhelpful training in the pop-psychology of interviewing). In addition, it is notable that the demeanour of interviewers is also scrutinised, although not to the same extent or through an identical lens.

Potential problems in making assessments of credibility based on observation of witnesses' demeanour in court have been recognised by courts:

> There is a growing understanding, both by trial judges and appellate courts, of the fallibility of judicial evaluation of credibility from the appearance and demeanour of witnesses in the somewhat artificial and sometimes stressful circumstances of the courtroom.[6]

In the same judgment, Justice Kirby acknowledged that 'demeanour is, in part, driven by culture'. Stereotypes affect evaluation. 'Distaste or prejudice can cloud evaluation.' He also noted the contribution of psychological research demonstrating 'the danger of placing undue reliance upon appearances in evaluating credibility'.[7] It has to be acknowledged that 'so-called common-sense assumptions about human behaviour may result in undue weight being attached to such things as a witness's demeanour' (Hunter et al. 2005:1116). Consequently,

> the law expects both appellate and trial judges when assessing factual matters to limit their reliance [on] witnesses' demeanour and instead rely 'as far as possible, on the basis of contemporary materials, objectively establish facts and the apparent logic of events'.[8]

---

[6] *State Rail Authority of NSW v Earthline Constructions* [1999] HCA 3. For analysis of this and other cases, see Hunter et al. 2005:1114–1119.

[7] Op. cit.

[8] Hunter et al. 2005:821, quoting Gleeson CJ, Gummow and Kirby JJ in *Fox v Percy* (2003) 214 CLR 118.

While the relevant reported cases have been concerned with evaluation of witnesses' credibility in court, their warnings are equally applicable to assessment of credibility in electronically recorded police interviews.

6.1.4   Control of police and protection of suspects

A significant minority of defence lawyers (25%) reported that control of police and protection of suspects were the major advantages to them of ERISP. While clearly overlapping with reducing allegations and integrity, control and protection were articulated in a way requiring separate treatment. As Table 6.2 showed, 31% of defence lawyers nominated suspects as the group which had benefited most from the introduction of ERISP. There was general agreement that ERISP prevents police malpractice during interviews: the simple verbal, assaults, and oppressive treatment were deterred during the taping of interviews. This may seem self-evident: however, we should remember the example cited in Chapter 1 of English police officers whose threats and profanity were not prevented by video-recording: as ever, the effectiveness of a device of accountability depends upon whether those responsible for holding officials to account do their job.

Table 6.16   'ERISP prevents police misconduct during interviews'

	Police (N=123) %	Prosecutors (N=71) %	Defence (N=77) %	Judges (N=49) %
Strongly agree	73	72	18	45
Agree	19	23	58	41
Neutral/ undecided	2	4	6	6
Disagree	2	1	13	2
Strongly disagree	1	0	4	2
Don't know	2	0	0	2
No response	1	0	0	2

Typically, a prosecutor commented:

ERISP generally speaking has been a great advance in fairness to both suspects and police: there is far less room for speculation and doubt about how an interview was conducted.

A more controversial question is whether police misconduct before interview is prevented by ERISP:

Table 6.17   'ERISP prevents police misconduct prior to interview'

	Police (N=123) %	Prosecutors (N=71) %	Defence (N=77) %	Judges (N=49) %
Strongly agree	22	4	3	10
Agree	32	48	6	18
Neutral/undecided	17	11	9	14
Disagree	19	22	52	27
Strongly disagree	6	8	26	22
Don't know	2	6	4	6
No response	1	0	-	2

While a variety of views amongst each group is apparent, most notable is that more than three quarters of defence lawyers (78%), almost half the judges (49%), and, perhaps more surprisingly one quarter (25%) of police did not believe that police misconduct before interview was prevented by ERISP. As indicated in Chapter 1, the failure to complement ERISP with an effective scheme of legal regulation of custodial interrogation has left room for doubt and concern about the pre-charge process.

6.2   Comparing ERISP with records of interview

In order to gain another perspective on ERISP, we asked participants what advantages (if any) they thought that typed interviews had over ERISP — i.e. what has been lost by the introduction of audio-visual recording. This was inviting answers which were largely hypothetical in that, since 1995, the law has made use of ERISP almost compulsory in indictable (and some other) matters.[9] Comparing pre- and post-1995 experiences, many participants provided some interesting insights on the process.

Table 6.18   Advantages of typed records of interview compared to ERISP*

	Police (N=152) %	Prosecutors (N=71) %	Defence (N=77) %	Judges (N=49 %
Better interviews	30	8	0	14
Immediate access to RoI	17	0	9	4
Time-saving	7	0	0	6
Easier to edit	0	7	1	0
Shorter/ more convenient	0	20	9	8
Demeanour not shown	0	1	14	0
More challengeable	0	0	28	0
None	26	55	28	47
No response	21	8	9	24

*   Other advantages mentioned by:
- police: some suspects will not do an ERISP interview (14); some suspects were more cooperative in naming co-offenders (7); better police control of interview, cheaper (6); some suspects were less intimidated, interviews possible away from station, less formal atmosphere (3); record easier to read (2); better if large volumes of documents are to be produced (1);
- one prosecutor's view was that they were 'less staged'.

It is notable that, with the narrow exception of prosecutors, only a minority of each group thought that records of interview had no advantages over ERISP.

Several police officers felt that ERISP had disturbed effective police practices, particularly challenging the interviewers' control over the situation. Typed interview records had several perceived advantages:

---

[9]   See n4, above.

Allows police a great deal of control over the content and context of the interview.

More time to think about questions asked — able to review previous questions/answers to ensure all proofs are covered, and clarification questions asked.

You can read an accused's answers and more fully ask questions about answers given. You get more time to examine and interrogate a suspect.

Interview can be more "directed" when typed.

Somewhat similarly, some prosecutors noted the advantages to their professional practice of dealing with typed records of interview:

At times, questions were more thoughtfully (and slowly) constructed by police. This is probably because of the absence of the pressure of being recorded, e.g. while taking a long time to think of the next question, etc. The camera 'demands' spontaneity and constant flow of questions.

More compact/specific. Less waffle.

They are easier to edit. They are clearer in that in taped interviews some parts are hard to understand and sometimes unintelligible.

A defence lawyer noted a benefit of typed interviews was that

Suspects don't give long rambling answers to equally long questions. The more a suspect says, the tighter the noose becomes.

Another commented that a typed interview provided more 'opportunity for discussion between accused and legal representative during the interview'. Given the extreme rarity of defence lawyers' presence during interview in NSW, this can hardly be regarded as significant. More interestingly, a defence lawyer commented that records of interview did not have ERISP's simulacra of completeness, which tends to draw attention away from police conduct before recording begins.

Typical judges' comments on typed interviews included

The answers as recorded are usually less ambiguous than in an ERISP.

They are short and much more to the point.

The police, having to type it all out, are more concentrated and economical with their questioning.

It is worth noting the judge's assumption in the final comment above that a record of interview is a full, contemporaneous record rather than a selective construction. Others were more sceptical:

ERISP records reveal the interview 'warts and all' — every pause, error, correction, action is recorded, whereas except for grammatical and spelling errors, a typed record of interview does not reveal everything and is, therefore, not necessarily true and accurate.

ERISP represents the whole interview rather than at best in part a summary of what transpired.

It provides the actual response, rather than suggested answer.

A Crown Prosecutor provided a perceptively sarcastic response:

Suspects don't seem to be quite as articulate on ERISP as they were before. Moreover, their grammatical skills have deteriorated noticeably with the advent of video/audio recording. These things make admissions more plausible, but often not that comprehensible.

Judges, defence lawyers, and prosecutors were asked whether, and in which respects, the evidence available from ERISP interviews was different from that in typed records of interview. Eighty per cent of judges, 73% of Crown Prosecutors, 86% of private defence lawyers, and 95% of public defence lawyers thought it was different. It was widely agreed that ERISP records were longer, more accurate, more reliable, and more complete, although sometimes more difficult to use than a concise typed record of interview. It would seem that the record of interview was bureaucratically convenient in many ways, but that it had to be replaced by ERISP because of the systemic strains associated with its use.

Legal professionals were asked about their comparative preference. All Crown Prosecutors and all but one (neutral) judge preferred ERISP to typed records of interview. Similarly, almost all prosecutors (67/71) thought a system like ERISP which includes video is preferable to a system (such as that generally used in England and Wales) which only records audio (with only 2 disagreeing and 1 undecided). There was a small dissenting minority amongst private defence lawyers: while 69% preferred video to typed records of interview, 9% disagreed. Similarly 42 of 46 responding judges thought video was preferable to audio, with three neutral, and one strongly disagreeing. While 55% of private defence lawyers preferred video to audio, 14% disagreed. The most negative comment came from a Crown Prosecutor, who stated

> *All ERISPs have done is move the emphasis of the defence attack from the confession itself to antecedent or collateral matters.*

6.3 The impact of ERISP on police practice

Three quarters of police (75%) reported that the way they prepared to interview suspects had been affected by ERISP. Almost all of these noted that ERISP interviews required more planning and preparation: questions had to be prepared, ripostes to possible responses had to be considered, and exhibits had to be organised. The pace of ERISP interviews is quicker: there is no time to collect thoughts while the typist catches up or to read through a record of interview to ensure points had been covered. Interviews are no longer 'ad hoc' or 'impromptu'. As one put it you 'must know contents of all victim/witness statements so you don't look like an unprofessional idiot on tape'.

> *It has become necessary for interviews to be prepared. This has led to a more professional interview, with greater accuracy and quality of content.*

> *You have to be more thorough in your preparation. It looks very unprofessional if you have to keep leaving the interview room for something you forgot. You can easily leave out important questions if not properly prepared.*

> *Police will have to be prepared to do a more complete investigation into inquiries prior to interviewing suspects.*

As previous chapters have shown, such comments are sometimes more aspiration than description.

While most officers thought that interviewers had to be better prepared, they were more divided on the issue of whether ERISP required different techniques *during* the interview. Forty-nine per cent thought the same were required, while 41% thought different techniques were needed. Of those (n=62) who thought different techniques were required, by far the most common reference (39%) was to a more conversational, spontaneous style. While a few (4) suggested that the ERISP interview was more formal, they were referring to the need to prepare and structure, rather than to the quality of the interaction during interview. Several (19%) mentioned the need to present oneself well in electronically recorded interviews. Others noted that more questions could be asked, but that interviewers had less time than in a typed record of interview to consider before asking a question. If the outcome is simpler questions, this may be a benefit. Typical comments from police were:

> *Simpler — less complex questions asked during ERISP and more questions able to be asked. In typed interviews — to reduce typing and time – more detailed questions asked.*

> *ERISP tends to be less structured and more spontaneous. Investigators' questions more determined by defendants' responses*

> *Easier for corroborating officer to participate in the ERISP.*

> *Questions tend to become 'less formal' and conversational, often a question which is somewhat 'leading' can be used very effectively. Courts appear to be more flexible in admitting this conversation than in the more formal RoI.*

> *On ERISP questions have to be put much more circumspectly, less demanding but more insistently, a difficult task often resulting in prevarication or resistance from suspects.*

> *In a non-ERISP interview, the interview technique is in the form of direct questioning and more often than not the whole of the interview is not recorded, by that I mean during the course of the interview the defendant may require clarification regarding some points which are not usually recorded.*

> *Your ability to conduct a professional and thorough electronic interview gives you more credit at court.*

> *Bearing in mind voice and vision of police are available to jury in ERISP interviews, it is important for police to present well and appear polished.*

As these comments indicate, these police officers appreciated that ERISP requires a substantial change in policing practice. They identified both beneficial and detrimental aspects of ERISP. Sometimes these ran together: if police have less time to construct questions, equally suspects have less time to think of answers. Numerous officers mentioned the benefits to police of spontaneity and speed of interaction in ERISPs. An area of concern is the uncertainty over how searching an investigator's questions can be: in commenting on difficulties in a recent case, one officer noted his frustration in 'not being able to cross-examine on matters I believed to be false'. As elsewhere (Dixon 1997:ch4), police officers are left with a difficult task of exploring the limits of acceptability (which are only vaguely set by the judiciary).

In order to focus our subjects' responses, we asked them for details of the most recent ERISP that they had conducted. While the range of offences was wide, because these were experienced detectives, their work tended to include a large proportion of more serious offences than those in our tape samples: 10% involved homicides and 11% involved sexual assaults. We asked whether the officer had questioned the suspect before the ERISP. Of the 152 answering, 37% said they had not. Of the rest, 25% had recorded questions and answers in a notebook, 30% had informally interviewed the suspect in the station, and 20% had interviewed him/her elsewhere. (Some had done more than one kind of pre-ERISP interview.) The suspect confessed in 40%, made partial admissions in 27%, and did neither in 32%. Most of these confessions/admissions had already been made when the ERISP began: while less than one third (31%) were made only during the ERISP, 19% were made at the crime scene, 12% at the suspect's house, 9% during a notebook interview at the station, and 24% in an informal interview at the station. (Unexpectedly given experience elsewhere, none was reported to have been made on the way to the station.) In the officers' broader assessment of ERISP, 35% agreed or strongly agreed that 'it is advisable to put the charges to the suspect in a pre-ERISP interview to prepare for the ERISP', but 42% disagreed or strongly disagreed.

We asked officers to imagine that the suspect in their most recent ERISP had been interviewed using a typed interview. Twenty per cent thought that more time would have been needed for preparation, 53% thought preparatory time would have been the same, while 24%

thought less preparation would have been needed. Despite the emphasis in training on the need to structure ERISP interviews, only a quarter thought ERISP required more preparation. As indicated in Chapter 4, this was perhaps reflected in the interviews in our tape samples in which some officers, freed from the constraints of typed questions and answers, wandered aimlessly around their subject matter. Nonetheless, 89% disagreed or strongly disagreed with the proposition that 'minimal training is needed to interview suspects effectively', and 75% agreed or strongly agreed that ERISP requires new interview techniques (with 21% disagreeing or strongly disagreeing). Perhaps more surprisingly, 93% thought that carrying out a typed interview would have been more time-consuming than an ERISP, with only 3% thinking it would be less. However, many officers (41%) thought that a typed interview would have taken less time to prepare for the DPP, while 39% thought the same and 19% thought it would have taken more.

In general, NSW police officers' attitudes towards electronic recording were similar to those found in other jurisdictions (Dixon 1997:151–152; Sullivan 2004:14). After initial hostility from some and wariness from many, ERISP had been accepted as a valuable tool:

> ERISP is a good thing. After being initially apprehensive about its introduction I am now fully in favour of it.

The problems (discussed below in the next section) were more than outweighed by the benefits, notably reducing allegations of misconduct.

Police officers' perceptions of the impact of ERISP on their practices may be compared with those of other participants.

Table 6.19   Has ERISP affected how police question suspects?

	Prosecutors (N=71) %	Defence (N=77) %	Judges (N=49) %
Yes	72	43	69
No	22	49	10
Undecided	6	8	18
No response	0	0	2

The most common change reported by Crown Prosecutors was that police had become less aggressive, less prone to cross-examination, and better prepared than before. However, not all change was for the good. According to two Crown Prosecutors,

> *Stage fright of police with little experience has meant vague rambling interviews.*

> *Police tend generally to ask more questions, some of which are irrelevant ... In many cases, they tend not to delve more deeply and do not go far enough.*

Private defence lawyers' views varied. While four thought there was more cross-examination, five thought the police were less overbearing. A number commented on increased preparation by police, and the number of questions asked. One noted that police were more likely to stay seated during interviews.

Given their specialist role, the Public Defenders' views carry particular weight.

> *The police are much more conscious of their responsibilities.*

> *Police are conscious that they are being observed by camera ... As a result they are more polite, more thorough, less aggressive and more measured.*

> *They are at great pains to word questions carefully and ask more detailed questions.*

> *In many cases the interviewing is more genuinely investigatory and likely to produce material which explores defences and explanations as well as material going to guilt.*

> *They are more cautious about their treatment of the suspect and are careful to obtain admissible material.*

> *They are much more careful to obey simple rules of procedural fairness. There are no more allegations of bullying during the interview.*

One noted that some problems may be a result of attempts to be more thorough:

> *Longer questioning — often less focused, sometimes repetition almost to point of cross-examination.*

There was, not surprisingly, a marked difference of opinion in response to a deliberately provocative statement about police practices:

Table 6.20   'ERISP is used by the police to record what they want to present as evidence, not the full interview'

	Police (N=123) %	Prosecutors (N=71) %	Defence (N=77) %
Agree/ strongly agree	3	7	35
Neutral/ undecided	2	11	25
Disagree/ strongly disagree	95	77	35
Don't know	0	3	5
No response	0	1	0

One Public Defender provided a balanced, if critical, view:

> *The ERISP procedure has been a huge improvement ... It has been my experience however that ... the advantages are being circumvented by some police who still do 'deals' of the old-fashioned kind, in which (for example) there will be a promise of bail (or some other inducement) in exchange for a series of stage managed admissions ('Do you agree you told me ...? Do you agree you told me ...? Do you agree you told me ...?') Ideally, particularly in more serious matters we still need a requirement that all discussions of whatever nature between suspect and police should be recorded otherwise not admissible. The verbal is not dead, just suffering a persistent infection - 'I'll tell you what happened but I won't go on that machine'. It's just harder to get a jury to believe it.*

In commenting on their most recent case which involved an ERISP, Crown Prosecutors noted that there had been few allegations of malpractice — only 3 in 46 cases. These concerned: illegal detention of juvenile interviewed in absence of parent/guardian; threats made during an interview break; and failure to record a statement made after adoption of the interview. Similarly, private defence lawyers reported such allegations in only 5 of 52 cases: these involved assault, threats and inducements during breaks in interview.

However, allegations about other aspects of detention and questioning were more common. One quarter of Crown Prosecutors

(12/49) whose most recent trial had involved ERISP evidence reported that the case included allegations about malpractice prior to the ERISP. (Eight of these had been dealt with in a voir dire.) These allegations were assault (4, including the traditional claim in one of bashing with a telephone book); inducements (2); 'loading up' with drugs; oppression; alleged fabrication of oral admissions; denied access to solicitor; injury while trying to escape police; unspecified (1 each). There were allegations of misconduct in 14 of the defence lawyers' 52 cases. Allegations included: assault (4), threats (4), inducements (2), 'suspect taken to a deserted area and threatened prior to making of ERISP'; refused access to legal adviser, 'retaining accused (woman) at Police Station whilst young children wailed in car, independent person (father of Aboriginal young person) drunk, pre-ERISP interviewing of juvenile in absence of independent person (1 each). Some cases included more than one type of alleged malpractice. Two private defence lawyers commented

> There is a tendency to over-emphasise the success which ERISP has had in eliminating police malpractice. 'Verbals' have been significantly reduced, but not eliminated. Also confessions can still be obtained by threats and intimidation.

> ERISP has not solved all the problems which we thought it would. Too much occurs pre-ERISP that influences the interview.

We asked participants if their perception of police interviewing had been affected by their experience of ERISP:

Table 6.21   Has using ERISP evidence changed your views about police interviewing practices?

	Prosecutors (N=71) %	Defence (N=77) %	Judges (N=49) %
Yes	44	30	26
No	48	64	55
Undecided	8	6	14
No response	0	0	4

A negative answer did not necessarily imply any complacency about police practices. On the contrary, several Crown Prosecutors felt that their doubts about previous practices had been supported by the contrast between typed records of interview and ERISP.

> *Very strongly indicates how false or at least artificial the old RoIs were.*

Similarly, a Public Defender commented

> *ERISP confirmed what I always knew, typed interviews were selective, biased and weren't a true record of what went on.*

As a private defence barrister pointed out,

> *I have never seen a RoI [typed] where a suspect is said to have made any complaints. I have frequently seen complaints or other comments on ERISPs ... I was not inclined to believe typed RoIs accurately represented the contents of interviews. Hence, I consider interviewing practices have changed with ERISPs because ... leading questions, threats (subtle or otherwise) etc are no longer used to the same degree.*

Importantly, Crown Prosecutors felt more confident that the evidence which police provided for use against defendants had been collected with propriety. Consequently, there was more trust between police and prosecutors. Similarly, a judge pointed out how double-edged the impact of ERISP had been:

> *My views have generally become more favourable towards the interviewing police, but I am more inclined than before to disbelieve claims that answers were recorded verbatim (in untaped interviews).*

> *Opportunities by police to stand over or cross-examine are very, very limited.*

However, another judge commented that

> *the style of questioning is now obviously far more discursive and often tends to cross-examination.*

Clearly, the issue is what one counts as cross-examination, and how realistic one is prepared to be about what went on before the introduction of ERISP. Some Crown Prosecutors commented critically on the quality of police interviewing

It is apparent in many interviews that police have not had sufficient time to prepare questions to assess significance of material available.

Some questions are not as free flowing and organised as they appeared to be on typed RoIs — police are now required to think about their interviewing techniques.

They don't seem to think the questions out as well and tend to ask more general and sometimes unclear questions when the discipline of typing it down had gone.

I have realised how bad they are at it.

ERISP has shown, particularly with older police, their lack of an interviewing style in the framing of appropriate questions. This shows that prior to ERISP there was employed a style which was totally different from the method now required.

A Crown Prosecutor pointed to the significance of the discrepancy between the time spent interviewing suspects and the length of typed records of interview.

Before ERISP it was obvious police edited interview evidence in a minor way — e.g. the 'ums' and 'ahs' weren't recorded. But ERISP really showed just how substantial this editing was. A half-hour typed record of interview used to amount to about 3 pages. Now a half hour interview occupies about 15 pages. Typing speeds of police officers wouldn't account for such a difference.

Some defence lawyers were more blunt:

I can't believe how illiterate interviewing police are and how ill-prepared they are to interview.

I didn't realise how hopeless police were at interviewing until I actually heard them on ERISP.

Many practices are still deviant and dishonest, many police will still try and [sic] mislead suspects, and misrepresent the evidence then available as more than it is. Many police are conducting unrecorded interviews to 'pinpoint' a series of admissions or a statement by the suspect ... and then recording it. A version of the unrecorded materials then appears in the officer's statement and notebook.

A Public Defender summarised his view of how practices changed with the introduction of ERISP:

> *More leading questions. Unfair questions — facts assumed by interviewer not admitted by suspect. Detailed instructions should be given to police as to proper questioning techniques.*

One defence lawyer's assessment was ambivalent:

> *Far fewer verbals are used although it has not entirely eliminated them. It has also made the police far more courteous to suspects.*

Some judges' comments were pointedly critical:

> *Such interviews highlight the inadequacy of the NSW police force to structure an interview and ask a simple question.*

> *The ERISP tends to be more discursive, more haphazard ... Many police have not mastered the art of interviewing.*

> *Much more detailed, though often irrelevant or trivial.*

> *Because police do not need to handwrite or to type the questions and answers, police ask longer questions, unnecessary questions, irrelevant questions, argumentative questions, questions based on incorrect or inaccurate information and questions based on hearsay just to obtain an answer from the suspected person.*

> *The principal problem since the introduction of ERISP is the change in attack from 'verbals' to inducement. The police are very poorly trained as to how to obtain worthwhile answers which will reduce the chance of making false allegations as to inducements. The standard question — 'Has there been any threat, inducement etc?' certainly does not produce such an answer.*

However, another judge summarised his view as being that interviews were now:

> *Less aggressive ... More courteous ... Fairer...*

Our question asked whether 'the style of questioning' had been affected by ERISP. Many respondents unselfconsciously compared records of interview to ERISP, with no apparent acknowledgment of the fact that the former were not, could not, be verbatim transcripts.

However, for some Crown Prosecutors, doubts about police practice had been dispelled:

> They have either changed overnight or they remain more dispassionate than I previously believed.

> Largely, I am impressed by the standard of interviewing displayed on ERISP.

6.4 The impact of ERISP on suspects

Opinion was divided over suggestions that suspects who have previously been interviewed by use of ERISP become reluctant to agree to electronic recording of subsequent interviews. Similar proportions of both prosecutors and defence lawyers agreed, disagreed, or were undecided about this suggestion. Of Crown Prosecutors, 28% agreed or strongly agreed with this suggestion, while 33% disagreed or strongly disagreed, with 23% undecided, and 6% saying they didn't know. Among private defence lawyers, 17% agreed, 21% were undecided and 17% disagreed. Of the Public Defenders, none agreed, 3 were neutral, 7 disagreed, and 9 did not know. Similarly, there was a similar division about the suggestion that it is rare for a suspect to make an incriminating statement and then refuse to acknowledge or adopt it in a subsequent ERISP.

As noted above, ERISP has made police concentrate in interviews on the suspected offence for which the arrest was made: 41% of police thought the amount of information about criminal activity involving other people and about other crimes involving the suspect had been reduced by ERISP (with 34% undecided).

Table 6.22   Has ERISP affected how suspects answer questions?

	Prosecutors (N=71) %	Defence (N=77) %	Judges (N=49) %
Yes	38	39	41
No	37	40	35
Undecided	25	21	22
No response	0	0	2

Crown Prosecutors who thought suspects' answers had been affected often commented that its effect varied:

> *'Experienced' suspects, not overawed by ERISP, are quite expansive sometimes, but others become very guarded.*

Similarly, one judge commented

> *[I]t depends on the defendant. Some are camera shy, some are theatrical; most look resigned.*

Another commented

> *Rambling questions elicit rambling answers. But recorded answers did not necessarily reflect all that was said by the suspect even where there was no dishonesty in the paraphrase.*

One Crown Prosecutor thought some suspects were more cunning:

> *As suspects appreciate the video is an absolute record of the interview, many now use the ERISP as a means of attacking Crown witnesses/complainants pre-emptively.*

Private defence lawyers, not surprisingly, worried about their clients saying too much:

> *Most people talk easier when being orally interviewed. Suspects can give a better account of themselves. Contra, suspects are less on their guard and have less time to think and fashion answers*

> *They say too much and generally do themselves more harm than good.*

Equally, they stressed that ERISP means that we can now know how suspects answered, removing the unhealthy speculation about malpractice in the past.

Public defenders commented:

> *Some people seem either to clam up or (less commonly) chatter on in an uncontrolled way.*

> *In typed records suspects would often cooperate with the police in 'working out' an appropriate succinct answer for police to type down – often to the disadvantage of the suspect. Now they simply respond without having to work out a summary.*

Clearly, suspects vary in their ability to cope with the pressures of police questioning.

Table 6.23   Do you think that any type(s) of suspect is disadvantaged in particular by ERISP?

	Prosecutors (N=71) %	Defence (N=77) %	Judges (N=49) %
Yes	28	75	65
No	65	16	24
Undecided	7	8	10

Two groups of such suspects were identified. First, there are those who do not appreciate the significance of the interview process. These include NESB suspects, those who are drug-affected, intoxicated, or inarticulate, and those with low intelligence or mental illness. A defence solicitor characterised these as

> *The novice suspect. The scared suspect. The young suspect. The verbose suspect. The uneducated suspect. The naïve suspect.*

Several Public Defenders emphasised the vulnerability of NESB suspects:

> *People with limited English who may look like they understand the questions but often are not aware of the implications of their answers.*

Secondly, there are those suspects whose appearance fitted stereotypes. Crown Prosecutors suggested

> *Those who look like law breakers.*

> *A suspect whose demeanour and appearance is consistent with that you would expect of someone who has committed that type of offence.*

> *Suspects who are overawed by the process of being involved with the police when they are otherwise articulate and thereby may appear to have a 'guilty' demeanour.*

A defence lawyer drew attention to

> *the unattractive suspect, either by appearance or demeanour.*

A District Court judge suggested that

anyone who is physically otherwise than normal, either through neglect, circumstances of arrest, time of arrest or condition at the point of arrest is at a disadvantage.

Some suspects — notably Aboriginal people — fitted both categories. A Public Defender drew attention to

Those who 'look guilty', are inarticulate or overwhelmed by the clinical surroundings, particularly Aborigines, juveniles and some ethnic clients.

It may be appropriate for juries to be warned about drawing conclusions from demeanour, although the record of judicial warnings' impact is not good (Dixon 1991). Perhaps it would be more effective to educate judges and lawyers about problems in assessing vulnerable suspects' responses to police interviewing.

One Crown Prosecutor pointed out that ERISP also disadvantages suspects 'who wish to fabricate allegations against police' — the kind whom, a judge said 'having made admissions, later seek to deny having done so'. Defence lawyers were blunt about some of their clients whom ERISP disadvantaged, pointing to 'bad liars' or 'The smart arse. The drunk. The nervous smiler'.

Judges pointed out that those advantaged by ERISP were the mirror image of the disadvantaged: the articulate, well-groomed, confident suspect has an advantage. However one judge also suggested that there is an advantage for

the recidivist who was more prone to verballing ... They cannot be verballed as easily — it is still possible for events to occur, or inducements to be offered off camera, but it is more difficult and dangerous for police to attempt it.

However, one Public Defender thought that the 'con-merchant and professional criminal' could be disadvantaged because 'their "performance" looks too slick'.

We asked defence lawyers if the introduction of ERISP has affected the advice they were likely to offer to clients who *have been* charged. Private lawyers were almost evenly divided: 48% said such advice had been affected, while 43% said it had not (with 9% undecided).

I'm less likely to advise them to challenge the ... police handling of the interview.

One no longer challenges admissions.

If admissions have been made in an ERISP, the advice to plead guilty is made easier.

If the suspect has confessed, I can tell him that a good plea is better than a bad defence.

Public Defenders divided two to one in favour of change: (11 to 5, with 3 undecided). They clearly connected advice to charged clients with the potential course of court proceedings. A suspect may make a statement in the ERISP, then decline to give evidence in court. It is an indication of change in criminal justice when a person accused of a crime might feel that they have more to fear from a prosecutor's cross-examination than from a police investigators' interrogation.

Our advice to clients now is largely predicated for [sic] the fact that they can no longer give a dock statement, and therefore an ERISP may be the main vehicle of getting a version to the jury. Traditional basic advice (say nothing) is not affected — police are too devious.

If presented with an opportunity, I would strongly consider placing a defence on record as an alternative to being forced to give evidence at trial.

You can more accurately assess the likelihood of success to any challenge to the interview, e.g. 'Yes I did it. I'm very sorry. I fucked up' — no challenge. 'No, you haven't threatened me but before my aunty arrived that policeman there threatened to beat the shit out of me' — challenge.

We focused on advice after charge because so very few suspects have access to lawyers before being charged. It was unfortunately clear that several lawyers answered as if the question related to pre-ERISP, pre-charge advice. While some of these recommended refusal to participate in ERISP, others advised on appearance, demeanour, and care in answering questions. Unfortunately, the lack of a *substantial* right to pre-charge legal advice means that such comments were largely hypothetical.

Questioning of some vulnerable suspects requires the attendance of interpreters. Around one third of both prosecutors and defence lawyers thought that ERISP had led to an increase in use of interpreters. Very few thought the number had decreased. Most of the remainder either did not know or thought there had been no change.

6.5   Legal professionals' use of ERISP

In 6.4 above, we analysed police detectives' experience in their most recent case involving ERISP. In this section, we examine the similar experience of prosecutors, defence lawyers and judges. Prosecutors reported that ERISP evidence was available in 69% of these cases, while the proportion for defence lawyers was 62%. As in the case of police officers, the subject matter of these cases was varied, but included a greater proportion of more serious alleged offences than those in our tape samples: for prosecutors, 20% involved homicides and 30% involved sexual assaults, while for defence lawyers the respective percentages were 30% and 28%.

Participants do not rely solely on the audio-visual record. Nineteen of 49 Crown Prosecutors and 27 of 36 defence lawyers had listened to the audio tape of the ERISP. Most (15/19 prosecutors, 16/27 defence lawyers) were satisfied or very satisfied with the sound quality. Almost all the prosecutors (47/49) had watched the video tape. Twenty-eight of the 36 defence lawyers had done so: this disparity presumably reflects the fact that defence lawyers normally have to arrange to see the ERISP at the DPP's office. Table 6.24 records the level of dissatisfaction with the technical quality of ERISP recordings.

Table 6.24   Dissatisfaction with ERISP quality

	Prosecutors %	Private Defence %	Public Defence %	Judges %
Audio tape	21	15	7	22
Clarity of picture	30	17	21	16
Visual field	45	26	36	24
Transcription	24	17	6	n/a

It is notable that prosecutors are more likely than other groups to express dissatisfaction with ERISP quality. Indeed, 45% were dissatisfied with the visual field. All 21 Crown Prosecutors who expressed dissatisfaction with the visual field referred to the suspect being too far away and/or out of focus. Surprisingly, given some judges' role in pushing for new technology (see above), only a quarter of judges were dissatisfied with the visual field. A typical complaint from this group was:

> *There is not an adequate view of the defendant's face. He is too far from the camera, so you can't discern facial expressions etc that help to evaluate responses.*

We asked judges how often they examined ERISP evidence in their chambers. Of 48 who replied, 27 never watched the video, 15 did so rarely, 4 occasionally, and 2 often. They listened to the audio tape even less frequently (3 never, 11 rarely, 4 occasionally).

A quarter of Crown Prosecutors (and only slightly fewer defence lawyers) expressed dissatisfaction with the transcript. Their complaints were generally about inaccuracies and omissions. A defence lawyer complained:

> *The transcript was inaccurate in many respects. As well, it was discovered ... that there was more material, questions and answers, than was typed up. One answer was vital.*

In NSW, transcripts are prepared by companies under contract to the police. Reliable accurate transcripts are vital: as one private defence lawyer remarked, 'juries, judges and counsel become very tired of watching them. An agreed transcript is essential.' One prosecutor identified a specific source of difficulty:

> *The transcript is prepared from the audio tape not the video tape. The audio tape is switched off and the video left running, therefore conversation on the video wasn't in the transcript.*

This accords with findings in our tape samples (see Chapter 4): there were some significant exchanges after the audio tape was stopped. It was suggested by prosecutors that investigating officers must take responsibility for checking that the transcript is complete and accurate.

Prosecutors reported that the tape was edited for presentation in court in 21 of the 47 recent cases involving ERISP. Typically, prejudicial references to previous convictions must be excised. Only one was dissatisfied with the quality of editing. (This was a case when there was not time to edit, so the expedient was adopted of turning down the volume when 'the offending material' was playing. No doubt, the jury wondered what they were missing.) Similarly, there was only one complaint about editing from defence lawyers. (There were some complaints about inaccessibility of editing facilities in non-metropolitan areas.) This was in contrast to complaints about the synopses sometimes compiled by police, which were often said to be biased. Similar problems were reported in England (Baldwin 1992c). NSW Police now rely on the transcript rather than attempting a synopsis.

Audio tapes were played in only 6 of 49 cases involving our Crown Prosecutors. It is the audio, not video tape that acts as the 'security copy', while the video is routinely shown in court: 80% of judges (40/49) reported that ERISPs were shown to the jury often or very often (4 said occasionally, 1 rarely, 4 no response). Almost all judges (45/49, with 4 non-respondents) thought the ERISP was advantageous to jurors, with many pointing to the jury's ability to assess the demeanour of the suspect. We asked whether the use of ERISP evidence was affected if the trial was by judge alone. (This procedure depends upon prosecution and defence concurrence.) Only a minority (7/49) said there was a difference: 4 of the 7 said that it was more likely that they would rely on the transcript and not watch the video.

An additional possible use of the ERISP transcript is to inform the decision on sentencing: pleas of contrition may, for example, carry more weight if the defendant can show signs of immediate remorse. The opposite is also possible: later expressions of contrition may be undermined by ERISP evidence that the suspect was callous and unapologetic when being interviewed. However, the judges reported that such use of ERISP was not common: in the preceding two years, 32 of 46 judges responding to this question had never seen an ERISP shown at sentencing (9 rarely, 4 occasionally, 1 very often). Of 47 responding, 22 judges agreed with the proposition that 'the ERISP is superfluous in sentencing hearings' (with 14 neutral, and 11 disagreeing). Typically, judges rely on a transcript which was accepted by both parties to a guilty plea. Pressures of time militated against requests for showing ERISP videos unless there were exceptional circumstances: a Public Defender commented

No practice of playing them on sentence has developed. On one occasion when I sought to play one to resolve a conflict on facts the application was rejected as 'time wasting'.

6.6   Media use of ERISP material

Visual images of suspects being questioned are very attractive to news media and there has been considerable discussion about the propriety of allowing the media to have access to such material. After some controversial incidents in the mid-1990s, there was some official interest in legislating to prevent the media showing ERISP material. However, concern died down and no action was taken.

We asked lawyers if they would have supported or opposed release to media of the ERISP tape in their most recent case.

Table 6.25   Attitudes towards releasing ERISP tapes to the media

	Prosecutors (N=49) %	Private Defence (N=36) %	Public Defenders (N=16) %
Support	16	8	0
Oppose	61	77	94
Undecided	22	14	6

The minority of prosecutors who would have supported release said, for example:

The public must see how frequently admissions are made by suspects, lest the mostly mythical spectre of police verbals is accepted.

The public have a right of access if appropriate.

The only justification offered by a private defence lawyer was 'They seem to get it anyway.'

However, these were minority opinions: most prosecutors would have opposed release. They gave a variety of reasons: the nature of the case (9), prejudice to future proceedings involving the defendant (5), potential effects on suspects' cooperation in other cases (5), distrust of media (5), privacy of suspect (3), 'no right' (3), 'rules' (2). Defence lawyers consistently considered release to be against their clients' interests and distrusted the media.

Judges were asked more generally whether they would support or oppose the release of an ERISP. Of 47 answering, 5 supported, 31 opposed, 11 were undecided. The opponents were concerned that material would be taken out of context (13), distrusted the media (8), considered it a breach of the suspect's right to privacy (5), might prejudice future proceedings (3), be sensationalised (3), or might adversely affect third parties (1).

> *The fact that people would no doubt still like to watch public hangings is no reason to permit them or those who pander to their tastes, such as the media, to do so.*

> *Have a look at the disaster in the USA.*

> *The media's incapacity or unwillingness to be fair in reporting.*

Those in favour considered that the public had a right to see the ERISP.

6.7 Perceptions and experiences of ERISP

In summary, ERISP has been successful in putting an end to the long debate about verballing,[10] and is perceived by many criminal justice professionals to have increased guilty pleas, reduced trial length, reduced challenges to the admission of confessional evidence, and increased public confidence in the justice process. This is not to say that complacency is appropriate. But instead of the public controversy over verballing, there is now a series of more specific concerns. Some of the respondents' comments raise concerns in themselves, notably the confidence of many judges that they can assess a defendant's truthfulness from his or her demeanour.

---

[10] See chapter 1, above.

CHAPTER 7

CONCLUSION: THE ROLE OF AUDIO-VISUAL RECORDING IN CRIMINAL JUSTICE

In this final chapter, we draw some broad conclusions from this study.

7.1   The impact of ERISP

From the perspective of police and prosecuting authorities, the ERISP program has been a considerable success. The issue of verballing has largely been resolved. There may be dispute about what a suspect said outside the interrogation room or about how he or she came to make a confession within it or about the truth of the confession: these issues are addressed below. But the simple question 'Did the suspect say what police claim he/she said in the interrogation room?' can now be answered with confidence. Given the trouble which verballing — actual or alleged — used to cause the criminal justice process, this must be regarded as a substantial achievement. Use of the term 'verballing' is dropping out of everyday discourse: one indication is that I now have to explain the term to my students, rather than being able to take for granted that they would be familiar with it.

Looking back, what is surprising is that electronic recording was ever so controversial and that its introduction was delayed so long. It involves the application of a relatively simple, familiar technology. As Chapter 6 has demonstrated, most of the benefits expected from electronic recording have eventuated, while few of the predicted problems have done so. The continuing resistance to comprehensive electronic recording in some US police departments is a reminder that technical or practical concerns about recording are often expressions of deeper concerns about police losing control of their affairs. Video-recording promises — or threatens — to open up the secret world of police interrogation rooms. To some, this accountability through openness is unwelcome. Perhaps the best response to such concerns is the experience of police officers in jurisdictions which have adopted electronic recording. When electronic recording is introduced, antagonism and opposition quickly fade away and is replaced by acceptance and enthusiasm (Aronson & Hunter 1998:334; Sullivan 2004:14).

7.2 Policing politics and policy transfer

Along with other Australian states, NSW has set the pace for the rest of the world in the development of audio-visual recording of police interviews. Indeed, it is unfortunate that this achievement has not been adequately recognised. Locally, good news about policing tends to be overlooked in the usually superficial and over-politicised 'debate' about law and order. This is particularly the case if the relevant initiative cannot be simply presented as a new power or resource for police in the 'war on crime'. A program like ERISP does not conform to the neat dichotomies that structure criminal justice politics — police powers or suspects' rights, crime control or due process. As I have argued at length elsewhere, these dichotomies (and their familiar representation through the metaphor of 'balance') can be misleading (Dixon 1997, 2006). Electronic recording of interrogation is an example of the broader potential for regulation to benefit both police and suspects, both crime control and due process.

A notable feature of recent discussions of video-recording in the United States is the (at best) minimal interest in and (more often) apparent ignorance of Australian experience in electronic recording. Several reasons may be suggested for this. First, there is the localised nature of Australian policing: each state and territory has its own policing and criminal justice system and each has developed its own system of electronic recording. While there has been some cooperation and collaboration, there has been a familiar insistence on local responsibility and development. Although some comparative (or competitive) benefit is produced by each jurisdiction developing its own electronic recording system, there is also much waste in this process of local wheel-invention, which is increasingly regarded as anachronistic and counterproductive in criminal law and justice generally. Diseconomy of scale is just one cost of this approach, notably as regards technical development and provision of recording equipment. The transfer from using video tape to digital recording would obviously benefit from a coordinated approach.[1] A less obvious

---

[1] Problems which need to be addressed include procuring and/or developing reliable economical equipment; providing an equivalent of the 'time line' on ERISP VHS tapes; training; dealing with the need to 'finalize' digital recordings when the end of a CD is reached in the middle of interviews; coordination with other users, e.g. defence lawyers and prosecutors; providing transcribing equipment which will pause CDs; and editing, storing and communicating data (Earle 2002; Newburn 2004).

cost is that rather than there being a single Australian model which overseas colleagues can notice and adopt, there is a confusing range of local developments which are less likely to receive international attention.

Equally important is the parochialism of so many international criminal justice practitioners and researchers. Despite the increasing interest in comparative criminal justice and the practical pressures for international cooperation to deal with organised crime such as drug trafficking and terrorism, lack of interest in other jurisdictions is still common. There is also in play the obverse of the Australian 'cultural cringe' — the assumption by British and American researchers and practitioners that Australia will follow, not lead.

7.3   Interrogation skills

As noted above, ERISP has achieved its objective of dealing with verballing. In most cases, we are now able to know whether or not a suspect confessed. But, in retrospect, that looks a relatively modest target. The world has moved on. The fact that a confession has been made is just first base. Ahead lie much more complex and contested questions concerning whether a confession is true. Commonsense assumptions about confessions have been cruelly exposed by a quarter of a century of miscarriages of justice in the United States and the United Kingdom (Gudjonsson 2003; Dixon 2006). The manner in which police interrogate suspects has emerged as a crucial issue. In NSW, officers were alert to developments in England, and sought to follow the lessons of investigative interviewing taught by the PEACE program. This achievement is perhaps better appreciated if one thinks what would have resulted had NSW Police chosen to follow the US rather than the English model (Williamson ed 2006).

However, the limited impact of the NSW version of the PEACE process has been outlined in Chapter 5. Comparable results have been reported in English research for the Home Office (Clarke & Milne 2001). This experience suggests the need for innovative approaches in teaching officers how to interview suspects. A key starting point may well be to present material relating to investigative interviewing not as 'training' — i.e. the passing on of technical skills — but as education. PEACE requires not just a set of skills, but an attitude towards the interviewing of suspects. This must be based on an understanding of the crucial lessons about interrogation which the miscarriage of justice cases teach. Common sense and schlock psychology do not provide an adequate basis: instead, police should draw on the extensive evidence-based research literature which is now available. Above all, it shows that innocent people do confess to crimes. They may do so not because they are mentally ill or seeking notoriety, but because of how police officers question them. Study of some of the crucial cases — the 'Cardiff 3', George Heron, and the Central Park jogger assault — would be useful in this respect (Gudjonsson 2003; Sekar 1997, 2005; Davies 2006; Leo et al. 2006; Kassin 2006). These cases should show that the issues are not hypothetical or 'academic', but of pressing operational concern. As suggested in Chapter 5, the skills which need to be taught are not highly technical: any officer should be able to learn the basic norms of social interaction which underlie good interviewing.

There is one exception which requires attention: the interviewing of difficult, resistant suspects. We are not convinced by the claims that intensive questioning produces inherently unreliable results. We do not accept the jump from the conclusion that suspects seldom crack to the assumption that they can never legitimately be made to do so. The miscarriage of justice cases of the 1980s and 1990s are taken by some as establishing that interviewers should not seek to press suspects to confess because of the potential unreliability of any resultant confession. Baldwin insists that

> there is little an interviewer can legitimately do to induce a suspect to confess, and it is therefore important not to foster this obsession (1992a:13).

> The simple truth is that it is extremely difficult to induce reluctant suspects to confess by methods that would nowadays be regarded as acceptable (1993:333).

Mortimer and Shepherd have expressed disquiet that PEACE interviewing does not adequately equip officers to deal with

> resistance, particularly frustrating and discrepant responses, e.g. indignation, anger, tears, arguing, diverting, 'blinding with science', non-cooperation, silence, verbal hostility or lying ... If officers construe PEACE as not preparing them for 'difficult' suspects its validity (and therefore credibility) is brought into question (1999:312).

It is important to note that officers responsible for the development of the PEACE program and investigative interviewing in England and Wales respond vigorously to such criticism, insisting that investigative interviewing is not a soft option (see Gary Shaw, quoted in Dixon 2006). However, it was acknowledged that 'serious crime demanded a higher level of interview technique that was both ethical and effective if convictions were to be obtained' and specialist interview training building on and developing PEACE has been introduced (Griffiths & Milne 2006:171).

Despite the development of other investigative methods, interrogation will continue to be necessary in investigating certain suspects. Some suspects need to be interviewed because sometimes getting a confession is the only way of solving a crime or establishing guilt — or indeed of obtaining information about other actual or potential offenders. There is of course no guarantee that intensive questioning will be effective, but so long as police believe that it may be (and many do), then there is a dangerous gap between cultural knowledge and policy, which is likely to promote deviance. If they are not trained how to deal with resistant suspects, 'frustration is inevitable and the pressures will be great to switch from investigatory to constraining/accusatory questioning' (Mortimer & Shepherd 1999:312). In other words, if departmental policy and training is perceived to be unrealistic, officers are likely to dismiss the approved mode of interviewing as unrealistic, and fall back on more traditional techniques. Alternatively, they could turn to manuals such as Inbau et al.'s (2001). These will teach officers how to make reluctant suspects confess: the problem is that the research literature shows that such techniques may produce false as well as true confessions, and consequently are unreliable (Gudjonsson 2003:26–27; Leo 2004).

Although far from the everyday police work which is the subject matter of this study, the interviewing of terrorist suspects has become a major issue for police departments and other government agencies. Simply waiting for the suspect to provide an account is unlikely to be productive. Again, failing to address this issue will mean that interviewing officers will be forced to find their own solutions. The controversies since 9/11 about coercive interrogation and torture of terrorist suspects illustrate the importance of the issues (Dixon 2006; Greenberg ed 2005). Crucial questions about the reliability of what coercive questioning produces and the effectiveness of non-coercive interviewing of terrorist suspects are being examined in ways which may be of general significance to police interrogation.

Accepting the need for intensive questioning does not entail ignoring Baldwin's warning about potential unreliability. Intensive questioning must be conducted taking account of the crucial rules of interviewing: be self-critical and reflexive about the development of case theories; develop a capacity for empathy; take care that definitive information about the offence is not leaked to the suspect; examine the post-confession narrative carefully; and rigorously check a confession to see if it is consistent with other evidence. If it is not, the response should be to re-evaluate the confession, not to try to interpret, adapt or ignore other evidence. A confession should include material known only to the suspect: if it does not do so, it should be treated by police (and subsequently by courts) as being of questionable value. This means keeping information about the offence from the suspect: specifically, it requires great care when a suspect is being questioned to ensure that interviewers do not leak information.

How does an officer know where is the line between what is acceptable and what is oppressive? There is some legislation and case law[2] but this does not amount to clear and detailed guidance. In NSW courts, a question must be disallowed if it

> (a) is misleading or confusing, or (b) is unduly annoying, harassing, intimidating, offensive, oppressive, humiliating or repetitive, or (c) is put to the witness in a manner or tone that is belittling, insulting or otherwise inappropriate, or (d) has no basis other than a sexist, racial, cultural or ethnic stereotype.[3]

This could be adapted for use as a guide to police interviewers. However, the courts continue to shy away from specificity, 'preferring instead a vague "whole context" approach' (Hunter et al. 2005:573).

Distilling the effect of British cases such as *Paris* and *Heron*, Zander concludes:

> It would be oppressive to repeat a question dozens of times in order to gain an admission. It would be oppressive repeatedly to use abusive language, to shout or bully the suspect, constantly to interrupt the suspect, or to pound him with allegations of guilt, with accusations that he is lying. It is legitimate to go over the same ground more than once but to do so for the umpteenth time becomes oppressive (2003:320).

---

[2]   Zander 2003:316–320; Hunter et al. 2005:ch12.
[3]   Criminal Procedure Act 1986 (NSW) s275A.

Being more specific is difficult. The courts hesitate to go further for a good reason. Suspects vary: for example, the tactics appropriate for an adult might be oppressive for a juvenile. In *LL*, searching, sceptical challenging of a juvenile's answers was found to be oppressive by the NSW Supreme Court.[4] Had the suspect been an experienced, mature adult, the result would have been different. In assessing the reliability of a confession, NSW courts must take into account 'any relevant condition or characteristic of the person who made the admission, including age, personality and education and any mental, intellectual or physical disability to which the person is or appears to be subject'.[5]

The frustration felt by officers with the uncertainty of the guidance provided to them is understandable.[6] It is not enough to tell police what they cannot do: they need to be told what they can do, and how to do it. Such information needs to be accumulated by appropriate research (e.g. Gudjonsson 2003).

It should be stressed again that miscarriages of justice are of concern not just because some innocent people suffer, but because those really guilty escape justice for so long. The Cardiff 3 and Central Park cases were exceptions in that the real offender was eventually discovered (Sekar 2005; Kassin 2006; Leo et al. 2006; Davies 2006). Much more commonly, the trail has long gone cold and no conviction is achieved. There is a good deal of complacency about these matters in Australia. Some knowledgeable officers have suggested to us that this will continue until a local version of these cases occurs, finally making people take the issues more seriously. It would be most unfortunate if we have to take this unnecessary (and costly, in many respects) step.

The focus of the research reported in this book has been on everyday, mundane offences, rather than the dramatic homicides which feature in the most-publicised miscarriages of justice. We would argue that the same pressures, albeit at lesser intensity, affect everyday cases. An investigator may not have the media demanding arrest, charge, and conviction of an offender, but he or she may well be under pressure to produce results. A suspect may not be so stressed or vulnerable, but may still put short-term gain above long-term cost. The cost of even a modest prison sentence will be underestimated only by the ignorant. Consequently, interview training

---

[4] Unreported, 1 April 1996: see Hunter at al. 2005:633.
[5] Evidence Act 1995 (NSW) s85(3).
[6] See e.g. Northumbria Police 1994.

should not be reserved for specialists. A useful approach is the five stage model of interview training developed in England and Wales (Burbeck 2003; Griffiths & Milne 2006).

7.4 Rehearsals, unrecorded questioning, and regulation

A major area of concern must be the incomplete recording of interviews with suspects which was discussed in Chapter 2. As we have shown, such pre-ERISP interviewing is usually a matter of routine. Nonetheless, it threatens the integrity of the system. ERISP shows that a suspect made confessions or admissions, not how he or she came to do so. What we know from other jurisdictions about deliberate misconduct and inadvertent influence by interviewers and about apparently irrational responses by innocent suspects indicates that there is no room for complacency. It is necessary to have as much questioning recorded as possible. Given the problems of recording field interrogation, this questioning should be conducted in police stations. This should not put unrealistic demands on police. Claims that spontaneous outbursts make recording impracticable echo arguments from the 1980s that electronic recording would be impossible. The response now should be the same as then: of course exceptions must be allowed, but these must be in defined circumstances and/or subject to rigorous scrutiny.[7]

The High Court's treatment of these issues has been inconsistent. Asked to decide on the admissibility of recorded confessions which followed sessions of unrecorded questioning, the High Court in *Pollard*[8] and *Heatherington*[9] interpreted the statutory regime as

---

[7]   For a good example of a statement which an officer could not record, but which was properly declared admissible, see *Taouk* [2005] NSWCCA 155. In this case, a man who had killed his wife and brother-in-law went to a police station and told the officer on duty at the counter, inter alia, 'I have just shot someone at my house.' Although not repeated in subsequent, recorded interviews, this statement was admitted into evidence. In *Donnelly* ((1997) 6 A Crim R 432), a man was in hospital after attempting suicide following the death of his wife. He confessed to his cousin, a police officer, that he had murdered her. He was subsequently cautioned and repeated the confession. The first confession was admissible. By contrast, in *Horton* ((1998) 45 NSWLR 426), a confession made at a crime scene was ruled inadmissible because an eye-witness had identified the offender to the police officer before the confession was made, notionally providing an opportunity for cautioning and electronic recording.

[8]   (1992) 176 CLR 177.

[9]   (1994) 179 CLR 370.

requiring only the recording of the session in which the confessions or admission was made, so long as the sessions could be substantively distinguished. Once again, the court's emphasis on specific circumstances obstructs the development of more general criteria or guidelines (Hunter et al. 2005:598–599). In *Kelly*,[10] the High Court insisted on a narrow interpretation of the phrase 'in the course of official questioning', allowing police to use in evidence their claim that, after a formal interview had ended, Kelly had made a (very dubious) incriminatory remark which was not electronically recorded. It was no coincidence that there was very strong circumstantial evidence against the defendant (as well as an earlier inadmissible confession, which Kelly agreed to having made, but now repudiated). *Kelly* was a particularly unfortunate vehicle for a crucial statutory interpretation. Subsequently, in *Nicholls & Coates*,[11] the High Court shifted from this narrow legalism in favour of a purposive approach which interpreted 'interview' to mean 'the entirety of a discussion between a police officer and a suspect carried out on a particular day for the purpose of eliciting statements from the suspect'.[12] The issue is by no means settled. *Nicholls & Coates* did not overrule *Kelly*. The High Court distinguished *Kelly* on the basis that differently worded legislation was involved (Hunter et al. 2005:610). This provides a good example of how continuing conflicts between narrow legalism and interpretative/purposive approaches make case law a problematic mode of regulating police interrogation (Dixon 2006). It is not clear which approach — legalism or a purposive approach — will be followed in respect of different pieces of legislation.

So long as much interviewing is conducted before the ERISP machine is activated, there will be room for controversy about what happened. Such controversy includes doubt about the reliability of recorded confessions, if what preceded — or prompted — them is unknown. The potential benefits of ERISP are dissipated if it is used to record rehearsed material. It should be stressed that, from all the evidence available, the costs and problems of comprehensive recording are minimal. If a police officer feels uncomfortable about using an interviewing technique on tape, the reliability of any resulting confession may be questionable. It should be noted that our suggestion

---

[10] [2004] HCA 12.
[11] [2005] HCA 1.
[12] McHugh J at para 104.

is that the costs are minimal, not that they do not exist. As explained above, there are going to be occasions when recording is impossible or inappropriate — e.g. when an admission is blurted out or when a suspect insists that he/she will not name an accomplice while being recorded. This is not an unusual dilemma in policing: the objective is the minimisation of problems, not some problem-free utopia. Police should record all questioning of suspects conducted within police stations and interviewing of suspects should only be done in police stations (except in cases of exceptional need which fall within specified categories).

Dealing with partial recording requires a more general remedy. What is needed is the legal regulation of policing by the development of rules, policies and standards (Dixon 1997:ch7; 2006. This does not mean more rules, a message which would find favour with no-one. It means having rules which (in the terminology of the Policy Studies Institute: see Smith & Gray 1985) become 'working rules' (i.e. part of the cultural and other norms which guide everyday working practice) rather than 'inhibitory rules' (which are effective only if there is an immediate prospect of their enforcement) or 'presentational rules' (whose main purpose is to placate a public audience).

NSW Police continues to have a traditional approach to legal regulation in which too many rules are largely presentational. When legislation providing a legal regime for pre-charge investigative detention was finally passed in 1997, the Crimes Amendment (Detention after Arrest) Act included a requirement that the Minister should review the provisions 'to determine whether the policy objectives of the Part (of the Act) remain valid and whether the terms of the Part remain appropriate for securing those objectives'. This review was to be 'undertaken as soon as possible after the period of 12 months from the commencement of this Part' and a report on the review was to be tabled in Parliament within 12 months thereafter. This legislation was brought into force in February 1998. At the time of writing, more than eight years later, it appears that the review is still 'incomplete'. Instead, the detention after arrest provisions were consolidated into the Law Enforcement (Powers and Responsibilities) Act 2002.[13] It is a regrettable indication of official attitudes towards

---

[13] It became operational in December 2005. This Act also has a review and report requirement in s243: it is to be hoped that it is taken more seriously than its predecessor.

legislative accountability that the obligation to review has not been fulfilled. This is another expression of the detrimental effect of law and order politics on criminal justice. In a climate in which being tough on crime and backing the police are the only politically acceptable stances, government has little apparent interest in detailed accountability.

This is unfortunate because, if conducted properly, such reviews can have great benefits for the police and others. A good example is provided by the way in which the Police and Criminal Evidence Act 1984 (and particularly its codes of practice) in England and Wales has been subjected to continuing scrutiny, consultation and research which has allowed the rules to be adapted in response to perceived needs. This kind of active, responsive legal regulation has potential benefits for all concerned. Of course, both a review and its eventual recommendations will require the government to provide funds. This could provide a good test of governmental commitment to good policing: is government prepared to fund developments which may not make news on the front-page (or on talk-back radio), but which could allow the NSW Police to develop a world-class system of questioning detained suspects — a task which is at the core of policing?

The lack of interest in the legal regulation of custodial interrogation is, in part, due to the success of ERISP. Its introduction took the wind out of the sails of calls for other measures to protect suspects' rights, such as a substantial right to legal advice, corroboration of confessions by independent evidence, and even the prohibition of custodial interrogation (all of which were on the agenda for consideration in the late 1980s: see NSW LRC 1990). Electronic recording should be regarded as just one element of a comprehensive package of regulatory measures. Unfortunately, it is all too often regarded as a panacea.

7.5 Interrogating images

In the report from which ERISP was developed, the Criminal Law Review Division acknowledged that using visual images in evidence could be problematic, considering whether 'a record of things such as tattoos, speech, mannerism, dress, demeanour and language' might be prejudicial to some defendants (1986:15). CLRD's view was that prejudice to the defendant was unverifiable and that it might be counterbalanced by advantages, such as showing the pressures on a suspect (1986:15). In retrospect, this conclusion appears to be justified, although the balance favours the prosecution. We found that police officers and prosecutors were routinely enthusiastic about the court being able to see the contrast between the neatly dressed, polite defendant in the dock and the scruffy, abusive suspect pictured on ERISP (see Chapter 6, above). On the other hand, our samples included several cases in which, to the defendant's benefit, the ERISP provided information not discernible from a transcript or audio tape, for example that the suspect was affected by drugs during the interview.

However, the CLRD did not foresee that the problem would be not responses to objectively identifiable matter such as dress and tattoos, but subjective interpretations of behaviour — the reading of 'body language' in order to draw inferences and, particularly, to detect deception. This meant that a potential difficulty involved in the use of video was underestimated.

NSW judges have shown considerable interest in interpreting the ERISP image, particularly for the detection of deception. A disturbing encounter early in our research was with a judge who confidently claimed to be able to assess the veracity of witnesses by observing whether they glanced to left or right. Judges' interest in detecting deception provided much of the pressure for the showing of ERISPs in court, the improvement in ERISP picture quality, and, most significantly, the introduction of technology providing an image alternating between a general picture of the interview room and those present to a close-up of the suspect.

Alternating images has both advantages and disadvantages. The most obvious advantage is that for the first time the viewer can see a large, clear image of the suspect's face during the interview. After years of (at times frustrating) attempts to make out how the suspect looks (Are his/her eyes closed? Is he/she falling asleep during some questions? How serious an injury is that mark on the forehead which is a blur from the distance? Is she visibly alcohol affected?), it is good to be offered such a large clear image of his or her face. The size and clarity of this image of the suspect greatly reduces what previously may have remained in the realm of guess work.

Among the disadvantages are that other persons present in the interview are only seen briefly, if at all. The ERISP camera records the whole interview table only for some 20 seconds every three minutes, before reverting to the face of the suspect. For most of the time, the interviewers are not on screen. If ERISP is to be used as a mechanism of supervision and accountability of interviewing officers, something is lost by focusing on the suspect. There is a relatively simple technological solution to this aspect of the problem. Replacing ERISP recorders with units including two cameras which could produce split image or 'picture in picture' images would allow simultaneous recording and presentation of both the suspect's face and the room as a whole. However, this would not deal with the problem of misinterpretations of images.

While both prosecution and defence may gain some advantage from the close-ups showing the suspect's condition, there are grounds for concern about potential interpretations of these images by both prosecutors and judges. ERISP 073 illustrated the potential problem. In close-up, the suspect appeared somewhat shifty as he moved his eyes from side to side. However, the brief wider focus showed that these eye movements were a normal mode of interaction with two interviewers who were both attempting to maintain eye contact with him. Seeing him reacting to questions rather than seeing him as one of three people exchanging questions and answers invited incomplete or inaccurate interpretation.

In our questionnaire study, a majority of both judges and prosecutors reported that they believed that demeanour is an indicator of veracity.[14] By contrast, more police disagreed than agreed with the statement (see Table 6.14, above). Direct experience of interviewing suspects and the Police Service's discouragement of pretensions to read deception from body language are presumably responsible for this.

This is not the place for a review of the extensive psychological literature on this topic. It is sufficient for present purposes to point out that the research evidence clearly establishes that, whatever a highly trained psychologist may be able to do in detecting deception, a judge (or indeed prosecutor, jury or police officer) cannot do so accurately, and that standard interview training does not increase the capacity to correctly identify deception (Memon et al. 1998; Milne & Bull 1999:64; Mortimer & Shepherd 1999:302; Vrij 1999). Indeed, 'special training in deception detection' may be positively harmful: it 'may lead investigators to make pre-judgements of guilt, with high confidence, that are biased and frequently in error' (Kassin 200:212). In the long

---

[14] For analysis of judicial decisions on how to interpret behaviour which apparently contradicts what the suspect says, see Hunter et al. 2005:623–624.

shadow of the Chamberlain case, those concerned with criminal justice in Australia should be particularly aware of the dangers of basing an assumption of guilt on a perception that a suspect's response to an event is inappropriate.

The widespread dissemination of schlock psychology through magazine articles or (as in the case of the judge noted above) brief professional education courses is a matter of real concern, indicating the need for a vigorous program of appropriate education and training for criminal justice professionals, including judges and prosecutors, in any jurisdiction considering the use of video to record interviews with suspects.

7.6   Regulating interrogation

Legal regulation should establish positions from which a variety of pressures are put on the investigatory practice of police officers. Audio-visual recording is just one of those potential pressures. Others include proficient, well-resourced legal advisers (and, for vulnerable suspects, social workers trained to take the role of support person); rules of evidence in the hands of judges and magistrates who are prepared to be active in the control of policing; and senior officers who are prepared to supervise in order to ensure that investigators work within the rules and use approved techniques for questioning suspects. None of these is a panacea or a silver bullet. Progress may be possible through the combination of various (admittedly flawed) mechanisms, of which audio-visual recording is one.

This assessment of ERISP has returned us to the much broader and more complex issue of regulating police practice. Audio-visual recording is not enough by itself: it must be used as a tool in a general regime of regulation. The recorded interview is just one stage in a suspect's detention. Its reliability and propriety depend substantially on legal regulation of the context in which interviewing takes place. Such problems can only be tackled by much more rigorous regulation of investigative practices and, in particular, by requiring that (with the caveats noted above) all interviews should be electronically recorded in full. There are obvious incentives for officers to question suspects before a formal recorded session. If electronic recording is to have a significant role in controlling police interviewing and ensuring the reliability of confessions by providing more than confirmation of what a suspect said in a rehearsed interview, then effective legal and supervisory regulation of investigative practices is necessary.

REFERENCES

ABS (2005) *Aboriginal and Torres Strait Islander Peoples: Contact with the Law* (Canberra: Australian Bureau of Statistics).

Alder, K (2002) 'A social history of untruth: lie detection and trust in twentieth-century America' *Representations* 80: 1–33.

Alderson, K (2001) *Powers and Responsibilities: Reforming NSW Criminal Investigation Law*, PhD thesis, University of New South Wales.

ALRC (1975) *Criminal Investigation* Report #2 (Canberra: Australian Government Printing Service).

Anderson, J, Hunter, J & Williams, N (2002) *The New Evidence Law* (Sydney: Butterworths).

Anderson, T (1992) *Take Two* (Sydney: Bantam).

Arantz, P (1993) *A Collusion of Powers* (Dunedoo: Arantz).

Aronson, M & Hunter, J (1998) *Litigation* 5th ed (Sydney: Butterworths).

Ashworth, A (1998) 'Should the police be allowed to use deceptive practices?' *Law Quarterly Review* 114: 108–140.

Baldwin, J (1990) 'Police interviews on tape' *New Law Journal* 11 May pp 662–663, 681.

—— (1992a) *Videotaping Police Interviews with Suspects – an Evaluation* Police Research Series Paper #1 (London: Home Office Police Department).

—— (1992b) 'Suspect interviews' *New Law Journal* 31 July pp 1095–1096.

—— (1992c) *Preparing Records of Taped Interview*, Research Study 2 (London: Royal Commission on Criminal Justice).

—— (1993) 'Police interview techniques: establishing truth or proof?' *British Journal of Criminology* 33: 325–352.

Bandes, S & Beermann, J (1998) 'Lawyering up' *Green Bag* 2: 5–14.

Beach, B (1978) *Report of the Board of Inquiry into Allegations against Members of the Victoria Police Force* (Melbourne: Government Printer).

Bennett, R (1993) 'Criminal justice', *London Review of Books* 24 June, 3–15.

Bennett, WL & Feldman, MS (1981) *Reconstructing Reality in the Courtroom* (New Brunswick: Rutgers University Press).

Bottomley, AK, Coleman, CA, Dixon, D, Gill, M & Wall, D (1991) *The Impact of PACE: Policing in a Northern Force* (Hull: Centre for Criminology and Criminal Justice).

Brown, D (1997) *PACE Ten Years On: A Review of the Research* (London: HMSO).

Bucke, T & Brown, D (1997) *In Police Custody: Police: Powers and Suspects' Rights under the Revised PACE Codes of Practice* (London: HMSO).

Bull, R (1999) 'Police investigative interviewing' in A Memon & R Bull (eds) *Handbook of the Psychology of Interviewing* (Chichester: John Wiley) 279–292.

—— & Milne, B (2004) 'Attempts to improve the police interviewing of suspects' in GD Lassiter (ed) *Interrogations, Confessions, and Entrapment* (New York: Kluwer Academic) 181–196.

Burbeck, J (2003) *Standard entry for ACPO manuals on investigative interviewing from the National Strategic Group on investigative interviewing* (London: Association of Chief Police Officers).

Caswell, R (1984) *Scales of Justice* (Sydney: Currency Press).

Central Planning and Training Unit (1992a) *A Guide to Interviewing* (London: CPTU).

—— (1992b) *The Interviewer's Rule Book* (London: CPTU).

Centrex (2003) *Training Curriculum for Tier 5 of the ACPO Investigative Interviewing Strategy* (Bramshill: Centrex).

Chan, J (1997) *Changing Police Culture* (Cambridge: Cambridge University Press).

Clarke, C & Milne, R (2002) *National Evaluation of the PEACE Investigative Interviewing Course* (unpublished, Home Office).

CMC (2004) *Listening In: Results from a CMC Audit of Police Interview Tapes* (Brisbane: Crime & Misconduct Commission).

Coulthard, M (1992) 'Forensic discourse analysis' in M Coulthard (ed) *Advances in Spoken Discourse Analysis* (London: Routledge) 242–258.

Criminal Law Review Division (1984) *The Use of Electronic Equipment to Record Police Interviews* (Sydney: CLRD).

—— (1986) *A Proposed System of Electronically Recording Police Interviews with Suspected Persons* (Sydney: CLRD).

Crowley, WD (1972) 'The interrogation of suspects' in D Chappell & P Wilson (eds) *The Australian Criminal Justice System* (Sydney: Butterworths) 419–428.

David, I (1995) *Blue Murder* (Sydney: ABC).

Davies, SL (2006) 'The reality of false confessions: lessons of the Central Park jogger case' *NYU Review of Law & Social Change* 30: 209–253.

Dixon, D (1990) 'Juvenile suspects and the Police and Criminal Evidence Act' in DAC Freestone (ed) *Children and the Law* (Hull: Hull University Press) 107–129.

—— (1991) 'Interrogation, corroboration and the limits of judicial activism' *Legal Service Bulletin* 16: 103–106.

—— (1997) *Law in Policing: Legal Regulation and Police Practices* (Oxford: Clarendon Press).

—— (1999) 'Reform, regression and the Royal Commission into the NSW Police Service' in D Dixon (ed) *A Culture of Corruption: Changing an Australian Police Service* (Sydney: Hawkins Press) 138–179.

—— (2005) 'Why don't the police stop crime?' *Australian & New Zealand Journal of Criminology* 38: 4–24.

—— (2006) 'Regulating police interrogation' in T Williamson (ed) *Investigative Interviewing: Developments in Rights, Research and Regulation* (Cullompton: Willan) 318–351.

—— (2006a) '"A window into the interviewing process"? The audio-visual recording of police interrogation in NSW, Australia' *Policing & Society* 16: 323–348.

——, Bottomley, AK, Coleman, CA, Gill, M & Wall, D (1990) 'Safeguarding the rights of suspects in police custody' *Policing and Society* 1: 115–140.

Donovan, D & Rhodes, J (2000) 'Comes a time: the case for recording interrogations' *Montana Law Review* 61: 223–249.

Dovey, W (1954) *Report of the Royal Commission of Inquiry into Certain Matters Relating to David Studley-Ruxton* (Sydney: Government Printer).

Drizin, SA & Reich, MJ (2004) 'Heeding the lessons of history: the need for mandatory recoding of police interrogations to accurately assess the reliability and voluntariness of confessions' *Drake Law Review* 52: 619–646.

Earle, R et al. (2002) *The Introduction of Visual Recording of Police Interviews with Suspects First Interim Report* (LSE/Kent University, unpublished).

Ericson, R (1994) 'The Royal Commission on criminal justice system surveillance' in M McConville & L Bridges (eds) *Criminal Justice in Crisis* (Aldershot: Edward Elgar) 113–140.

Fenwick, H (1993) 'Confessions, recording rules and miscarriages of justice' *Criminal Law Review* 174–184.

Finnane, M (1994) *Police and Government* (Melbourne: Oxford University Press).

Fitzgerald, T (1989) *Report of an Inquiry into Possible Illegal Activities and Associated Police Misconduct* (Brisbane: Government Printer).

Fletcher, GP (1976) 'The metamorphosis of larceny' *Harvard Law Review* 89: 469–530.

Fox, G (1993) 'A comparison of "policespeak' and "normalspeak"' in JM Sinclair, M Hooey & G Fox (eds) *The Techniques of Description* (London: Routledge) 183–195.

FPT Heads of Prosecutions Committee (2004) *Report on the Prevention of Miscarriages of Justice* (Ottawa: Ministry of Justice, Canada).

Geller, WA (1992) *Police Videotaping of Suspect Interrogations and Confessions: A Preliminary Examination of Issues and Practices* (Washington DC: National Institute of Justice).

Gibbons, J (ed) (1994) *Language and the Law* (London: Longman).

—— (2003) *Forensic Linguistics* (London: Blackwell).

Grant, A (1987) *The Audio-Visual Taping of Police Interviews with Suspects and Accused Persons by Halton Regional Police Force* Ontario, Canada. Unpublished report for the Law Reform Commission of Canada.

Greenberg, KJ (ed) (2005) *The Torture Debate in America* (New York: Cambridge University Press).

Griffiths, A & Milne, B (2006) 'Will it all end in tiers? Police interviews with suspects in Britain' in T Williamson (ed) *Investigative Interviewing: Developments in Rights, Research and Regulation* (Cullompton: Willan) 167–189.

Gross, SR, Jacoby, K, Matheson, DJ, Montgomery, N & Patil, S (2005) 'Exonerations in the US 1989–2003' *Journal of Criminal Law & Criminology* 95: 523–560.

Gudjonsson, GH (1993) *The Psychology of Interrogations, Confessions and Testimony* (Chichester: Wiley).

—— (1994) 'Investigative interviewing' *International Review of Psychiatry* 6: 237–245.

—— (1999) 'Police interviewing and disputed confessions' in A Memon & R Bull (eds) *The Psychology of Interviewing* (Chichester: Wiley) 327–341.

—— (2003) *The Psychology of Interrogations and Confessions* (Chichester: Wiley).

—— & MacKeith, JAC (1994) 'Learning disability and the Police and Criminal Evidence Act: protection during investigative interviewing: a video recorded false confession of double murder' *Journal of Forensic Psychiatry* 5: 35–49.

Haldane, R (1986) *The People's Force: A History of the Victoria Police* (Melbourne: Melbourne University Press).

Hall, P (1998) *Do you agree that you said, "It's like this, she did fall down the stairs...": Electronic recording of interviews with suspect persons (ERISP): Register or merely situation?* BA (Hons) thesis Macquarie University.

Hodgson, J (1997) 'Vulnerable suspects and the appropriate adult' *Criminal Law Review* 785–795.

Holmes, M & Boni, M (2001) *The Cognitive Interview as a Tool in Australasian Policing* Paper Series #6 Payneham, SA: Australasian Centre for Policing Research.

Home Office (1992) *Principles of Investigative Interviewing* Home Office Circular 22/1992.

—— (1993) *Investigative Interviewing: National Training Package* Home Office Circular 7/1993.

Huff, CR (2002) 'Wrongful conviction and public policy: the American Society of Criminology 2001 Presidential address' *Criminology* 40: 1–18.

Hunter, J, Cameron, C, & Henning, T (2005) *Litigation* (Sydney: Butterworths).

Inbau, FE & Reid, J (1953) *Lie Detection and Criminal Interrogation* (Baltimore: Williams & Wilkins).

——, ——, Buckley, JP & Jayne, BC (2001) *Criminal Interrogation and Confessions* 4th edition (Gaithersburg, MD: Aspen).

Inglis, KS (1961) *The Stuart Case* (Melbourne: Melbourne University Press).

Iraola, R (2006) 'The electronic recording of criminal interrogations' *University of Richmond Law Review* 40: 463–479.

Irving, B (1980) *Police Interrogation: A Case Study of Current Practice* (London: HMSO).

—— & McKenzie, I (1989) *Police Interrogation* (London: Police Foundation).

Johnson, D (1997) 'False confessions and fundamental fairness: the need for electronic recording of electronic recording' *Boston University Public Interest Law Journal* 6: 719–751.

Kable, J (1989) 'Williams to Carr – where now?' *Current Issues in Criminal Justice* 1: 9–31.

Kamisar, Y (2006) *On the 40th Anniversary of Miranda* University of San Diego Law School Reseach Paper.

Kassin, SM (1997) 'The psychology of confession evidence' *American Psychologist* 52: 221–233.

—— (2002) 'False confessions and the jogger case' *New York Times* 1 November 2002.

—— (2003) 'The Central Park jogger case', paper presented to the Psychology & Law conference, Edinburgh, July 2003.

—— (2006) 'A critical appraisal of modern police interrogations', in T Williamson (ed) *Investigative Interviewing: Developments in Rights, Research and Regulation* (Cullompton: Willan) 207–228.

—— & Kiechel, KL (1996) 'The social psychology of false confessions' *Psychological Science* 7: 125–128.

—— & McNall, K (1991) 'Police interrogation and confessions' *Law & Human Behaviour* 15: 233–251.

Kidston, RR (1960) 'Confessions to police' *Australian Law Journal* 33: 369–372.

Kirby, M (1979) 'Controls over investigation of offences and pre-trial treatment of suspects' *Australian Law Journal* 53: 626–647.

—— (1991) Miscarriages of justice – our lamentable failure?' *The Child & Co Lecture* 1991, unpublished.

Lassiter, GD, Slaw, RD, Briggs, MA & Scanlan, CR (1992) 'The potential for bias in videotaped confessions' *Journal of Applied Social Psychology* 22 1838–1851.

—— & Irvine, AA (1986) 'Videotaped confessions: the impact of camera point of view on judgments of coercion' *Journal of Applied Social Psychology* 16: 268–276.

Lee, JA (1990) *Report of the Royal Commission of Inquiry into the Arrest, Charging and Withdrawal of Charges Against Harold James Blackburn and Matters Associated Therewith* (Sydney: Government Printer).

Leng, R (1993) *The Right to Silence in Police Interrogation* Royal Commission on Criminal Justice Research Study # 10 (London: HMSO).

—— (1994) 'A recipe for miscarriage: the Royal Commission and informal interviews', in M McConville & L Bridges (eds) *Criminal Justice in Crisis* (Aldershot: Edward Elgar) 173–185.

Leo, RA (1992) 'From coercion to deception: the changing nature of police interrogation in America' *Crime, Law and Social Change* 18: 35–59.

—— (1994) 'Police interrogation and social control' *Social & Legal Studies* 3: 93–120.

—— (1996a) 'Inside the interrogation room' *Journal of Criminal Law & Criminology* 86: 266–303.

—— (1996b) 'Miranda's revenge: police interrogation as a confidence game' *Law & Society Review* 30: 259–288.

—— (2001) 'False confessions: causes, consequences and solutions' in SA Westervelt & JA Humphrey (eds) *Wrongly Convicted: Perspectives on Failed Justice* (New Brunswick: Rutgers University Press) 36–54.

—— (2004) 'The third degree and the origins of psychological interrogation in the United States' in GD Lassiter (ed) *Interrogations, Confessions, and Entrapment* (New York: Kluwer Academic) 37–84.

——, Drizin, SA, Neufeld, PJ, Hall, BR & Vatner, A (2006) 'Bringing reliability back in: false confessions and legal safeguards in the twenty-first century' *Wisconsin Law Review* 2006: 479–539.

Lucas, GAG (1977) *Report of Committee of Inquiry into the Enforcement of Criminal Law in Queensland* (Brisbane: Government Printer).

Magid, L (2001) 'Deceptive police interrogation practices: how far is too far?' *Michigan Law Review* 99: 1168–1210.

Maguire, M (2003) 'Criminal investigation and crime control', in T Newburn (ed) *Handbook of Policing* (Cullompton: Willan) 363–393.

—— & John, T (1996) 'Covert and deceptive policing in England and Wales' *European Journal of Crime, Criminal Law & Criminology* 44: 316–334.

Maher, L, Dixon, D, Swift, W & Nguyen, T (1997) *Anh Hai: Young Asian Background People's Perceptions and Experiences of Policing* (Kensington: Faculty of Law, UNSW).

Masters, C (2002) 'Interview with Ray Beattie, an ex Detective Sergeant' ABC TV 4 Corners 22/7/02 at www.abc.net.au/4corners/stories/s609299.htm.

McClintock, I & Healey, A (1987) 'Getting it taped: recording police interviews' in G Zdenkowski, C Ronalds & M Richardson (eds) *The Criminal Injustice System: Volume 2* (Sydney: Pluto) 5–41.

McConville, M (1992a) 'Videotaping interrogations: police behaviour on and off camera' *Criminal Law Review* 532–548.

—— (1992b) 'Video taping interrogations' *New Law Journal* 11 May pp 960, 962.

—— & Hodgson, J (1993) *Custodial Legal Advice and the Right to Silence* Royal Commission on Criminal Justice Research Study # 16 (London: HMSO).

——, Sanders, A & Leng, R (1991) *The Case for the Prosecution* (London: Routledge).

McGurk, BJ, Carr, MJ and McGurk, D (1993) *Investigative Interviewing Courses for Police Officers: An Evaluation* Police Research Series Paper # 4 (London: Home Office Police Department).

McKenzie, I (1994) 'Regulating custodial interviews: a comparative study' *International Journal of the Sociology of Law* 22: 239–259.

McNab, D (2006) *Dodger: Inside the World of Roger Rogerson* (Sydney: Macmillan).

Memon, A (1999) 'Interviewing witnesses: the cognitive interview' in A Memon & R Bull (eds) *The Psychology of Interviewing* (Chichester: Wiley) 343–355.

Milne, R & Bull, R (1999) *Investigative Interviewing: Psychology and Practice* (Chichester: Wiley).

Mitchell, R (1974) *Second Report of the Criminal Law and Penal Methods Reform Committee of South Australia* (Adelaide: Government Printer).

Mortimer, A & Shepherd, E (1999) 'Frames of mind: schemata guiding cognition and conducting the interviewing of suspected offenders' in interview' in A Memon & R Bull (eds) *The Psychology of Interviewing* (Chichester: Wiley) 292–315.

Moston, S & Engelberg, T (1993) 'Police questioning techniques in tape recorded interviews with criminal suspects' *Policing and Society* 3: 223–237.

——& Stephenson, GM (1993a) *The Questioning and Interviewing of Suspects Outside the Police Station*, Royal Commission on Criminal Justice Research Study #22 (London: HMSO).

——& —— (1993b) 'The changing face of police interrogation' *Journal of Community & Applied Social Psychology* 3: 101–115.

——, ——, & Williamson, TM (nd) *Police Interrogation Styles and Suspect Behaviour* Summary Report to the Police Requirements Support Unit (London: Home Office).

——, ——, & —— (1992) 'The effects of case characteristics on suspect behaviour during police questioning' *British Journal of Criminology* 32: 23–40.

——, —— & —— (1993) 'The incidence, antecedents and consequences of the use of the right to silence during police questioning' *Criminal Behaviour and Mental Health* 3: 30–47.

Murakami, A, Edelmann, RJ, & Davis, PE (1996) 'Interrogative suggestibility in opiate users' *Addiction* 91: 1365–1373.

National Crime Faculty (1998) *A Practical Guide to Investigative Interviewing* 2nd edition (Bramshill: NCF).

Newburn, T et al. (2004). *The Introduction of Visual Recording of Police Interviews with Suspects* LSE/Kent University, unpublished.

—— & Hayman, S (2002) *Policing, Surveillance and Social Control* (Cullompton: Willan).

—— & Sparks, R eds (2004) *Criminal Justice and Political Cultures* (London: Willan).

New Jersey (2005) *Report of the Supreme Court Special Committee on Recordation of Custodial Interrogations* (New Jersey: Supreme Court).

New Zealand Law Commission (1992) *Criminal Evidence: Police Questioning*, Preliminary Paper #21 (Wellington: Law Commission).

—— (1994) *Police Questioning* Report # 31 (Wellington: Law Commission).

Norris, C & Armstrong, G (1999) *The Maximum Surveillance Society: the Rise of CCTV* (West Sussex: Berg).

Northumbria Police (1994) *Report of an Enquiry into the Practices and Procedures adopted by Police Officers during Interviews with George Robert Thomas Heron following the murder of Nikki Davie Allan* (Ponteland: Northumbria Police, unpublished).

NSW LRC (1990) *Police Powers of Detention and Investigation after Arrest*, LRC #66 (Sydney: NSW Law Reform Commission).

NSW Police (1992) *ERISP Instructions and Guidelines Manual* (Sydney: NSW Police).

—— (1998) *Code of Practice: Custody, Rights, Investigation, Management, Evidence* (Sydney: NSW Police).

Ord, B & Shaw, G (1999) *Investigative Interviewing Explained* (Woking: New Police Bookshop).

PAG (Prisoners' Action Group) (1989) 'Will video stop verbal?' *Current Issues in Criminal Justice* 1: 81–83.

Pearse, J (1995) 'Police interviewing: the identification of vulnerabilities' *Journal of Community & Applied Social Psychology* 5: 147–159.

——., Gudjonsson, GH, Clare, ICH & Rutter, S (1998) 'Police interviewing & psychological vulnerabilities' *Journal of Community & Applied Social Psychology* 8: 1–21.

—— & —— (1996) 'Police interviewing techniques at two South London police stations' *Psychology, Crime and Law* 3: 63–74.

Phillips, C & Brown, D (1998) *Entry into the Criminal Justice System* (London: HMSO).

PIC (2001) *Operation Florida* (Sydney: Police Integrity Commission).

Porter, C (2003) *Walking on Water: A Life in the Law* (Sydney: Random House).

Powell, M (2000) 'Practical guidelines for conducting investigative interviews with Aboriginal people' *Current Issues in Criminal Justice* 12(2): 181–197.

Presser, B (2001) 'Public policy, police interest: a re-evaluation of the judicial discretion to exclude improperly or illegally obtained evidence' *Melbourne University Law Review* 25: 757–785.

RCCJ (1993) *Report of the Royal Commission on Criminal Justice* Cm2263 (London: HMSO).

Reiner, R (2000) *The Politics of the Police* (Oxford: Oxford University Press).

Rutherford, ML (1975) *Submission to the Australian Law Reform Commission inquiry on criminal investigation* (unpublished).

Sanders, A (1987) 'Constructing the case for the prosecution' *Journal of Law & Society* 1: 229–253.

—— & Young, R (2000) *Criminal Justice* (London: Butterworths).

Scheck, B, Neufeld, P, & Dwyer, J (2000) *Actual Innocence* (New York: Doubleday).

Sekar, S (1997) *Fitted In: the Cardiff 3 and the Lynette White Inquiry* (London: The Fitted In Project).

—— (2005) 'The downfall of cellophane man' *Web Mystery Magazine* 3: 1–10 (http://lifeloom.com/I2Sekar.htm).

Shearing, CD & Ericson, R (1991) 'Culture as figurative action' *British Journal of Sociology* 42: 481–506.

Shepherd, E (1986a) 'Interviewing development: facing up to reality' *Police Journal* 59: 35–44.

—— (1986b) 'Conversational core of policing' *Policing* 2: 294–303.

—— (1993a) 'Resistance in police interviews: the contribution of police perceptions and behaviour' in Shepherd ed 1993: 5–12.

—— (1993b) 'Ethical interviewing' in Shepherd ed 1993: 46–56.

——, Mortimer, A & Fearns, B (1989) 'The best-laid schemas' *Police Review* 6 January 1989, pp 8–19.

—— (ed) (1993) *Aspects of Police Interviewing* Issues in Criminological and Legal Psychology #18 (Leicester: British Psychological Society).

Shorter Trials Committee (1985) *Report on Criminal Trials* (Melbourne: Victorian Bar/Australian Institute of Judicial Administration).

Shuy, RW (1998) *The Language of Confession, Interrogation and Detection* (Thousand Oaks: Sage).

Simon, D (2001) *Homicide* (New York: Ivy Books).

Skolnick, J & Leo, RA (1992) 'The ethics of deceptive interrogation' *Criminal Justice Ethics* 11: 3–12.

Slobogin, C (2003) 'Toward taping' *Ohio State Journal of Criminal Law* 1: 309–322.

Smith, D & Gray, J (1985) *Police and People in London* (London: PSI).

Stephenson, GM & Moston, SJ (1993) 'Attitudes and assumptions of police officers when questioning criminal suspects' in Shepherd ed 1993: 30–36.

Stevenson, N (1980) *A Study of Evidence Presented to the District Court in NSW* (Sydney: Bureau of Crime Statistics & Research).

—— (1982) 'Criminal cases in the NSW District Court – a pilot study' in J Basten, M Richardson, C Ronalds, & G Zdenkowski (eds) *The Criminal Injustice System* (Sydney: Australian Legal Workers Group) 106–145.

Stockdale, JE (1993) *The Management and Supervision of Police Interviews* Police Research Series Paper # 5 (London: Home Office Police Department).

Sturgess, D (2001) *The Tangled Web* (Brisbane: Bedside Books).

Sullivan, TP (2004) *Police Experiences with Recording Custodial Interrogations* (Chicago: Center on Wrongful Convictions, Northwestern University School of Law).

—— (2005) 'Electronic recording of custodial interrogations' *Journal of Criminal Law & Criminology* 95: 1127–1144.

Talbot, R (2005) *Judicial regulation of police investigative practices* Unpublished LLM thesis, Flinders University.

Thomas, GC & Leo, RA (2004) 'Interrogating guilty suspects' in G Yeffeth (ed) *What Would Sipowicz Do?* (Dallas: Benbella).

Tillam, CR, Collins, RW, Fitzgerald, L & Sanders, N (1986) *Recording Police Interviews* NSW Institute of Technology, appendix to CLRD 1986.

VLRC (1986) *Criminal Responsibility: Intention and Gross Intoxication* Report No 6 (Melbourne: Victorian Law Reform Commission).

Vrij, A (1999) 'Interviewing to detect deception' in A Memon & R Bull (eds) *The Psychology of Interviewing* (Chichester: Wiley) 317–326.

—— (2000) *Detecting Lies and Deceit* (Chichester: Wiley).

Walker, C & Starmer, K (eds) (1999) *Miscarriages of Justice* (London, Blackstones).

Walkley, J (1987) *Police Interrogation: A Handbook for Investigators* (London: Police Review).

Westervelt, SD & Humphrey, JA (eds) (2001) *Wrongly Convicted: Perspectives on Failed Justice* (New Brunswick: Rutgers University Press).

Westling, WT (2001) 'Something is rotten in the interrogation room' *John Marshall Law Review* 34: 536–555.

—— & Waye, V (1998) 'Videotaping police interrogations' *American Journal of Criminal Law* 25: 493–543.

White, WS (1979) 'Police trickery in inducing confessions' *University of Pennsylvania Law Review* 127: 581–629.

Williamson, T (1990a) 'Are nice cops winning? Trends in police questioning', paper presented to the British Psychological Society.

—— (1990b) 'Strategic changes in police interrogation', PhD thesis, University of Kent.

—— (1991) 'In search of truth' *Police* March, 27–28.

—— (1993a) 'Review and prospect' in E Shepherd (ed) *Aspects of Police Interviewing* Issues in Criminological and Legal Psychology #18 (Leicester: British Psychological Society) 57–59.

—— (1993b) 'From interrogation to investigative interviewing: strategic change in police questioning' *Journal of Community & Applied Social Psychology* 3: 89–99.

—— (1994) 'Reflections on current police practice' in D Morgan. & G Stephenson, G (eds) *Suspicion and Silence: The Right to Silence in Criminal Investigations* (London: Blackstone Press) 107–116.

—— (2006) 'Towards greater professionalism' in Williamson ed 2006: 147–166.

—— (ed) (2006) *Investigative Interviewing: Developments in Rights, Research and Regulation* (Cullompton: Willan).

Willis, C Macleod, J & Naish, P (1988) *The Tape Recording of Police Interviews with Suspects* (London: HMSO).

Wood, JRT (1996) *Interim Report of the Royal Commission into the NSW Police Service* (Sydney: Royal Commission).

REFERENCES

—— (1997) *Report of the Royal Commission into the NSW Police Service* (Sydney: Royal Commission).

Worden, R (2004) *The Role of False Confessions in Illinois Wrongful Murder Convictions since 1970* (Boston: Center on Wrongful Convictions).

Zander, M (2003) *The Police and Criminal Evidence Act 1984*, 4th edition (London: Sweet & Maxwell).

Zdendowski, G & Brown, D (1982) *The Prison Struggle* (Ringwood: Penguin).

Zuckerman, A (1991) 'Miscarriages of justice and judicial responsibility' *Criminal Law Review* 492–500.

Index

Alderson, K 3, 10, 13, 15, 16

ALRC 16

Arantz, P 3-4, 5, 6, 7

Audio-visual recording

Alternating images 32, 37, 106

As a benefit for suspect 106

As a panacea 2-3, 11

As a problem for suspect 46-7, 106, 227

Australian development of 2-3

Benefits 23, 30, 224-38

Confession rate, effect on 227-8

Controlling police 237-8

Court use 33

Delay in introduction 17-19

Digitalisation 32, 263

False allegations, effect on 224

Guilty pleas, effects on 228-9

Image of suspect 32, 35, 36-7, 256-8

Interviewing, effect on 242-5

Introduction 20-4

Judicial attitudes 219-61

Media use of 260-1

Police objections 18-19

Public confidence in 228

Refused participation 61, 137, 184

Sentencing, use in 259

Sound 40-2

Audio-visual recording (cont.)

Supervision 44-5

Suspects' response to 100-1, 252-7

Technical problems 38-40, 42-5, 257-8

Technology 14, 32, 263, 273-4

Transcripts 32, 257-8

Typed records, vs 238-42, 244

Baldwin, J 45, 49, 55, 88, 136, 137, 167, 175, 176, 194, 216, 265, 267

Beach Inquiry 13, 14, 18, 134

Body language 232-7, 272-5

Canada 2, 20

Cases

Alladice 125

Anunga 102n4

Blackburn 206n7

Blades 56n16

Blake 121

Burke 11

Burns 10n11

Carr 15

Central Park jogger 265, 268

Chamberlain 275

Clarke 187n4

Donnelly 269

Dumoo v Garner 102n4

Esposito 111

Fox v Percy 236n8

Hawkins 67

Heatherington 269

Cases (cont.)

    Helmhout 124

    Heron 67, 187, 265, 267

    Hill 61n17

    Horton 269n7

    Kelly 150n6, 270

    Kiszko 198

    Lattouf 11

    LL 268

    Mason 67

    McKinney & Judge 15, 19

    Miranda 1n2, 138

    Mohammed 112

    Molinari 14n17

    Nicholls & Coates 61n17, 270

    Paris/Cardiff 3 275, 267, 268

    Percerep 125n23

    Phung & Huynh 53, 123n19

    Pollard 269

    Reid 54n14

    Sophear Em 100-1

    Stagg 67

    State Rail v Earthline 236n6

    Stuart 7, 50

    Tang 123n19

    Taouk 269n7

    Vinh Ngoc Phan 187n2

    Waters 47

    Williams 15

Caution 136-9

CCTV 2, 63-4

Charging 211-13

Clarke, C & Milne, R 215

Confessions 91-2, 221

Courts 8-11

CRIME Code of Practice 52, 54, 110, 116, 134

Criminal Law Review Division 13, 20-3, 272

Culture

    Police 5, 6

    Public attitudes to criminals 6, 10

Deane, W 15

Deception

    Detection 21, 49, 68, 232-7, 272-5

    Obtaining evidence by 65-8

Defence lawyers 9, 11, 115

Delay in criminal process 231

DNA 1-2

Dock statements 201, 220, 256

Dowd, J 18

Drugs & drug offences 24, 30, 31, 85, 90-1, 92, 99, 199, 207

England 24, 45-7, 52, 62, 68, 123-4, 174, 215-16, 241, 259, 264

Evidence legislation 23-4, 66

Fitzgerald Inquiry 5

Hall, P 62-3

High Court of Australia 15, 269

Hodgson, J 119, 124

Hunter, J 187

Inbau, F & Reid, J 64, 174, 266

Interpreters 111-14, 115, 116, 153, 256-7

Interrogations/interviews

Account giving 140-4, 198-201

Adopting earlier answers 52-3, 54, 61-2, 99

Allegation, response, challenge 160-6

Bail bargaining 46

Breaks 150-4

Case theories 206, 228

Caution 136-9

Challenges 144-8, 201-6

Closed questions 154-60, 207-8, 210

Closure 211-13

Deception by police 65-8

Demeanour/body language 40, 235-6, 261, 272-5

'Do you agree?' questions 136, 138, 139, 158, 162, 167-72, 182, 192, 199, 209-10, 214, 247

Employment, questions about 80

Engage/explain 188-98

Gap arrest-interview 30-1

Hypothetical questions 163, 204

Interruption 142-4

Investigative interviewing/ PEACE 140-4, 174-218, 264-5

Judicial control of 53, 68-9

Leading questions 158-9, 249, 251

Legal closure questions 82-3

Length 28-9

Interrogations/interviews (cont.)

Listening skills 147, 194-8

Modes 154-73

Notebooks, use of 150

Offence types 29-30

Oppression 267

Persuasion 64-5

Physical evidence, use of 149, 180-1

Practices & props 149-50

Preparation for 177-80, 242-5

Rapport 136, 190-1

Read-backs & rehearsals 22, 49, 52-64, 244, 269-72

Regulation 52, 68-9

Seating 33-6, 38, 116

Training 175-6, 215-16, 217, 264-6

Unrecorded 46-9

Violence in 4

Witness statements, use of 181

See also Suspects, Verballing

Interviewers 70-80

Gender 71

Manner 72-4

Partners 71, 74-80

Ranks 70

Response to silence 97-8

Judges 221-61

Kirby J 236

Law & order politics 272, 263

Legal advisors 115, 125-6, 180, 189, 200-1, 219-61

Legalisation 55, 166-73, 181-8, 240

Legislation

Crimes Act (Cth) 54, 102n4

Crimes Act (NSW) 220

Crimes Amendment (Detention after Arrest) Act (NSW) 8n10, 14n15, 97, 271

Crimes Sentencing Procedure Act (NSW) 46n7

Criminal Justice Act (England & Wales) 52n10

Criminal Justice and Public Order Act (England & Wales) 92, 96n2

Criminal Procedure Act (NSW) 24n25, 53n11, 220n4, 267

Evidence Act (NSW) 93, 102n4, 110, 137n1, 220, 231n5, 268

Law Enforcement (Powers & Responsibilities) Act (NSW) 8n10, 53, 102n4, 115n15, 271

Law Enforcement (Powers & Responsibilities) Regulation (NSW) 103n6, 116n16, 123

PACE (England & Wales) 1, 46, 52n10, 62, 63, 67, 68, 110, 121n18, 123, 272

Leo, R 4, 64

Lucas Inquiry 14, 19

McConville, M 45, 49, 51, 82

McGurk, B 175-7, 215-16

Miscarriages of justice 1-2, 7, 68, 102, 174, 177, 198, 264, 268

Mortimer, A & Shepherd, E 265

Moston, S 175

NSW Crime Commission 21

NYPD Blue 64-5

Peattie, R 4-5, 6, 8

Police

Adopting officers 36, 40, 48, 97, 112, 127-35, 153

Attitudes to ERISP 221-61

Custody officers 104-5

Private 142

Police powers

Commonwealth 21

England & Wales (PACE) 1, 46, 62, 63, 67, 68, 110, 121n18, 123

NSW 8, 14-15, 22, 53

'Police speak' 83-4, 196-7

Porter, C 4, 9

Prisoners' Action Group 19, 46

Prosecutors 219-61

Queensland 4, 5, 7-8, 13, 14, 19, 20, 24

Regulation 271, 275

Research methods 26-8

Court study 28, 51, 58-9

Observation 51

Problems 45

Quantifying right to silence 92-3

Samples 26-8

Right to silence 92-3, 187, 190

Rogerson, R 4, 6, 11

Royal Commission on Criminal Justice 63

Royal Commission on Criminal Procedure 174

Shaw, G 266

Stevenson, N 10, 17

Stuart, M 7

Support persons 114-26

    Absence of 103-4

    Family members as 114, 120-2

    Fire-fighter as 122

    Intervention by 84-5

    Police attitude to 116, 118, 123, 129-30

    Role 118, 124-5

    Social workers as 122, 124

Suspects

    Aboriginal 7, 50, 101-2, 106, 124-5, 255

    Alcohol affected 30, 39, 41, 86, 88, 105-11, 142, 180, 183, 191, 193, 233, 235, 254

    Drug-affected 88, 105-11, 138, 180, 183, 193, 233, 235, 254

    Employment status 80

    Gender 80

    Intellectually disabled 24, 86, 102-5, 124, 183

    Juveniles 80, 102, 268

    Manner 87-90

    Mentally ill 102-5, 124, 254

    NESB 94, 111-14

    Resistant 265-6

    Response to allegations 90-2

    Response to ERISP 100-1

    Silent 65, 91, 92-9, 102

    Sleeping 95

Suspects (cont.)

    Terrorist 266

    Understanding of questions 81-7

    Witness/suspect 188

Tasmania 20

Trial length 231

USA 1-2, 4, 24-5, 64-6, 174, 262-3

Verballing

    Practices & causes 3-12, 69

    Reaction against 13-17, 223, 261, 262

Victoria 13, 14, 18, 20, 22

Voir dires 17, 224, 229-31, 248

Walkley, J 174

Western Australia 24

Wood Royal Commission 6, 9, 69, 134-5, 220